# Airbus Industrie

# Airbus Industrie

## THE POLITICS OF AN INTERNATIONAL INDUSTRIAL COLLABORATION

DAVID WELDON THORNTON

St. Martin's Press
New York

AIRBUS INDUSTRIE
Copyright © 1995 by David Weldon Thornton
All rights reserved. Printed in the United States of America. No part of this book may be used or reproduced in any manner whatsoever without written permission except in the case of brief quotations embodied in critical articles or reviews. For information, address St. Martin's Press, Scholarly and Reference Division, 175 Fifth Avenue, New York, N.Y. 10010

ISBN 0-312-12441-4

Library of Congress Cataloging-in-Publication Data

Thornton, David Weldon, 1957-
    Airbus industrie : the politics of an international industrial
collaboration / David Weldon Thornton. — 1st ed.
        p.    cm.
    Includes bibliographical references (p.        ) and index.
    ISBN 0-312-12441-4
    1. Airbus Industrie.  2. Aircraft industry—Europe—International
cooperation.   I. Title.
    HD9711.E884A348   1995
    338.8'8729133349—dc20                                94-43407
                                                              CIP

First Edition: August 1995
10  9  8  7  6  5  4  3  2  1

*To Dr. Donald J. Puchala and the staff of the Institute of International Studies at the University of South Carolina.*

# CONTENTS

## Part I
### The Context of Collaboration

## Part II
## The Structure and Operation
## of Airbus Industrie

# LIST OF FIGURES AND TABLES

# ACKNOWLEDGMENTS

My thanks first to Dr. Donald J. Puchala for his guidance and encouragement over my entire graduate school career, especially on my dissertation. I also am indebted to the rest of my committee for their support throughout and for insight at crucial stages of the project.

Thanks to the European Community Studies Association (ECSA) for their generosity in granting me a dissertation fellowship in 1992, which made the European phase of the research possible.

At Airbus Industrie of North America (AINA), my appreciation to Sandy Smith and especially to Alan S. Boyd for granting me his valuable time and for supporting my request to conduct interviews in Europe.

At Airbus Industrie, thanks to all those who helped me to understand the complex business of designing, building and selling aircraft within a multinational framework. My special thanks to Michel Dechelotte for his time and insight, and especially for introducing me to so many accommodating people throughout the Airbus organization.

Thanks to Don Lang of Pratt and Whitney, who has spent numerous hours educating me about the politics and economics of the airliner business.

Special thanks to both of my parents, Barbara and Weldon Thornton, for their consistent support for all my endeavors.

My deepest appreciation to my wife, Diane Conner, whose love and attention has given me strength.

David Weldon Thornton
February 1995

# LIST OF ABBREVIATIONS

| | |
|---|---|
| AFVG | Anglo-French Variable Geometry |
| AI | Airbus Industrie |
| AINA | Airbus Industrie of North America |
| AP | Arnold and Porter |
| APU | auxiliary power unit |
| BA | British Airways |
| BAC | British Aircraft Corporation |
| BAe | British Aerospace |
| BSE | Bristol-Siddeley Engines |
| CEC | Commission of the European Community |
| CFM | Commercial Fan Moteur |
| CRS | Congressional Research Service |
| DASA | Deutsche Aerospace |
| DOC | direct operating costs |
| EFA | European Fighter Aircraft |
| FAA | Federal Aviation Administration |
| FADEC | fully authorized digital engine control |
| FFCC | forward-facing cockpit crew |
| FLA | Future Large Aircraft |
| GATT | General Agreement on Tariffs and Trade |
| GE | General Electric (U.S.) |
| GIE | Groupement d'Intérêt Économique |
| GPA | Guiness Peat Aviation |
| GRA | Gellman Research Associates |
| HSA | Hawker-Siddeley Engines |
| IAE | International Aero Engines |
| JAA | Joint Airworthiness Authority |
| JAEC | Japan Aero Engine Corporation |

| | |
|---|---|
| JET | Joint European Transport |
| MBB | Messerschmitt-Boelkow-Blohm |
| MRCA | Multirole Combat Aircraft (Tornado) |
| MTV | Motoren und Turbinen Union |
| NASA | National Aeronautics and Space Administration |
| NATO | North Atlantic Treaty Organization |
| OPEC | Organization of Petroleum Exporting Countries |
| P&W | Pratt and Whitney |
| RAF | Royal Air Force |
| RPM | Revenue Passenger Miles |
| SFCC | side-facing cockpit crew |
| SNECMA | Société National d'Étude et Construction des Moteurs d'Aviation |
| SST | Supersonic Transport |
| USTR | United States Trade Representative |
| WEU | Western European Union |

# INTRODUCTION

*My aim is to place* in historical and theoretical context the creation and development of Airbus Industrie (AI) as an important new actor in the global commercial airframe industry. Now the world's second largest manufacturer of large airliners, AI brings together the design and construction skills of Europe's premier aerospace firms. Formed under French law in 1970 as a Groupement d'Intérêt Économique (GIE), AI is jointly owned by Aérospatiale of France (37.9 percent), Deutsche Aerospace of Germany (37.9 percent), British Aerospace of the United Kingdom (20 percent) and CASA of Spain (4.2 percent). Having developed a family of seven technically sophisticated designs, AI has delivered aircraft to 110 customers worldwide and now claims approximately 30 percent of new orders in a highly competitive global market.

At the most fundamental level, I see Airbus Industrie as an instrument forged by European states and industrial interests in response to a challenge embodied in American dominance of the post–World War II aerospace industry. The genesis and evolution of Airbus Industrie as a tool of a sophisticated yet essentially mercantilist European strategy is ultimately rooted in the dynamics of the Cold War, specifically in the central role played by aeronautical capabilities in that sustained confrontation. In harnessing the material means to deter feared Soviet aggression, the United States government had directed the creation of formidable technological and organizational capabilities that gave U.S. firms a dominant position in the era's leading economic sector, aerospace. Government and business leaders in postwar Western Europe thus were placed in a paradoxical situation; in assuring its own ability to guarantee the security of the Atlantic Alliance, the United States threatened to relegate its allies to a position of perpetual economic and political subordination.

Faced with the dilemma of simultaneous geopolitical alliance and economic competition with the world's premier superpower, European leaders responded by rationalizing and strengthening national capacities across a broad range of industrial sectors. Aerospace assumed a central place in these adaptive strategies, but as European leaders restructured their respective industrial capabilities, they soon realized that national efforts alone would remain inadequate to the challenge posed by the volume of U.S. resources and the continental scale of the American market. In hopes of reestablishing their competitive position in this high technology industry, the Europeans undertook the daunting challenge of international industrial collaboration. Herein I analyze the collective European effort to redress an imbalance that epitomized and perpetuated American dominance of transatlantic relations after World War II. As I explain the result was a unique mechanism of cooperation that preserves national control of key industrial assets while insuring their effective combination in order to realize a specific objective, the resurrection of a truly autonomous European capacity in civil aeronautics.

## IMPLICATIONS FOR THE STUDY
## OF INTERNATIONAL POLITICAL ECONOMY

Set within this framework of challenge and response, the emergence of Airbus Industrie as an important actor within the highly competitive commercial aerospace industry has direct relevance to the theory and practice of international economic relations. More specifically, the creation of AI by European political and industrial elites calls into question commonly accepted notions of state, market and the relationship between them. By showing how European governments have engaged in sustained collaboration in creating an effective instrument of commercial strategy, I challenge the view, prevalent in much of the current literature on international political economy, that political authority and market forces should be understood as competing modes or contending logics of resource accumulation and allocation.[1]

Rather, I argue that, in order to understand clearly the historical development and essential nature of the relationship between market forces and governments as providers of direction and incentive to productive activity in the modern context, it is necessary to conceive of their influence upon one another as interactive in nature and cumulative in effect. In this conception, market forces or relative prices do not emerge automatically from "objective" material conditions or from the "natural" propensity of individuals to barter, truck and trade. Rather, markets are the reflection of larger social priorities that make current and manifest the cumulative impact of a whole series of past decisions and actions, especially those of governments.

Just as important for framing this study, I use a realist perspective to explain the interactive effects of state behavior on the development of markets and industries.[2] I emphasize that states inhabit a world populated by similarly self-interested actors and that the environment created by their interaction can be quite challenging if not thoroughly hostile to their very survival.[3] The profound insecurity of states stems from the fact that they must provide for their own well-being in an anarchic situation where "no one can chose that the struggle for power shall cease."[4] This existential feature of the international system means that once confronted by the threat of another state able and willing to use force to impose its will, a state must find a way to adapt, or perish.[5]

It follows from this realist line of argument that states take many of the most economically significant decisions and actions in confronting the security dilemma. This is especially true in the past 200 years, since the unrelenting competition among states occurs in a context whose most salient feature has been industrialization–the application of inanimate sources of power and mechanization to all aspects of resource transformation. Since industrial and technological capability has become sine qua non of military power and political influence, the adoption of an industrial economic system in one country confronts friends and foes alike with a drastically changed situation in terms of power relations. Facing what is so easily construed under conditions of anarchy as a new threat, it is "the insecurity of territorial states that motivates them towards the achievement of industrialization and economic self-sufficiency once other industrial nations appear in the international system."[6]

Therefore, beyond the relatively passive role played in providing the legal infrastructure for market-based accumulation and allocation, states are also important in shaping economic activity and technological change because of the unique position they occupy as authoritative actors in both the international and domestic realms of social organization. The conflictual situation facing states in the modern international system dictates an inherently dynamic interaction of international political competition and industrial change.[7]

The economic and industrial salience of states has only been enhanced by the demands placed upon governments and societies in this era of protracted war, both hot and cold. Procurement of the material means of self-defense in the twentieth century has compelled national governments to take a permanent stake in mobilizing societal resources. Mechanization, industrialization and bureaucratization together have generated a modern form of interstate conflict of unparalleled scope and lethality, integrating state and society to an unprecedented degree. Indeed, the interests, relationships and bureaucratic structures formed under the pressure of interstate (and indeed intersocietal) competition have created a new economic and political reality. But the main theoretical point here is that the most important force binding these new actors together has been the necessity of maintaining the technological, industrial and organizational capacity required to meet the challenge of other, competing state/society partnerships in a period of intense geopolitical competition and accelerating innovation.[8]

Much of the so-called market information relating to the costs and benefits of undertaking a given productive activity, especially in the most sophisticated and technologically advanced industrial sectors, is actually the result of the past actions of states taken in response to pressures from their counterparts. The cumulative effect of governmental credit, purchasing, subsidy and taxation policies implemented under the pressure of international political and military competition is to create a set of material conditions and relationships that are reflected in the relative prices of a wide range of industrial inputs and products. Therefore, what becomes manifest in the form of market signals, relative to a given set of resources, has been so powerfully conditioned by past and ongoing state action that little or nothing is gained analytically by conceiving of these signals as categorically distinct from some other concrete evidence of state priorities.

## TRANSLATING POLITICAL PRIORITIES INTO ECONOMIC FACTS: AEROSPACE

Thinking about production and trade is now increasingly informed by the recognition that governments play a significant role in creating the conditions that prevail in many important markets and industries; the idea of "competitive advantage" has begun to displace the notion of "comparative advantage." Rather than seeing business organizations as responding to a given set of market-driven possibilities or constraints, important research is now directed toward explaining how firms are able to generate substantial and enduring industrial and technological advantages over their rivals.[9] This approach has been recognized as especially relevant to capital- and technology-intensive industrial sectors in which research and development costs are large and recurrent. Firms successful in gaining market power in such sectors gradually may achieve a dominant market position that becomes increasingly secure behind formidable barriers to entry. Consistent with this perspective and indeed implicit within it is the notion that states that wish to have firms based on their territory enter a particular business may well be justified in taking direct action to remedy the accumulated imbalances; "the more dominant the existing the organizations and the greater the capital investments required to enter the global industry, the more necessary will it be for a national strategy to give privileged access to public resources to those national business organizations that can best develop and utilize these resources."[10] The rationale for intervention is strengthened by the increasingly tight linkages among economic sectors, which insure that the effects of such initiatives will not remain confined only to targeted industries.[11]

Thus, as the result of state policies, new technologies, production processes and goods can be made available for both intermediate use and direct consumption, stimulating the rise of industries and markets where none existed before. In such situations, privileged firms are able to gain positions of influence and even dominance in these emerging sectors. In deference to this "new" reality of economic and industrial development, novel and increasingly formalized theories of trade and competition are gaining an audience among academicians and policymakers alike.[12] Rather than assuming the existence of atomistic "perfect competition," among small, dispersed producers unable to affect the market or their competitor's behavior, these models emphasize that much of what is observed in industry and trade today "seems to reflect arbitrary or temporary advantages resulting from economies of scale or shifting leads in close technological races."[13] The search for the sources of these "market imperfections" has led analysts to give explicit consideration to the role of states in creating these advantages: "If government targeting of one of several sectors has spillover effects on other sectors, then the overall effects on the economy and on its competitive position in a whole chain of related sectors could be widespread and profound."[14]

These points (which will be developed more fully in chapter 9) are made to place in proper context our discussion of the emergence of Airbus Industrie as an important actor in what is perhaps the most dynamic, technologically advanced and organizationally complex industrial activity ongoing in the world today, aerospace. Due to its military and economic salience, the aeronautics industry is the point at which the logic of political authority and state power intersects (or collides) most directly with the logic of the market in shaping the character of economic activity and technological change. Due to huge economies of scale, steep learning curves, the "dual use" nature of aeronautical technology, and its impact as a leading sector, aerospace is an inherently oligopolistic industry that squarely occupies the nexus of political power and economic development. But in this sector, concerns for national military and economic security confront a technological and industrial reality whose scope and scale creates demands on resources and organization beyond the capacity of all but the most generously endowed countries. It is therefore no accident that aeronautics has been and will remain both a focal point of international political and economic rivalry, as well as an industry in which the pressure for transnational industrial collaboration are especially intense.

In tracing the evolution of this modern strategic sector, I argue that the aerospace industry's entire configuration, including the size, strength and competitive position of the firms within it, along with the prevailing level of technological and product development, has been and continues to be shaped primarily by the cumulative effect of governmental policies conceived and implemented in response to the security dilemma. More specifically, the rapid development of aeronautical capabilities in the context of the Cold War dramatically altered the very nature of interstate political and military competition, and created a new set of technological and organizational challenges for those states wishing to remain in the first rank of powers. The economic and social impact of the new technologies when applied to the commercial realm was no less dramatic, and the combined technological and industrial effects represented formidable challenges to governments hoping to reap benefits from the era's leading sector.

Clearly, such a theoretical perspective has direct relevance for the aerospace industry and the emergence of AI within it, just as the case of Airbus Industrie provides a powerful example of how states can create important new economic and technological conditions and actors. By interpreting the creation and development of AI as the primary instrument of the European response to an American challenge in an industry so crucial to security in the modern international system, I argue that the motive force of national interest need not preclude the judicious use of commercial or market incentives in achieving distinctively political objectives. Rather, in the context of today's tight links between state and market, the commercial has become inherently political, and in aerospace as well as other advanced industrial sectors, the notion of the "market" as something that can be "distorted" by state "intervention" is based on a fundamental misunderstanding of the forces at work in today's international political economy.

However, viewed from the perspective of an outmoded economic liberalism, Airbus Industrie cannot be conceptualized as an understandable and perhaps even legitimate European response to a powerful partnership of U.S. government and industry. Rather, the European governments that created and continue to fund the new entity are seen as violating rules which dictate that government regulate business, not support it. But such a conception likely reflects the American desire to retain a favorable position in an ongoing and essentially mercantilist international competition rather than a sincere attempt to arrive at an accurate understanding of the historical and contemporary reality of competition among states in a context increasingly dominated by industry, science and technology.

## THE CREATION AND DEVELOPMENT OF AIRBUS INDUSTRIE

From my theoretical perspective, therefore, I view European collaboration in civil aerospace through the Airbus venture as a response to an actual and perceived threat to the economic well-being and political autonomy of the nations involved. But understanding why the eventual partners chose to cooperate in meeting the U.S. challenge neither explains the choice of Airbus Industrie as the mechanism for collaboration nor accounts for the consortium's success in breaking the American monopoly. A thorough assessment of Airbus Industrie as a successful multilateral response by European nations to the U.S. challenge in commercial aviation must address both why this novel entity was created and how it has been able to accomplish its objectives.

In so doing, this book will develop complementary themes whose explication entails examination of both practical aspects and theoretical implications of this singular case of international industrial collaboration. The first and most important of these central ideas is that the context in which AI was conceived would subsequently condition both the organizational structure and operational procedures that proved so effective in responding to the American challenge. While driven by technological and economic necessity to combine their efforts in civil aviation, none of the partners was willing to cede control over industrial assets crucial to both the economic and military dimensions of national security. Rather, each sought to use industrial collaboration as a means to achieve distinctive political goals; specifically, to augment national aeronautics capacities and reap the associated employment and technological benefits. Still, the partners had to make their collective effort responsive to market realities and insure that differences of culture, language and distance did not become insurmountable barriers to designing, producing, marketing and supporting a commercially viable product. Therefore, describing and analyzing the mechanism by which the consortium's members found a workable compromise between national interest and commercial necessity is a primary task of this study.

Second, and precisely because it represents such a compromise, AI is the continually evolving product of political will and functional necessity. The launching of a viable product line in a technically advanced and highly competitive industry dominated by established firms is a remarkable commercial achievement, made even more so since it has been accomplished through a collaborative effort. But successfully meeting these technical, commercial and organizational challenges also has required an enduring willingness on the part of the respective national governments to provide the necessary backing. Thus, the creation, development and significance of AI also must be examined from a political perspective, with special attention paid to the intergovernmental agreements and funding arrangements that have provided the financial means by which to meet the challenges of the market.

Third, since Airbus Industrie has emerged as a key actor in what is arguably today's definitively strategic industry, the significance of its inception, development and eventual success can be fully appreciated only by examining implications beyond the interfirm and intergovernmental levels. As outlined, AI's penetration of the global market for large airframes represents an important case for both the theory and the practice of international economic competition and trade. The emergence of AI as the second largest producer of airliners has altered the very structure of that crucial industry, and the political effects of this commercial success continue to reverberate. Policymakers and theorists alike discuss the impact of AI on transatlantic and international economic relations, but often without a clear understanding of why the consortium was created or how it actually functions. In addressing these closely connected questions, I aim to clarify these contentious issues of trade and competition, especially concerning the role of government subsidies in AI's success.

Finally, and in keeping with my general theoretical orientation, both the history of the aerospace industry in general and the creation and development of the Airbus consortium in particular provide a lens through which to view the dynamics of international political economy in the post–World War II era. Indeed, this study is based on the proposition that the cumulative effect of states confronting the security dilemma in an increasingly industrialized context has been to shape technological and organizational possibilities available to other societal actors. In acting out the ancient dynamic of challenge and response, national governments continue to revolutionize economic activity and social relations; recent developments in telecommunications, information processing and powered flight are but a few of the more important examples of this process. This volume proposes to enhance understanding of how the unfolding of this ancient dynamic in the modern context continues to create powerful forces and potent actors that shape today's international relations.

## ORGANIZATION OF THE STUDY

This book is based on a variety of secondary sources as well as on interviews with executives of the AI consortium, both at the subsidiary in the United States (Airbus Industrie of North America in Herndon, Virginia) and at major design and production sites in Europe. I have also benefited from the unique perspective and insight of executives of American aerospace firms who act as suppliers to the Airbus consortium as well as the U.S. airframers. To clarify the analysis, an appendix contains relevant figures and tables.

The book is divided into two major parts. Part I, comprised of chapters 1 through 5, deals with the background to and initial stages of the collaborative effort. Part II, which encompasses chapters 6 through 9, deals with the subsequent development of the consortium. The first part thus provides the conceptual and factual context for the more focused analysis of the second. The conclusion, chapter 9, summarizes the analysis, addresses both theoretical and policy implications of the case, and then assesses the consortium's prospects for the future.

### *Part I*

Chapter 1 examines the dynamics of Cold War confrontation that led to American political, economic and industrial dominance of its European allies in the Atlantic alliance. It argues that the situation in the aerospace industry epitomized this unbalanced relationship and, in analyzing the development of the aviation industry in the United States, emphasizes the impact of U.S. government procurement policies upon this crucial sector. The discussion concludes by documenting the extent of American technological and commercial dominance of postwar aeronautics, thus setting the stage for a detailed examination of the strategies pursued by European leaders in meeting this formidable challenge.

Each of the next three chapters is devoted to the principal national partners in Airbus Industrie: Great Britain, France and Germany. These analyses emphasize throughout how the international political and economic environment of the Cold War era influenced the restructuring of national industrial capabilities in general and of the aeronautics sector in particular within each country. Each includes discussion of important historical and institutional factors affecting the relationship between the political authorities and economic actors, with particular emphasis on the respective aerospace firms. Finally, the place of international collaboration in these distinctively national strategies is analyzed.

This comparative analysis of economic, industrial and aerospace policies is relevant, indeed essential, to understanding both why AI was created and how it has become successful, because the very character of the actors involved in the collaborative effort was shaped by the nature of the connection between state and industry in each country. While each national political and industrial elite would conclude that cooperation among them in civil aerospace was necessary if not inevitable, both the motives and means of the firms eventually involved in the Airbus project would be strongly conditioned by the specific nature of their relationship to their respective governments and national economies. As a result of these relationships, each prospective partner would bring to the negotiating table its own particular set of priorities and capabilities, all of which would have to be reconciled with those of the others. Convergent at some points and divergent at others, these distinctive interests and abilities would be reflected in the organizational structure and operational procedures created to manage cooperation. Whether these compromise arrangements might fail or succeed would be determined by the extent to which the partners could turn national differences into collective advantage in meeting the technical and commercial challenges posed by American dominance. But without an appreciation of the distinctive political and industrial positions of the national partners, it is impossible to understand the structure, operation or especially the significance of the subsequent cooperative effort.

As discussed earlier, a major premise is that the creation and development of Airbus Industrie as a mechanism of international industrial collaboration represented a compromise between the economic and technical imperatives imposed by American dominance of the world aeronautics market and the dictates of the national interests of the partners involved. Having provided the background to the American challenge in civil aerospace and outlined the separate national responses to it, chapter 5 concludes Part I by examining how these two sets of forces interacted in the inception of the Airbus consortium. In contrast to other cooperative arrangements, the way in which this tension was addressed at the outset provided the foundation for the development of AI as a uniquely successful project.

## *Part II*

Part II explores in greater detail how the contending forces of commercial imperative and national interest embodied in the Airbus consortium shaped both the form and content of the subsequent collaborative effort. It does so through an analytical chronology: by examining the most important aspects–new product development, changes in membership, modifications in structure and operation–of the consortium's development from its inception to the present. Therefore, chapter 6 deals with the creation in December 1970 of Airbus Industrie as a corporate entity, a Groupement d'Intérêt Économique (GIE), and its subsequent efforts to develop and market its first product, the A300B. It shows how the eventual sales success led to the emergence of the consortium as an important force in civil aircraft manufacture and also to a transatlantic struggle in the industry for British technological, industrial and financial assets. Chapter 7 examines the evolution of the consortium after British reentry in 1979 and focuses on the tensions generated within AI by continued expansion of the product line, in particular with the introduction of the single-aisle A320 in the mid-1980s. Chapter 8 addresses the international political and industrial consequences of AI's subsequent commercial success, with emphasis on the transatlantic dispute (which eventually went before the General Agreement on Tariffs and Trade) over continuing European government subsidies to the consortium, concerning especially the new A330/A340 aircraft. Finally, chapter 9 assesses the theoretical and policy implications of AI's entry into the global market for large civil aircraft, stressing its significance for the theory and practice of international trade as well as for prevailing conceptions of state and market that inform contending approaches to international political economy.

The emphasis throughout Part II is on how distinctive national political and industrial priorities have interacted with technological and commercial considerations in the design, development, production and sale of these sophisticated and expensive machines. In attempting to negotiate a middle course between political interests and market imperatives, a mechanism of collaboration was devised that effectively placed the industrial partners in roles simultaneously cooperative and adversarial. The result has been the emergence of a collective system of business control that, while sometimes cumbersome, compensates by setting up a creative tension among the members, thereby generating innovative and effective solutions to technical and commercial challenges. Description and analysis of these unusual arrangements is thus a second major focus of Part II, throughout which special attention is given to how the structure and operation of the consortium have addressed potential obstacles to effective collaboration, such as logistics, language, culture and national interest.

The point of examining these various aspects of the consortium's complex structure and operation is to show that Airbus Industrie continues to be very much a creature of the environment from which it emerged. Created by powerful industrial states as a response to a challenge that was a direct result of Cold War conflict, both its inception and subsequent development reflect nationalistic concerns. But unlike so many other politically motivated projects, this collaborative effort has been able to meet technical and commercial demands of the highest order. In responding to the imperatives of the market, the partners have woven competitive incentives into the very fabric of the collective enterprise, and success on the international market has followed. Yet problems remain, as critics both in Europe and especially the United States demand that the consortium be more open and accountable in the financing of its activities. Even within AI, it is recognized that in order to remain competitive in times like these, no organization can afford to ignore pressures for rationalization, efficiency and cost-reduction. While I assess the consortium's prospects herein, it is as yet unclear how these pressures will shape the future of AI as a mechanism for industrial collaboration.

Finally, while I describe and analyze the workings of the AI consortium, my most fundamental concern is to demonstrate how the dynamic of interstate challenge and response that is so basic to the operation of the global political economy continues to be played out in the late twentieth century. I use the case of the Airbus Industrie consortium, analyzing its history, structure, operation and future prospects, to argue that states acting under the pressure of international competition are very potent actors who shape the economic, industrial and technological environment around them. Further, the creation and development of Airbus Industrie, while embodying the tensions among national actors, shows that states are also capable of submerging their differences and are willing and able to provide enduring political support and financial capital to economic actors who seek to realize larger national objectives through their activities. These same states also have been willing to defer to the technical expertise and commercial judgement of the collaborating firms in achieving these objectives, thus allowing market forces to operate in shaping the eventual outcome.

The case of Airbus Industrie provides compelling evidence that the sustained application of state funding and political will can be a powerful force shaping both existing and emerging economic and technological capabilities, indeed creating entirely new actors, industries and markets. These new conditions in turn set the menu of choice for other societal actors, both domestic and foreign, thus opening up additional possibilities for both competition and collaboration among states and firms. In this important case, political authority and market forces have been combined effectively to produce an entity capable of fundamentally and irrevocably altering the structure of the environment in which it operates. The technical and commercial achievements of AI thus represent the realization of a long-term European strategy and the successful response to a difficult and pressing challenge.

# Part I

THE CONTEXT OF COLLABORATION

# 1

## Cold War and Atlantic Community:
## Geopolitical Alliance and Economic Rivalry

*In recent years*, one of the more contentious debates among students of international relations concerns whether the United States has entered a period of absolute or at least relative economic eclipse. While I neither address directly nor resolve this question, that debate is relevant to my argument concerning the nature of the relationship between the United States and the nations of Western Europe in the post–World War II era. Despite wide differences in both diagnosis and prescription, proponents of both sides of the "decline debate" have no problem agreeing that, in the decades following World War II, the United States was the dominant force in the world economy.

Paul Kennedy, one of the most credible proponents of the "relative decline" thesis, notes that even before the actual end of hostilities, "it was becoming clear that the global balance of power after the war would be totally different from that preceding it."[1] Indeed, the crushing of the Nazi threat in Europe and the defeat of Japan in Asia created an entirely novel set of political and economic arrangements amounting to a qualitative shift in the systemic character of international relations. The U.S. role in the new order was of particular salience for the former Great Powers because "in the new system the European states found themselves dependent in varying degrees on one or the other superpowers."[2] Few could fail to see the implications of Cold War superpower bipolarity: "All the efforts of the British and French governments to the contrary, there was no doubt about 'the passing of the European age.'"[3]

Forged in industrial combat, the material superiority of the postwar United States was manifested in a variety of ways. As Kennedy notes, one particularly revealing indicator is that, even as late as 1950, the manufacturing output of the United States still accounted for half of the world's total. In accordance with this new status, U.S. political and business leaders immediately set out to reconstruct the international economic system, and relations with Europe were the centerpiece of these efforts. U.S. government aid and private capital would repair and rebuild the foundations of material prosperity and social stability, while U.S. strategic forces would provide the ultimate guarantee against Soviet aggression; all of this in exchange for European acquiescence to U.S. leadership on global political questions. But while allowing for the foresight or even the altruism of some American statesmen, the essentially self-serving nature of these arrangements should not be forgotten. As Benjamin Cohen has noted, "The United States was the hegemonic power in 1945, the bargain with Europe was a way of organizing economic space in terms of its own interests and purposes."[4]

Despite the philosophical and ideological commonalities that supported and sustained the military and political structures of the Atlantic Alliance, specific and persistent features of the economic relationship gave European leaders legitimate cause for concern. Particularly worrying were patterns of trade and investment between the ostensible partners. David Calleo and Benjamin Rowland have noted that "if the flow of trade were really the determining indicator of an economic community, then it would be more proper to see the United States in an American hemispheric bloc than in an Atlantic Community. . . ."[5] The authors also note that "America's international investment has been far more significant in the post-war era than America's trade"[6] and that Europeans had good reason to be concerned by not only the dramatic increase in U.S. overseas investment volume but also by shifts in both the geographic location and sectoral allocation of these flows. In 1950 the bulk of U.S. foreign direct investment went to Latin America and Canada, with Europe lagging far behind in third position. But by 1970 this pattern had been inverted; "Europe's relative share had doubled in two decades–from roughly one-sixth to roughly one-third the total."[7] Perhaps more worrying for their European competitors was that the composition of overseas investment by U.S. firms had been changing as well, with much less being devoted to extractive and raw materials industries and more to manufacturing of capital and consumer goods.

Trends in trade and investment served to reinforce the growing sense in Western Europe of being overwhelmed, materially and even culturally, by the ugly Americans. By the early 1960s concerns were being voiced in both government and business circles about the ability of European companies to compete even at home, much less in rapidly globalizing overseas markets. But even before the call to European economic arms was made so cogently by a prominent French observer, efforts already were under way to restructure and rationalize basic industrial and infrastructural capacities in many European countries.[8] These economic and industrial policies can be understood as government-led attempts to adapt to a drastically altered economic environment, of which the most salient characteristic was the overweening influence of American corporations; their scale of operation, innovative manufacturing strategies and aggressive management style set the standard for postwar economic competition.

## TRANSLATING GEOPOLITICAL IMPERATIVES INTO ECONOMIC FACTS: THE DEVELOPMENT OF THE AEROSPACE INDUSTRY IN THE UNITED STATES

In the years following World War II there arose a growing fear among the nations of Western Europe of becoming an economic colony of the United States. As the precise industrial implications of the situation became clearer, by the 1960s it was recognized "that a broad capability in high-technology was more than a necessary requisite to military power; it had become essential to status as a first-rate economic power."[9] Especially in France, sectoral policies in energy, electronics and transportation were undertaken to address the new reality, and selected firms were designated as national champions to compete in the international arena.

Particularly disturbing for the Europeans was the situation in aerospace, which epitomized the marked imbalance in the overall economic relationship between the United States and Western Europe. Not only was the industry deemed crucial by Americans and Europeans alike to their continued success in confronting the military challenge of the Soviet Union, the allies both quickly identified it as a sector whose technical and commercial characteristics would lead economic development for decades to come. In short, in Europe it was recognized that: "Aerospace industries are strategic elements of national industrial capabilities. This strategic position extends beyond the obvious military significance of such industries to overall considerations of international status and predominance in the future development of science and technology."[10]

Before outlining the response of the leadership in each major European state to the perceived threat to national security in its largest sense, it is important to examine both the sources and extent of American dominance in both the military and commercial sides of the postwar aerospace sector. While I cannot provide a comprehensive history of the aviation industry or its techno-logical evolution, several aspects of its early development bear directly on the issues addressed here. First, from the latter decades of the nineteenth century there had been strong interest, both in Europe and the United States, in the theory and practice of powered flight. Aviation pioneers and entrepreneurs on both sides of the Atlantic inspired competition and fired public interest in this uniquely thrilling and inherently risky new venture. Indeed, the early 1900s saw nothing less than a veritable mania for flight, which took innumerable, if mostly ineffective, mechanical forms.

But although the exploits of individuals such as the Wright brothers, Louis Blériot and Charles Lindbergh are of intrinsic interest and quite significant to the rapid development of early aviation, of even more relevance here is that national governments always have played a crucial role in shaping its economic and tech-nological growth as well. Specifically, the evolution of powered flight was inevitably bound up in, for better or worse, the industrialization of interstate con-flict that has so powerfully shaped events in this century. Indeed, these two devel-opments have been so interdependent and mutually conditioning that it is impossible to tell the story of one without making constant reference to the other.

Although aviation and aircraft played a minor (though highly visible) role in determining the outcome on the battlefield in World War I, the conflict stim-ulated governmental interest, both in Europe and the United States, in devel-oping the products of an infant industry. In the United States, the results were less than auspicious. Despite the war's stimulus to the U.S. aircraft industry, the belated attempt to meet the rapid increases in demand exposed serious flaws in its very structure. The proliferation of designs and patent holders from the early days of powered flight were inappropriate and inadequate to the demands of producing working aircraft in large numbers. Legal wrangling combined with insufficient scale and a marked lack of coordination to frustrate government and business leaders in their efforts to rationalize the industry and bring its latent strengths to bear on the war effort.[11] Also, the mass-production techniques of American automobile manufacturing proved inapplicable to the still-artisanal task of building aircraft. Finally, from the perspective of the U.S. aviation indus-try, hostilities in Europe ended too quickly. Despite substantial spending, the Aircraft Production Board could claim only the belated deployment of the Liberty engine as a success, while "no useful airframes were developed, and not one American attack plane or heavy bomber reached the field of battle."[12]

Perhaps unfairly, the U.S. aviation industry emerged from World War I publicly discredited and without a clear mission or future.[13] Although the

National Advisory Committee on Aeronautics (NACA, later NASA) had been formed in 1915 to undertake research basic to all aspects of aviation and flight, its mission became more militarily oriented as time passed, and its budget was small.[14] Recognizing the dangers posed by the rapid postwar contraction of military orders, the industry sought to increase public and governmental awareness of the importance of its products, primarily through the Manufacturers Aircraft Association set up during the war to coordinate production. Its chairman, Samuel Stewart Bradley, led a delegation to Europe in the summer of 1919 and came back convinced of the necessity for the United States (like every industrial nation) to maintain a viable capacity in aviation, both civil and military.

Throughout the "dark years" of 1919 to 1926, Bradley (also head of the Aeronautical Chamber of Commerce formed in January 1922) and others, such General William "Billy" Mitchell, stressed the need for the government to finance and manage a revitalization of both the military and commercial sides of the industry. Their efforts were rewarded as the Morrow Board (appointed by President Coolidge) in its report of 30 November 1925 advised Congress to act. The result was the Air Commerce Act of 1926 to regulate and rationalize the air freight business and accompanying five-year procurement plans for both the army and navy. With the act, aviation was recognized explicitly as a strategic industry in the United States.

The solo flight of Charles Lindbergh from New York to Paris in 1927 did more than any single event up to that time to stimulate public interest in flight and the aviation industry. His accomplishment (not an isolated or even terribly daring feat by the time) created the so-called Lindbergh boom, an explosion of investment in aviation projects and the firms undertaking them. The massive influx of capital initiated a period of rapid consolidation and vertical integration within the U.S. aviation industry, with four firms emerging to control virtually all aspects of aircraft production and air travel. Their position was strengthened further in 1930 when the largest three conglomerates were awarded all but two of the 20 contracts for air mail delivery in the United States. The conglomerates were a formidable oligopoly: "The important point is that the Army and the Navy, and the Post Office Department, were all paying the same companies, although dealing with subsidiaries of the large groups."[15]

Their high profits were widely seen as an abuse of public funds, and in 1934 Congress passed the famous Air Mail Act, which split the aviation business into its two more or less natural halves, manufacturing and transport. Thrown into confusion by this restructuring and suffering from the continuing recession, the manufacturers had only to wait until later in that same year for governmental help in the form of authorization for the army and navy to purchase 1,200 and 2,320 planes respectively. Though there was substantial demand for commercial aircraft during this period, these military orders provided the bulk of sales and profits for the next several years. Government data show that, while 2,281 civilian aircraft were sold in 1937 for a total value of $19 million, 949 military aircraft were sold in the same year for a total value of $37 million. These same data also show that none of the major prime aviation contractors realized less than 59 percent of their sales from military contracts, and that most drew 75 percent or more of their revenue from this single source; the figure for one contractor was 100 percent.[16]

Although exports to Europe and Asia, due to rising international tensions in the 1930s, made an important contribution to the sales and profits of the major American aeronautics manufacturers in the late 1930s, it would again be U.S. government demand that would transform the organizational, geographic and technological shape of the industry in the 1940s.[17] Responding to Premier Paul Reynaud's call after the Nazi invasion of France in the spring of 1940 for "clouds of warplanes," President Roosevelt demanded that the U.S. industry be able to turn out at least 50,000 planes a year. Any lingering hesitancy on the part of politicians or industrialists to expand production was dispelled for good on 7 December 1941: "After the destruction of the American battleships at Pearl Harbor and the British battleships off Malaya, the airplane became the striking arm of the Navy."[18]

Airpower assumed a crucial new role in World War II by giving U.S. and Allied military leaders the means to fight a two-front war. "Flying the hump" over the Himalayas into China gave experience and credibility to tactical innovators such as General William H. Tunner, while an indispensable throng of engineers built runways and airfields around the world and gave the United States a truly global reach. At home, tremendous increases in productive capacity were attained; an aviation industry workforce of fewer than 49,000 in 1939 grew to over 2.1 million in 1943. Branch plants, licensee and subcontractor arrangements all were used to create the necessary production and assembly space; the major airframe and engine builders became primarily designers and assemblers of parts and sections built elsewhere. Labor and capital were combined effectively; from January 1940 to the Japanese surrender in August 1945, U.S. manufacturers produced some 300,317 military aircraft.

But unit numbers alone mask the importance of the continual increases in aircraft size and weight, which meant that much of the new productive capacity, in terms of tools, skills and organization alike, literally had to be invented on the shop floor. Flexibility and coordination were the watchwords in ascending steep production learning curves. Output per employee increased from 21 pounds in January 1941 to 96 pounds in August 1944, while the cost of producing a four-engine, long-range bomber fell from $15.18 to $4.82 per pound.[19]

The cessation of hostilities in 1945 brought a drastic, if predictable, drop in the level of government orders that had so expanded and transformed the U.S. aviation industry. Although winding down for some time already, 90 percent of existing contracts, totaling over $9 billion, were summarily canceled in that year alone. Industry sales fell from $16 million in 1944 to $1.2 million in 1947. Plants closed and workers, especially women, moved on to other jobs, or more often to begin the business of raising a family. But fears of repeating the disorderly contraction after World War I that had been so damaging to the industry were not to be realized, because both international politics and the conduct of warfare had been changed irrevocably in the interim.[20]

Most of the military leadership the United States recognized what their German and Japanese counterparts knew all too well: that American air power had been decisive in defeating the Axis. Even before the promulgation of the Truman Doctrine and the signing of the National Security Act (NSA), plans had been laid by General Henry H. "Hap" Arnold, General George C. Marshall (then army Chief of Staff) and others to recognize the impact of this contribution by removing the air forces from under the army's direct control. Therefore, among the many important provisions of the NSA of 26 July 1947 was the creation of the United States Air Force (USAF) under the newly formed National Military Establishment, later the Department of Defense. Billy Mitchell's long-standing dream of air forces as a separate and equal military service arm was finally a reality.

One of the most pressing tasks falling to the first secretary of defense, former secretary of the navy James V. Forrestal, was to clarify the role of air power in the emerging U.S. strategic doctrine and to delineate how this new power would be shared among the respective services. Predictably, the navy and air force had conflicting notions of how U.S. military assets should be config-ured and utilized, but the newer service proved convincing to the Air Policy Commission, appointed by President Truman in July 1947. Chaired by Thomas K. Finletter (who later would succeed W. Stuart Symington as the second secretary of the air force), an economic analyst with the U.S. Department of State, in December 1947 the Finletter Commission issued its report entitled "Survival in the Air Age," which concluded that United States military strategy should be based primarily on air power. Included in the report were recommendations to increase substantially the strength of the air arm, ideas that General Curtis LeMay, appointed head of the newly created Strategic Air Command (SAC) in October 1948, was quick to champion.

Events only confirmed the validity of these views; indeed, the situation in Berlin provided a challenge that seemingly could be met only through the effective application of air power. Rising tensions between the Soviet Union and the United States over the status of the divided city (and in particular the introduction of a new currency in the zone controlled by the Western powers) led Joseph Stalin to declare Berlin off limits to the Allies in June 1948. The blockade of land and water access into Berlin prompted the U.S. military governor of Germany, General Clay, to recall Tunner's "flying the hump" success in supplying the nationalist Chinese in World War II, and thus initiate on 25 June 1948 an unprecedented "airlift" to supply the beleaguered city. General Curtis LeMay, then commander of U.S. forces in Europe, was quick to respond with around-the-clock transport capacity that delivered provisions in the face of Soviet harassment. The supply of the city throughout the winter and the Soviets' eventual abandonment of their adventure on 12 May 1949 were crucial not only in creating confidence in the American commitment to Berlin, Germany, Europe and the defense of the West, but also in establishing the importance and credibility of the USAF.

The intensity of Cold War conflict was decisive in transforming the technological and organizational features of the U.S. aviation industry, not least because it "marked the watershed between piston and jet production."[21] After the triumph of the Berlin Airlift, events continued to conspire to encourage an increasing U.S. reliance on air power for both strategic deterrence and tactical capability. The explosion of a Soviet nuclear device in August 1949 confirmed the need for the U.S. military to maintain and improve its ability to deliver atomic weapons into the heart of the USSR. The resulting contracts for the development of large conventional bombers soon were augmented by demands from the USAF and especially the navy for jet aircraft with much improved tactical bombing and close air support capabilities. The movement toward the new jet technology was given further impetus by the outbreak of war on the Korean Peninsula, especially over the feared "MiG Alley," where Soviet MiG-15s demonstrated formidable power and agility.

For all of its advantages in simplicity of design and the accompanying savings in power-to-weight ratios and aerodynamic efficiency, the development of the jet engine was perhaps the single most important factor behind the rapid increases in the complexity and cost of developing new aircraft. Deceptively straightforward in their method of providing thrust, jet engines require unparalleled materials integrity and engineering exactitude for successful operation. Actual performance is not readily predictable from design projections, necessitating frequent and exhaustive testing followed by reworking, with the emphasis always on peak performance and flawless reliability.[22] Taken together, the rapid changes in the nature of the postwar threat and the technological responses to that challenge meant that U.S. military planners became enmeshed in a procurement process involving the research, design and development of highly complex industrial products. It was the symbiotic relationship between the imperatives of the international situation, as perceived by the U.S. political and military leadership, and the technological and organizational characteristics of the aeronautical industry, that provided the impetus for eventual American dominance of this crucial economic sector.

## A ROSE BY ANY OTHER NAME: THE EFFECTS OF COLD WAR INDUSTRIAL PLANNING ON THE UNITED STATES AEROSPACE INDUSTRY

The new reliance on air power in assuring national security meant that the newest of the armed services would take the lead in issuing large, long-term contracts to firms for the development and manufacture of what had now become expensive and complex weapons systems. Through the procurement practices of the air force, the political and military leadership of the United States exerted strong influence on both sides of the aeronautics market, providing not only final demand for the products but also insuring it a steady stream of research and development (R&D) financing. As noted earlier, the Korean conflict provided an especially dramatic fillip to the industry: "the Pentagon's spending on the aerospace industry shot up from $2.6 billion in 1950 to $10.6 billion in 1954."[23] In fact, for the 1945 to 1969 period, "the defense portion of total R&D expenditures never fell below 65 percent,"[24] and during that period the air force spent over 70 percent of its funds on product development.

Along with the rapid development of a massive industrial capability built on an extensive subcontractor base, the procurement of expensive and complex military aircraft also developed exceptionally tight links between government and industry in contract administration. Indeed, the economic and organizational impact of these capital outlay and procurement policies was so great that the U.S. government had a de facto industrial policy toward the aerospace sector. Under the intense geopolitical pressures of the Cold War, "the air force could not rely on market forces to maintain the world's largest and most technologically advanced aircraft industry. National security had become equated with industrial planning."[25]

But the impact of the procurement policies was to be felt far beyond the core of the emerging military-industrial complex. The nature of the technologies and manufacturing processes in aeronautics insured that the effects of government research and procurement policies would be felt in related sectors on both the military and commercial sides of the industry. The development and construction of modern aircraft require the assembly of several subsystems that are themselves extremely complex and whose successful integration is made even more difficult by their highly interactive nature. Propulsion systems, aerodynamics engineering, construction materials and guidance systems are only the most obvious examples of the large number of distinct industrial sectors stimulated by the inherently eclectic nature of aircraft design and manufacture. As observed in a recent study on the impact of military procurement policies on the economic geography of the United States:

> The cold war initiated a new era of industrial progress, nourished by government-financed, military-led research and development, with guaranteed government markets. The new dominant industries, arrayed around the aerospace complex, faced qualitatively new demands–to make small batches of experimental or innovative gear, with disproportionate numbers of scientists and engineers and dwindling numbers of blue-collar workers.[26]

But since "the history of technical development in commercial aircraft consists largely of the utilization for commercial purposes of technical knowledge developed for military purposes at government expense,"[27] the effects of the massive government R&D effort were transmitted rapidly into the civilian arena as well. Firms quick to capitalize on the translation of capital, technology and production process knowledge into commercial ventures could position themselves and their products at a crucial nexus connecting the military and economic domains of national security. Exemplifying this trend, Boeing Aircraft Co. gained substantial advantage over its domestic and international rivals alike by converting its KC-135 tanker (developed for in-flight refueling of bombers) into the 707 commercial airliner that was to dominate the passenger traffic market for ten years. In fact, the aircraft owed so much in design and process technology to the military version that the original prototype rolled out in Seattle had no windows in the fuselage. The same was even truer regarding engine development: "military supported research on power plants for the giant C-5A transport led to the development of the high by-pass ratio engines that now power the wide-body commercial transports."[28] So, by converting funding and expertise gained on military contracts to civilian applications, certain U.S. firms were able to derive products that would effectively create entirely new markets as their use was adopted. (Figure A.1 depicts in comparative context the gradual domination of the civil airframe market by the fewer and fewer U.S. firms that, as time passed, were able to afford to develop and market new civil airliners.)

Not that American firms were ready to rely solely on the emerging market for mass civilian air travel made possible by the new technology; profitable military sales remained crucial sources of capital and innovation for future product development. Neither did they intend to confine themselves to the U.S. domestic defense market; pressure on their European competitors were intensified as the U.S. government stepped up its efforts to sell overseas weapons developed for its own use. Used both as a means of extending political influence in the Cold War contest and to lower the unit cost of increasingly complex and expensive systems, stiff American competition compelled European manufacturers "to set initial prices which would require sales of 250 to 350 aircraft in order to reach the break-even point."[29] Having themselves long resorted to aggressive overseas sales campaigns to reduce procurement costs to their own armed services, French[30] and British governments and manufacturers alike found their traditional markets in Asia and the Middle East targeted by U.S. producers that benefited in their sales efforts from substantial Pentagon support.

The U.S. companies and the Pentagon were not hesitant in attacking markets in Europe itself, nor were they shy about reminding their allies of the political virtues of purchasing U.S. aircraft. The story of Lockheed's success in winning the 1959 German order (and subsequently those of the Belgians, Dutch, Italians, Canadians and Japanese) for F-104 Starfighters is an exceptionally spicy mix of international business and politics, but the deal's long-term effects were more significant than the revelations of scandal.

It is tempting to speculate how different might have been the subsequent development of Europe if the French plane [Mirage III] had been chosen instead of the American; a common European fighter might have brought much else in its flight path, in terms of technical and political collaboration, providing the basis for a much more competitive industry independent of America.[31]

The competition for the so-called Deal of the Century in the early 1970s involved similar but even higher industrial stakes; "the same issues arose as a decade earlier; the nature of the Atlantic alliance, the need for a common European technology, and the problem of standardisation."[32] And again a U.S. aircraft, the F-16, was chosen in June 1975 by four European nations to replace the Starfighters (as well as Tigers and Phantoms). Despite the reluctance and inexperience of its builder in competing for international business, General Dynamics received the historic contract in large measure because the "Pentagon had been relentless in making the connection between the commercial and diplomatic choices. . . ."[33]

## CONCLUSIONS AND IMPLICATIONS

It should be clear from this sketch that "aerospace is a highly competitive industry operating in a highly politicized international environment [and] is an unusual market where 'market forces' are constantly superseded by pervasive state intervention."[34] The principal firms in the United States aviation indutry were able to combine advantages provided by the scale of U.S. government procurement contracts and the Pentagon's aggressive overseas marketing efforts with the huge size of the U.S. market for civilian aircraft to attain unquestioned leadership in world aeronautics. Given the industrial and commercial impact of the enormous material and financial support channeled into the aeronautics industry by the U.S. government, it is understandable that the "West European governments and their aerospace industries have seen themselves as the victims of an overly powerful U.S. industry."[35]

The postwar disparity in scale between the U.S. and European aerospace industries was striking. Although the Europeans once had been leaders in both basic research and its practical application—even the first commercial jet airliner was the British-built Comet—by the early 1970s American dominance was complete:

> Sales of military and space products by the U.S. industry to the U.S. government were well over ten times the corresponding British and French sales combined. This disparity is reflected in the relative sizes of the leading U.S.

and West European firms. The average sales of the five largest U.S. firms were over five times the average sales of the first five European firms. Even the sales of the second five firms in the United States were 6.5 times larger than those of the second five European firms.[36]

From the European perspective, the situation was especially bleak in the world market for commercial aircraft. By the late 1960s U.S. manufacturers set cost and performance standards and their products essentially defined the large commercial airframe industry. Of the 2,136 jet aircraft in service on U.S. airlines in 1971, 2,076 had been produced by U.S. manufacturers.[37] More recent developments only continued the trend; of the 1154 jet airliners delivered in 1969 to 1971, 998 were U.S.-built, leaving 156 for all other manufacturers.[38] While U.S. dominance of the aerospace industry made the European task daunting, the industry's importance to both the military and economic dimensions of national security left little time for indecision or miscalculation. It was fully realized that:

> Faced with increasingly uneconomic national military markets and shrinking military exports, the major European industries either would have to increase their share of the civil transport market or would be reduced to a point at which competition with US firms would be out of the question.[39]

Moreover, inherent aspects of the technology and the production process continued to work to the disadvantage of the Europeans. As noted earlier, the extent of "technical borrowing" inherent in aircraft design and manufacture meant that innovation in any number of sectors would affect the complexity and expense of the component subsystems as well as the difficulty of integrating them into a coherent whole. Much of this innovation was military in origin and, particularly because of the increasing importance of electronic components in aircraft flight control and guidance systems, the complexity and cost of producing viable aircraft (military or commercial) was fast becoming prohibitive for all except the most well endowed.

Realizing the futility of attempting to match the United States in either the basic research or military procurement expenditures that were driving the rapid pace of technological change, government and industry in European countries would conclude that international collaboration was the only effective answer to the American challenge. But before considering in detail these collective European efforts, among the most important and successful of which has been Airbus Industrie, we will examine how each of the eventual partners in the consortium came to recognize that industrial collaboration in commercial aircraft production was in their national interest. This would be of direct relevance to the form and content of future collaboration, since each member was to bring to the subsequent arrangements a particular set of priorities and distinctive capabilities, both products of national experience and of the internal political and economic structure. By highlighting the national similarities and differences in how the American challenge was perceived and eventually met, the following profiles will provide the basis for analysis that illuminates the actual dynamics of intergovernmental cooperation and industrial collaboration.

# 2

## BRITISH ECONOMIC, INDUSTRIAL AND AEROSPACE POLICY, 1945–1975

*This chapter examines* British policy relative to commercial aerospace in the post–World War II period. It begins by identifying the most salient economic and industrial challenges facing British political and business leaders after the war and then examines the most important reasons for the uniquely British response to them. It shows how these priorities were manifested in the restructuring of the British aerospace industry and also in the checkered record of British participation in European collaborative ventures, especially regarding the Airbus project.

Two major themes are developed in this discussion. First, that enduring institutional and cultural aspects of the British political economy combined with the events of World War II and its aftermath to make an effective British response to the economic and industrial challenges of the Cold War era particularly difficult. I argue that victory on the battlefield prevented the British elite and public alike from reassessing policy priorities in the fundamental way required by the systemic changes wrought by the war. Second, that British politicians and business leaders in the period after the war were divided over whether to maintain the "special relationship" with the United States or to pursue an explicitly "European vocation." Taken together, these two fundamental aspects of British policy produced responses inadequate to the economic and industrial challenges at hand.

More specifically, this misperception and ambivalence were mani-fested quite clearly in British policy toward the aerospace industry, especially regarding the engine builder Rolls-Royce and its simultaneous (and ultimately disastrous) pursuit of American (Lockheed L-1011) and European (Airbus A300) contracts. This lack of clarity and consistency in policy relative to aerospace,

European collaboration, and the Airbus project itself quite nearly cost Britain a role in what would become the most successful example to date of European industrial collaboration.

## A PROBLEM OF PERCEPTION: BRITISH ECONOMIC AND INDUSTRIAL POLICY IN THE POST–WORLD WAR II ERA

In understanding both the challenges to and results of British economic and industrial policy in this period, one cannot underestimate the significance of victory in World War II. Having by immense sacrifice stubbornly resisted a fierce attempt to break both the body and spirit of the British people, its leadership and public alike concluded that British institutions and practices had been tested and found solid. It is instructive to contrast this experience and perception with that of the French, especially in terms of the impact upon the postwar economic policies of the two countries. As one observer has noted, "the failure of the war economy had forced the French to re-examine their national economic and industrial policies; the British successes encouraged them to believe that existing policies and techniques were sufficient for peacetime purposes."[1]

Although confronted by the accelerating collapse of their colonial empire, British governments after World War II wanted nothing more than to reestablish the nation's preeminence in international affairs.

> Again and again, British citizens were told by their government that they were living beyond their means and that they would have to accept cutbacks in services, higher taxes and slower economic growth if the nation were to remain solvent in its international competitiveness. But it was not in its domestic life that the country was living beyond its means. It was living beyond its means in trying to support an international life style to which it could no longer be accustomed.[2]

The tendency of the British to address what were arguably symptoms rather than the root causes of declining productivity and international competitiveness can thus be seen as an unfortunate result of wartime victory. In trying to retain an influence in international politics befitting a nation victorious in global war, the British used demand management tools in seeking balance-of-payments equilibrium and currency stability, thus hoping to restore international credibility. Sterling was "a symbol of Britain's international virility,"[3] and successive chancellors took the lead in using "the external strength of the pound as the principal regulator of activity in the domestic economy."[4] Again the comparison with the French experience is instructive; the latter showed themselves willing to sacrifice price stability and the external value of the franc to restructure the supply side of the national economy and restore competitiveness in markets at home and abroad. In Great Britain, however, pressing domestic needs, such as improving productivity or raising levels of capital investment, were subordinated to the chimera of regaining a forever vanished prewar international status.

Not that the dominance by the Treasury and the so-called sterling lobby of macroeconomic policy precluded direct government involvement factor markets; nationalizations along with a variety of physical and financial controls were important policy tools in postwar Conservative and Labour administrations alike. Never used with full effectiveness, however, nationalization of key industries gradually was abandoned as a tool of economic restructuring. Result: "There was no very apparent gain in efficiency, no revolution in industrial relations, no real reinforcement of the government's grip on the economy."[5] Reliance on exchange and interest rates as the primary tools of economic management meant that "the state was actually dismantling the institutions that might have allowed it to reorganize British industry."[6] It is ironic that "the nation that most avidly embraced Keynesianism also adopted the most arms-length industrial policy in Europe."[7]

Yet by the early 1960s, French success in modernizing their national economy inspired understandable emulation, both elsewhere on the Continent and even across the Channel. Conservative prime minister Harold Macmillan was an avid proponent of indicative planning, but the National Economic Development Council (NEDC, or "Neddy") formed 25 July 1961 was "fundamentally different from the French Planning Commission"[8] and failed to accomplish comparable results since the British Treasury still called the shots. Employed in the institutional context of the British political economy, the tripartite forum of government, business and labor produced perverse results since the employers were able to dominate the voluntaristic and consensual process. This only "reinforced the ability of existing firms to resist market pressure for reorganization and . . . tended to enhance rather than reduce the structural rigidities in many markets."[9]

The Labour government that took office in October 1964 had campaigned on the dramatic initiatives they would take in altering the international competitive position of British firms.[10] Prime Minister Harold Wilson and his cabinet set about the immediate reorganization of the NEDC, created the Department of Economic Affairs and a new Ministry of Technology and commissioned a comprehensive National Plan. But wholly consistent with past British economic theory and practice, "beneath the surface of the 1965 National Plan lay the assumption that the growth of productivity was *demand determined* and could be raised simply by the expansion of capacity . . ."; thus these efforts too failed to produce gains in productivity necessary to alter relative competitiveness.[11] The plan was ignominiously abandoned anyway in July 1966, and the episode damaged the public perception of the entire approach in Britain for years to come: "Indicative planning has never recovered from this setback."[12]

Not to heap blame on Labour; most observers stress the essential continuity of the reactive and ad hoc nature of British economic and industrial policy during this period. Overall, the unfortunate result was a pattern of "stop-go" gyrations that alternately sought to expand and contract the economy through the manipulation of interest rates in response to balance-of-payments dictates. For example, the Conservative attempt to reverse Labour "interventionism" was itself subject to an abrupt volte-face when two major British manufacturing firms, Rolls-Royce and Upper Clyde Shipbuilders, were found financially insolvent in 1971 and placed under government directorship. Again in contrast to the aggressively dirigiste style of economic management practiced in France, these bailouts were the epitome of defensive industrial policy. Rather than HMG ministers picking winners, "it was losers like Rolls-Royce, British Leyland and Alfred Herbert who picked Ministers" and "the main damage this phase of policy did was to confuse politicians and the public alike."[13]

## AEROSPACE: BRITISH POLICY AT THE FOCAL POINT OF ATLANTIC ECONOMIC AND INDUSTRIAL RIVALRY

This brief sketch of the priorities and policy responses of successive British governments to the economic and industrial challenges confronting the nation after World War II provides the background necessary to more detailed examination of developments in the aerospace industry. Given its military and economic significance, the industry occupied a prominent place in British efforts to adjust to the new Cold War environment. This centrality was reflected in government expenditure on research and development; "by far the largest proportion of government aid for innovation has been allocated to the space and aircraft industries or to nuclear power."[14] But despite significant early advantages in basic technology, the dedication of substantial governmental resources to the industry failed to arrest the erosion of Britain's relative position in aerospace.

The origins of this failure can be found in the history of the aviation industry as it evolved in the British context. As described in chapter 1, World War I insured that the theory and practice of powered flight would become an integral part of national security for all industrialized nations. In Britain as in other nations, the immediate aftermath of the Great War precipitated a dramatic decline in the industry, but the Air Ministry continued to support a relatively large number of selected firms. Agglomeration rather than true consolidation was the rule in the interwar period, as exemplified in the formation of the Hawker-Siddeley Group in 1935; "the net effect was to emphasize design at the expense of production and obstructed the development of firms of equivalent size and scale to those emerging in the US."[15]

Limitations of space do not permit even a cursory recounting here of the heroic role played by the Royal Air Force (RAF) in preventing Hitler from realizing his dream of European hegemony. As World War II drew to a close, the aircraft industry in Britain (as well as in the United States and France) was further transformed from a military necessity into an economic and political priority. On the recommendation of the 1943 Brabazon Commissions, the new Labour government began allocating civil aircraft development projects so as to offset the decline in military orders.[16] But as industry employment shrank from 1 million at the height of the war in 1943 to around 170,000 in 1945, the state failed to capitalize on the opportunity to use procurement policy to rationalize the fragmented industry. Successive governments continued instead to support "too many individual design centers and companies whose average size was far below those of the more important American firms."[17] Result: "From 1945 to 1950, nine British firms were in production on fourteen different types of large civil and military aircraft,"[18] even though only three of these firms— de Havilland, Gloster and Hawker—produced over 1,000 aircraft apiece during the period. As in the larger economic picture, it is possible to see in this dispersal of scarce resources the perverse effects of the British wartime victory. Too many companies were kept afloat on government contracts since "dissolution was hardly a reward for valiant wartime service."[19]

In keeping with the Brabazon strategy, the government sought to compel the nationalized airlines to "buy British," even though the carriers felt "that their interests were being sacrificed to build a British aircraft industry."[20] This nationalistic policy need not necessarily have undermined the commercial prospects of the British manufacturers or carriers, since the 1940s and early

1950s were not a period of rapid technological change in aircraft design and technology, and the serious American challenge had not yet emerged.[21] In fact, Great Britain held a substantial lead in jet engine design and production, and the market for long-range passenger travel was only just developing. But although de Havilland was able in 1952 to successfully incorporate British skill in propulsion technology into the world's first jet airliner, fatal crashes undermined the aircraft's chances for commercial success.[22] This hiatus and the accompanying loss of confidence and momentum allowed American firms, especially Boeing and Douglas (Convair fared less well), to apply the funding and experience of military production to the huge potential of the American markets for passengers and freight. With an initial order from Pan Am in 1955, Boeing launched the 707. From this point forward the British (and everyone else) would play catch-up with U.S. producers in the military and commercial sectors alike.

Although commercial air travel was developing into a major industry in the dawning jet age, in the late 1950s military sales still accounted for around 70 percent of British aerospace production. But despite the temporary boost given to the industry by American purchases of European and British fighter and transport aircraft at the height of the Korean conflict, lucrative military markets soon would come under competitive and financial pressures. The successes of the de Havilland Vampire, Hawker Hunter and English Electric Canberra notwithstanding, by the end of the 1950s "rising development and procurement costs proved too much for the British Treasury."[23] The British market could not generate the economies of scale necessary to compete with the Americans; "Between 1955 and 1961, US military production runs were three times greater than Britain's and four and a half times greater in transport aircraft."[24] As we have seen, the U.S. firms were quick to turn these discrepancies into commercial advantage.

The declining fortunes of British aviation firms relative to their American counterparts took place in a context of continuing economic malaise as successive governments sought to balance commitments (both domestic and international) and resources. While ministers had for some time been stressing the need for cuts in military spending and an accompanying restructuring of the entire defense industry, "the Sandys' Defense White Paper of 1957 provided the catalyst for the rationalisation of the aircraft industry."[25] The report called for a drastic shift in British military strategy toward an almost complete reliance on nuclear weapons and guided missile delivery systems at the expense of manned aircraft, which were deemed too expensive and obsolete. It was hoped that civil orders would take up the resulting slack in aircraft orders, but this optimistic view failed to appreciate what the American firms knew full well: that "civil aircraft projects were funded in part from the profits earned form defense contracts and helped by the inter-relationship between military and civil R&D."[26]

Even though the attempt to develop an effective British missile delivery system (Blue Streak) eventually was abandoned because of its own technical obsolescence[27] and the continued need for manned aircraft later acknowledged, the abrupt cancellation of numerous projects placed the aircraft manufacturers in financial straits. Minister of Supply Aubrey Jones[28] hoped to turn potential disaster into opportunity and to use the funding of any new projects as a lever to force consolidation in the industry. But his efforts would bear fruit only after the general election of October 1959 under Duncan Sandys, head of the new Ministry of Aviation for Macmillan. Sandys pressed on business leaders his view that the industry could accommodate only two major groups in both the airframe and engines sectors and that henceforth government would provide financial support for specific projects only after explicit consideration of the overall economic, industrial and commercial context.

Between November 1959 and January 1960, the new policy led to government-encouraged restructuring of the British aerospace industry. (See Figure A.2 for a diagram depicting the pattern of aeronautical industry consolidation in Britain.) It resulted in three major airframe manufacturers: the Hawker-Siddeley Group (called HSA and now including de Havilland), British Aircraft Corporation (BAC) and Westland Aircraft (helicopters); plus two engine producers, Bristol-Siddeley (BSE) and Rolls-Royce. Yet while the resulting industrial entities were stronger in financial terms, "rationalisation did not lead to improvement in the scale of production. . . ."[29] Design sites and factories remained small and dispersed, especially in comparison to their American counterparts. Thus failing to address the root cause of slipping rates of productivity—a fact quite consistent with British economic and industrial policies more generally—"the weakest aspect of the government's policy was that it appeared to have little overall concept of an optimal shape of an industry capable of taking on the Americans of staying in front of its European competitors."[30]

As the Conservative government pressed on with efforts to fund development of increasingly complex and expensive aeronautical weapons systems, it found itself the target of Labour opposition and public criticism concerning cost overruns and excessive contractor profits. Exemplifying the perceived failures was the TSR 2, a proposed multirole fighter aircraft to be built by BAC, which proved wholly unable to contain its cost or to guarantee its performance. The project became a focal point in the general election of 1964, and Labour came into power in October determined to set matters right. The new Aviation minister, Roy Jenkins, quickly axed three existing programs (including the ill-starred TSR 2) and appointed a commission to investigate the situation in the entire industry.[31]

The resulting Plowden Report,[32] commissioned in December 1964 and published in December 1965, was pessimistic in concluding there was little prospect of Great Britain ever again developing a completely new aircraft using solely national assets. In order to attain economies of scale, it saw the need for further rationalization of the industry, even under some form of direct governmental ownership. The report also recommended that the most expensive and complex weapons systems be purchased from the United States, while Britain should cooperate with other European nations toward the eventual goal of establishing a genuine European aerospace industry based on a unified market.

Predictably, the report received less than universal acclamation in Britain from either politicians or industrialists. First, it seemed to concede an insurmountable British weakness in aviation and appeared too ready to relegate its firms to the role of supplying simple and cheap components to dominant American producers. Second, it was feared that such a frank admission of unwillingness and inability to pursue a national policy of development and procurement undercut the leverage of governments and industrialists alike in negotiating with both prospective allies and competitors.

The Plowden Report and the way in which it was received reflected the confusion and lack of direction in British policy, especially toward the aerospace industry. Its publication provoked a period of introspection as both leaders and public recognized that the failure of past policies to respond effectively to economic and technological pressures for industrial reorganization threatened British jobs and indeed the very future of the crucial sector. At this juncture, calls to use international collaboration in strengthening the industry and improving its competitive position took on a new urgency, and a number of cooperative programs with European nations were launched. But while rational as a strategy for preserving vital industrial assets, these initiatives eventually would bring to the fore the essential tension in British postwar foreign policy between a "European vocation" and the Atlanticist "special relationship" with the United States.

## THE CHALLENGES OF COLLABORATION

Following publication of the Plowden Report, both the Labour government and aerospace firms began casting about for suitable opportunities for European collaboration. Given the spate of recent cancellations, military projects had special urgency and cross-channel contacts bore immediate fruit. The Memorandum of Understanding signed 17 May 1965 between the French and British governments actually linked two separate projects: the Jaguar and the AFVG (Anglo-French Variable Geometry). As was typical of other European collaborative ventures in military aviation, firms in each country were designated as "leaders" in the airframe and engine segments of the respective programs. Bréguet was to direct BAC in the development of the Jaguar airframe,[33] while Rolls-Royce would lead Turbomeca in designing its Adour engine. On the AFVG project, BAC would lead Dassault on airframe design, while SNECMA would direct engine development with BSE.

The Jaguar program proved a success; costs were contained, both national air forces were reasonably satisfied with the plane's performance and it even sold well abroad. The industrial partners worked together well and all derived benefits from the project, even after Dassault had taken over the French half of the program by merging with Bréguet in 1967. But perhaps more important than any immediate industrial or financial benefits was that "the collaborative framework would provide a model for future international programs."[34]

The AFVG story was a less happy one; differences in national perception of the project's ultimate purpose were behind its collapse in 1967. Great Britain, in particular BAC, saw the aircraft as a replacement for the TSR 2 and as a chance to develop expertise in advanced variable geometry technology. It soon became clear that the French government and especially Dassault had a much different view; "To the French, the AFVG seems to have been little more than a politically useful balance to the Jaguar, and interest was sustained in the AFVG no longer than it was required to commit the British to the Jaguar and the 1967 helicopter package."[35] Citing rising costs, the French withdrew in June 1967. The affair left gaps in the plans of both the industry and the RAF, was highly embarrassing to the British government and therefore "cast a pall over collaboration, especially with the French."[36] Critics, including the Society of British Aerospace Companies (SBAC), were confirmed in their belief that collaboration could succeed only if the British retained the capacity to "go it alone," so as not to be held hostage to the interests of foreign partners.

But collaboration as a strategy for increasing British industrial competitiveness was not abandoned, even if the French were deemed less than perfect partners. Following up on the relative success of Jaguar, the British government took the initiative in approaching the Germans and the Italians on a much more ambitious program, coproduction of the multirole combat aircraft (MRCA), or Tornado. Launched in December 1968, the partners used organizational structures similar to SEPECAT (formed to manage the Jaguar program) to link the industrial partners. Two separate holding companies were established to oversee airframe and engine development: Panavia joined together BAC, Messerschmitt-Boelkow-Blohm (MBB) and Fiat (which later became AerItalia), while TurboUnion pooled the capabilities of Rolls-Royce, MTU and Fiat. Initial work shares were assigned on the basis of projected purchases, giving Germany the lead role (to the irritation of some in Britain). As German procurement estimates fell, shares in Panavia were accordingly adjusted: 42.5 percent each for Britain and the Federal Republic of Germany (FRG), with the Italians taking the remaining 15 percent. Despite disputes and the fact that eventual production numbers failed to meet initial (perhaps unreasonable) expectations, both structures "have proved particularly effective in diluting question of design leadership and forging lasting transnational links between the six firms involved."[37] Export orders raised the total number of Tornados produced to around 1,000 aircraft, a heretofore inconceivable number for European manufacturers, "offering economies of scale approaching those of the United States."[38]

The successes of the Jaguar and Tornado military programs were not matched in civil aviation, as evidenced in the most famous (or infamous) example of European cooperation in civil aerospace, the Concorde. Despite a long-standing British industrial interest in supersonic technology, it was not until the new Macmillan administration (elected October 1960) had undergone a full "conversion" (the head of the new Ministry of Aviation, Duncan Sandys, was an ardent European) and decided to apply for European Economic Community (EEC) membership that concrete negotiations on collaboration began.[39] The June 1962 summit meeting of de Gaulle and Macmillan went so well that "the aviation project had quickly climbed on the agenda as a potential British contribution to European cooperation."[40] Therefore, "in the case of the SST—the Concorde—it was the coincidence of national industrial interests, technological ambitions and a major British foreign policy goal"[41] that led to the 29 November 1962 signing of the agreement between the two nations. Whatever its subsequent problems, it is fair to say that Concorde's "very scale and political importance was a vital catalyst in overcoming domestic resistance to the idea of collaboration, especially in the United Kingdom."[42]

But the cooperative arrangements had a basic flaw. Not a mere Memorandum of Understanding (MoU), this was a formal treaty under international law lacking completely in exit provisions and committing the partners to develop and produce a very complex aircraft. This binding aspect may have been directly responsible for keeping the project alive even when rapid cost escalation had pushed the British to try to withdraw from the program in 1964 and again in 1967. From the outset, therefore, political considerations were to dominate the project's immensely difficult technical, administrative and financial aspects. On the one hand, Concorde had become "a symbol of British good faith as a 'truly European nation,'"[43] while on the other France sought national technological and industrial gains along with international prestige. Beyond this not necessarily unbridgeable divergence in aims, the major shortcoming of the project was the unwillingness or inability of either partner to control costs, which would escalate rapidly throughout the project's life and be a fruitful source of recrimination, both between the governments and firms themselves.[44]

Among the industrial partners, negotiations between BSE and SNECMA concerning the engine went fairly smoothly, mainly because the French were happy to concede British leadership so that SNECMA might benefit from BSE's experience in developing the Olympus engine for the cancelled TSR 2. Negotiations on the airframe proved much more problematic; neither BAC nor Sud Aviation "was prepared to concede any aspect of design or industrial leadership to the other."[45] Throughout, the two companies retained divergent notions of the nature of the aircraft, but "under intense political pressure from the two governments, BAC and Sud simply agreed to differ."[46]

The core of the problem was that the governments had made effectively unlimited financial commitments while failing to insure that the contractors had any direct incentive to control costs. As if the project were not already of sufficient technical complexity to create tremendous difficulties, by guaranteeing a minimum level of profit, the governments virtually assured cost escalation.[47] Technical problems, environmental and noise restrictions, and the rapid fuel cost increases in the early 1970s sealed the project's commercial fate; eventually production was limited to 16 aircraft. Both Air France and British Airways would operate their small fleets of Concordes at a loss, not least because of the unfriendly reception the aircraft received in the world's largest air travel market, the United States.

Assessments of the ultimate value of the Concorde project vary widely, as would be expected in a project of such expense, complexity and political salience. For critics, the Concorde epitomized all that was wrong with politically driven collaborative projects: wildly expensive boondoggles with no commercial merit. For others, however, "the Concorde really unlocked the door to a new deal which will become the basis for all programs in the future."[48] The truth lies somewhere between these extremes, but it is clear that for future collaborative efforts, the Concorde provided as many negative lessons as positive ones.

## CONCLUSION: THE PRICE OF AMBIVALENCE

Overall, the British experience with European collaboration in aviation projects, both civil and military, was a mixed one. The real successes of the Jaguar and Tornado programs were offset by the unseemly AFVG affair, while Concorde's exploding costs rapidly consumed any remaining reservoir of British goodwill toward a cooperative European approach, especially involving a French partner. But, as we shall see, neither the failures nor the successes would provide adequate guidance concerning the second major program in European civil aviation during this period, the Airbus. Here British policymakers found themselves contemplating a project that would expose the latent political and industrial tensions existing between the "Europeanist" orientation and the constant "Atlanticist" temptation of casting the British lot with the massive American market.

But this moves ahead of the argument developed in this chapter. Confronting the implacable logic that flowed from the American-driven pace and direction of industrial and technological change in aerospace, successive British governments had found it impossible to retain national control over an economic sector crucial to national security. The scale of both the supply and demand sides of the American aeronautics market generated cost and learning curves so steep that European states could hope to climb them only with one another's help. Most British political and industrial leaders reached this conclusion only reluctantly and then found themselves confronting the necessity of collaboration fundamentally divided in their counsel. Lacking a clear set of objectives and handicapped by a dearth of policy tools to use if goals were ever defined, time was wasted and precious assets squandered in pursuing incompatible objectives.

As will be examined in detail in chapter 5, the events culminating in the British withdrawal from the Airbus project and the bankruptcy of Rolls-Royce (and Lockheed) show clearly the fundamental ambivalence in British policy toward perhaps the most crucial sector in the post–World War II national economy. Not only allowed to gobble up its rival BSE, Rolls-Royce was actively encouraged by the British government to pursue both the American and European markets simultaneously. Indeed, "the events surrounding the launch of the RB211 and the Airbus showed the increased politicisation of civil aerospace during the 1960s. . . . What was absent, however, was any clear sense of policy coherence."[49] HSA was left to negotiate its own terms with its Continental counterparts, while for its part, BAC continued to harbor hopes of launching a competing product with government support. And to this day, British Airways has not purchased an Airbus and shows no sign of changing its policy.[50]

As our more focused treatment of the creation and development of Airbus Industrie will show, the consensus of the British elite on the value of European collaboration in civil aerospace was a long time coming, and even today is not complete. There was little improvement in this regard during the 1970s: Despite the dire warnings by the director of Trade and Industry, Michael Heseltine, of the American challenge to British interests, Edward Heath's Conservative government did nothing to persuade Rolls-Royce or BAC of the virtues of a European orientation. The protracted and controversial process (finally concluded on 29 April 1977) of merging HSA and BAC into a single firm, British Aerospace, failed to clarify matters immediately, at least until the new company's directors openly expressed their fear of embracing the American octopus, Boeing, in a proposed joint venture. While James Callaghan's Labour government, and especially the Treasury, remained keen on transatlantic industrial ties, gradually "BAe became convinced that its future lay with Europe."[51] It received permission to rejoin the Airbus Industrie consortium in September of 1978 and launch the new A310. "Now at last all three major industries were partners in permanent commercial organisation whose aim was the development not of a single project, but a family of aircraft."[52]

But that would not come until nearly ten years after the creation of Airbus Industrie. The effect of the initial British ambivalence was to insure that Britain could exert only minimal influence over the eventual structure of this important European collaborative effort. While HSA would play a crucial role in the consortium's early success, it would do so as a subcontractor rather than as a voting member. The collaborative framework would instead reflect the interests and relative capabilities of its primary partners, France and Germany.

While neither could predict the consortium's later success, subsequently both would use quite effectively their roles in AI to strengthen their respective aeronautics capacities, especially relative to their cross-Channel rival. Britain's belated return to full membership and enthusiastic participation in the Airbus consortium has repaired this self-inflicted damage only partially.

# 3

## FRENCH ECONOMIC, INDUSTRIAL AND AEROSPACE POLICY, 1945–1975

*A major theme developed* in chapter 2 was that victory in World War II blinded the political and industrial elite in Great Britain to the necessity of fundamental reform. The British wartime experience and its impact on future policy stands in sharp contrast to that of the French, who suffered the most shocking and humiliating defeat in their nation's history. With bewildering speed the early 1940s brought defeat, occupation, collaboration, resistance and liberation—a wrenching experience that divided the country and destroyed faith in past institutions and practices. But by demanding a painful reassessment, the trauma of World War II and its aftermath also provided a unique opportunity for France to establish new national priorities and devise novel ways to realize these goals.

### NATIONALIZATION, PLANNING AND THE ÉCONOMIE CONCERTÉE OF THE FOURTH REPUBLIC

Although belated, French participation in the Allied victory over the Nazis and the success of the Resistance gave the provisional government (established in September 1946 under the leadership of General Charles de Gaulle) a mandate to carry out a thorough restructuring of discredited political and social institutions. As a result, the period of liberation and the inception of the Fourth Republic saw a fundamental realignment of the relationship between business and government in France. While the major political forces in the country did not share a common vision of ultimate goals, they did agree that the national government should take an active role in reshaping the economy. The initial postwar reforms thus entailed the nationalization of key sectors of the economy, especially energy, transport and credit. But despite the popular support enjoyed by the Communist Party (PCF), the assertion of governmental control over the "commanding heights" of the national economy was "less a breakthrough to socialism than an advance toward state economic management and technocratic overhaul."[1]

There was wide recognition that the problems plaguing the French economy (a low standard of living, balance-of-payments deficits) were the cumulative effect of the failure of French industry to invest in modern plants and equipment. Again in contrast to Great Britain, "what was distinctive about France was the compelling sense of economic backwardness."[2] State ownership thus was seen as a central component of a comprehensive effort to improve productivity by modernizing the industrial base and reorienting the French economy toward the competitive international environment. So, while decidedly not representing collective ownership of the means of production, state ownership of big business was far from symbolic either. In France "the nationalized enterprises subsequently became important instruments of the reconstruction and capital accumulation in basic sectors. . . ."[3]

But as was seen in the British case, nationalization alone need not necessarily translate into a coherent economic or industrial policy. In France, unity of purpose and efficacy of method in economic reform were given invaluable impetus by Jean Monnet as head of the Commissariat Generale du Plan (CGP), created in 1946. Monnet and his team overcame resistance from both the Treasury (the traditional fount of economic and financial policy in France) and industrial leaders in creating active political support for the CGP and the theory and practice of the économie concertée.[4] Monnet used his earlier experience as a government purchasing agent in the United States to help establish the credibility of the French economic recovery plan, thus assuring the success of Leon Blum's mission in May 1946 to secure vital American financing. With the aid of pragmatic young technocrats, many of them trained at the new École National d'Administration (ENA), "the plan became a rational investment program nourished by American aid, and planners became non-bureaucratic experts who coordinated and cajoled rather than commanded economic actors."[5]

The effect of the new *dirigisme*, whose only ideology was that of economic growth, was to shape the environment in which private business operated, and, through government direction of investment, "reconcile the market with an interventionist state."[6] By gradually improving both statistical proficiency through the Institut National de la Statistique et des Études Économiques (INSEE) and administrative capacity in economic planning, Monnet and his cadres combined indicative techniques and the skillful manipulation of rewards and penalties to turn the First Plan into a "cooperative venture between the managers of big business and the managers of the state."[7]

The Ministry of Finance and the Treasury within it played a crucial role in this strategy through the allocation of credit to chosen industrial sectors. Its head from 1947 to 1952, François Bloch-Lainé, was a primary spokesman for the theory and practice of the économie concertée. His policies demonstrated that he clearly "preferred the risk of overspending to letting the economy stagnate at a level of underdevelopment."[8] Quite different from British policy, the French strategy was to trade off domestic price inflation and stability in the external value of the franc for high rates of economic growth across a range of key industrial sectors. As the results would show, by the mid-1950s the French state had become an active and effective partner in the business of managing national economic growth.[9]

Another important effect of these efforts was to create an elite "techno-structure," in effect, "a new social group at the pinnacle of private and public sector management with a distinct set of shared attitudes, backgrounds and interests."[10] Indeed, it has been argued that in France "the inter-penetration of administrative and industrial technocracies has no equivalent in the western world, not even in Japan."[11] Although the CGP would play a less significant role under de Gaulle's Fifth Republic, it is clear that the technocratic, apolitical professionalism that Monnet and the plan engendered in the French bureaucracy was of immense importance in initiating and sustaining an economic performance that contemporaries viewed as little short of miraculous.[12] Yet it is important to remember that this new and self-conscious class of "administrative entrepreneurs" could exercise its influence only through actual companies competing successfully for market share both in France and abroad: "The key actors of industrial policy are of course the firms themselves, especially the large corporations who operate in high-technology sectors."[13] Therefore, under the Gaullist governments of the early Fifth Republic, selected firms would become the "national champions" representing France in the arena of international competition.

## INDUSTRIAL POLICY AND NATIONAL CHAMPIONS: THE GAULLIST STRATEGY OF INTERNATIONAL COMPETITION

By the late 1950s, the French state had responded to defeat and collaboration by forging both a broad political consensus and an enhanced administrative capacity in redirecting the economy toward success in international competition. Considerable continuity in economic philosophy and policy between the Fourth and Fifth republics can be detected, since the leaders of both clearly assumed that "France's role in the global division of labor should be determined as much by the nation's goals as by it natural endowments."[14] Thus, the industrial policies of the governments of the Fifth Republic can be understood best as key elements in a larger political and economic strategy, designed and implemented by a coherent elite, aiming to restore and enhance French power and influence in Europe and abroad. Yet it is clear, at least in retrospect, that these goals would be realized only on the foundation built by the very regime whose institutions and personalities de Gaulle and his followers so completely reviled. In the words of one particularly astute observer, "the Fourth Republic laid the industrial, scientific and technological foundation for France's emergence as a nuclear power, an independent arms producer, and a global arms supplier."[15]

Informed by the twin concepts of independence and grandeur, Charles de Gaulle rejected the hegemonic pretensions, whether military, political, industrial or financial, of the Russians and Americans alike. He sought to create by various means a space between *les Grands* in which Europe (led of course by France) would again play its proper role in world affairs. The idea of *défense à tous azimuts*, the development of the *force de frappe*, the withdrawal of French territory and armed forces from the integrated military command of North Atlantic Treaty Organization (NATO) in 1966, the aggressive sale of French arms abroad, the attempts to maintain a francophone and francophile African connection: All of these were complementary aspects of de Gaulle's unique vision of France in the postwar world.[16]

In the economic sphere, this Gaullist outlook was manifested in a growing "concern for the competitiveness of individual firms rather than the growth of entire sectors."[17] Successive Fifth Republic governments initiated an intense wave of consolidation across a variety of industries. Whether these industries were owned by the state outright or retained at least nominal independence, "with its merger policy the state essentially created the new social partners with whom it was to ally."[18] It is important to appreciate the extent to which the success of these proactive, "positive" industrial policies depended on the extremely close links forged between the staffs of the government ministries and the firms producing for government use as well as for consumption at home and sale abroad. Not only did these ministries provide funding for research and development and subsidies for export, through large and long-term contracts, these officials were able to "shape the key industrial decisions, such as the technical standards of the equipment purchased, the prices, the structure of the industry, the export strategy, etc."[19]

Not that the criteria for the selection of national champions were entirely of French choosing; it must be kept in mind that economically and industrially, "the needs of France were defined largely in terms of what existed in countries considered to be major rivals."[20] For example, perceived national deficiencies in steel and especially oil and telecommunications were measured against their American rivals, and policies then were devised to achieve the scale necessary to compete.[21] Indeed, one of the most striking aspects of French economic and industrial policy during this period is that a large number of "new government-backed ventures were undertaken as a response to the American challenge".[22]

## AEROSPACE: A CENTRAL COMPONENT IN FRENCH INDUSTRIAL STRATEGY

As we have seen, the aerospace industry occupied a pivotal place in the geopolitical and economic dynamics of the Cold War. Given the larger aims of French policymakers, especially of the Gaullists during the 1960s and early 1970s, it is no surprise that both military and commercial aviation received the special attention of successive governments. In fact, the state would take a particularly direct role in shaping an industry crucial to the reestablishment of French influence and prestige both in Europe and abroad.

British difficulties in turning substantial postwar endowments of talent and resources in aeronautics into national competitive advantage stand in contrast to French success in restoring a damaged and demoralized industry. Europe's early leader in the theory and practice of aviation, France even in the early 1930s could still claim a leading role, despite the growing competition from new technologies and burgeoning markets in Britain, Germany and especially the United States.[23] But although nationalized along with the rest of the armaments industry by Leon Blum's Popular Front government in 1936, the consolidation of French aviation under Pierre Cot's leadership failed to prepare it for the stiff production demands of the Axis threat.

The French aviation industry paid dearly for defeat and occupation in World War II. The portion of its capital and skilled labor allowed to remain in France was shackled to the service of the Luftwaffe, especially after the full occupation beginning on 8 November 1942. As the war dragged on and German resources were stretched, more and more French capacity was expropriated and moved across the Rhine. While meeting Nazi demands preserved a large measure of French design and production capability, the moral repugnance of collaboration discredited many business leaders and thus gave the Resistance victors an unparalleled opportunity to restructure the politically sensitive industry.

De Gaulle's appointment of the Communist Charles Tillon to head the Air Ministry reflected the PCF's popularity as well as that of the Resistance more generally, but Tillon's attempt to balance strident demands to maintain production and employment levels against rapidly declining demand for the industry's products proved ineffective. After the Communists departed from the fragile coalition governing France in May 1947, the Ramadier government and new air minister, André Maroselli, followed the Pellenc Report in creating a long-term plan for the industry based on very limited prototype design and development. Nationalized firms were central to this strategy of industrial streamlining, but private firms also were allotted a central role.[24]

Entrepreneurs such as Marcel Dassault (only at the last moment liberated from the Buchenwald concentration camp in 1945) and Louis Bréguet flourished in the new climate where the distinction between private and public ownership counted for less than a demonstrated willingness and ability to contribute to the resurrection of the industry. The state used procurement contracts (some for licensed products) in creating specialized capabilities resting on a broad and technically competent subcontractor base. The stage was thus set for France to regain its leading role in European aviation:

> By the early 1950s a new institutional structure for aviation, with a mixture of public and private firms, a division of decision-making responsibility between companies and the ministries, and an enduring set of reasonably stable trade unions, had emerged that would change only marginally in the two decades that followed.[25]

But while the situation in aeronautics reflected the *dirigiste* and technocratic character of relations between French government and industry, any prospects for the sector's revitalization would rely on effective demand for the products, whether nationalized or private. The American aid so important in rebuilding the French productive base and infrastructure (and in financing balance-of-payments deficits and the doomed attempt to maintain the Indochinese empire) also would prove essential in resurrecting the French arms industry, especially the aeronautics sector. Besides licensed production of the British Vampire jet fighter under the name Mistral, French industry had only one viable military program in progress, the Dassault Ouragan, which would enter series production in 1952. But the shock of the invasion of South Korea by the Communist Democratic People's Republic of Korea (DPRK) in June 1950 impelled the United States to seek an immediate revitalization of European military capabilities and to initiate the large-scale purchase of weapons from European manufacturers.

As a result of this massive procurement, Dassault was able to sell 225 Mystères, giving his firm the financing and expertise necessary to launch the Mirage series of fighters; clearly "the offshore program was a breakthrough in the development of France's military aircraft industry."[26] The aircraft's success not only in supplying the French air forces but in gaining export orders as well (India and Israel were prominent Mirage buyers) convinced the French government to grant Dassault an effective monopoly. By canceling or refusing to fund proposed development contracts, the French state gradually pushed the nationalized firms out of military airframe production. Dassault's remarkable success[27] in developing the Ouragan, Mystère, Super Mystère and Mirage jet fighters led to further concentration when Bréguet merged with its more aggressive rival in 1967, cementing Dassault's monopoly position.

In the commercial sector as well, "the role played by the government in rewarding the successful entrepreneur was a significant factor in strengthening the industry."[28] These entrepreneurs need not be private capitalists; the nationalized firm Sud-Est (SNCASE) under George Hereil won the contract to design and build an intermediate-range jet, the Caravelle. Meeting the needs not only of the state airline Air France but those of the commercially oriented Scandinavian Air Systems (SAS) as well, the Caravelle became a symbol of French technical competence. Moreover, this commercial success would be used to further the process of industrial rationalization, as the state encouraged Sud-Est to absorb its nationalized rival Sud-Ouest and form Sud-Aviation in 1957.

By the time of the Fifth Republic in the late 1950s, tight funding and selective procurement had encouraged the rationalization of the French aerospace industry around a core of four major nationalized firms (including the engine builder SNECMA[29]) and two large private producers. During the mid-1960s, the heyday of the Gaullist drive to establish French national champions in a variety of strategic industries, state-led rationalization of the industry continued. Following the pattern of earlier mergers, rationalization in the state-owned sector continued in 1970 as Sud-Aviation was merged with Nord-Aviation to form SNIAS, or Aérospatiale. By 1970 the French aerospace industry was comprised of one major firm specializing in civil and military airframes respectively, and SNECMA, specializing in both types of engines. (See Figure A.3 for a depiction of the pattern of French aeronautical industry consolidation.)

In comparing the pattern of government-industry relations in the British and French aerospace industries, M.S. Hochmuth observes that "though both industries have a history of gradual consolidation, the resemblance is superficial."[30] He and other observers argue that, on the whole, French governments of the period were more explicit in establishing goals for the industry and more consistent in their means of pursuing them. Edward Kolodziej notes that the French efforts drew additional coherence from the exceptionally tight links created by the Gaullists between the state and its military contractors.[31] This is not to make the French policy relative to aerospace seem more prescient or calculating than it actually was; it is more accurate to speak of a strategy that evolved in response to ongoing developments: "Each successive consolidation has been prompted by conjunctural opportunities, seized upon by the government, to advance its long-term goal of consolidation."[32] Neither did the existence of a reasonably coherent state-led plan render the French industry immune from the technological and economic pressures generated by the rapid pace of innovation being set by the United States. Rather, the same imperatives that drove industrial rationalization also pressed French industrialists and political leaders alike to seek resources on a scale much larger than national capabilities alone could provide.

## FRENCH PARTICIPATION IN
## COLLABORATIVE AEROSPACE PROGRAMS

Since the mid-1950s and up to the present day, France has been a leading participant in cooperative European efforts to develop both military and civil aircraft. Although such binding commitments might seem antithetical to French insistence on national prerogative, industrial collaboration has served as an important means of achieving larger French political and economic aims. Confronted in the military arena by rapidly rising development costs for all armaments (especially jet aircraft, which required additional expensive electronic components with each new generation), French planners sought to reduce unit costs through a variety of techniques, including the export of even quite advanced systems. But these efforts created problems of their own,[33] and proved ultimately ineffective in addressing the basic problem confronting the industry: the inadequate scale of the French resource base and market. Given the extent of American dominance in aircraft design and manufacture, a nationally based strategy could not prevent the eventual erosion of the French position in this crucial industry. "Ironically, to maintain broadly based and independent aerospace capabilities France had to seek some form of collaboration with foreign powers."[34]

In the late 1950s French politicians and industrialists alike found that their most fundamental interests could be served by approaching allies, especially in the newly created European Economic Community (EEC), concerning the joint development and procurement of both civil and military aircraft. Not only would procurement costs be reduced, industrial collaboration in military aviation with a rearmed and economically dynamic Germany seemed a good way both to assert French (and ultimately European) independence and to keep a close eye on developments across the Rhine in this crucial sector. For their part, the Germans, anxious to rebuild their own aeronautical capabilities after a forced ten-year hiatus, saw licensed production and cooperative projects as ways to establish both industrial competence and political credibility.[35]

Two major projects linking French and German interests and capabilities in military aviation were launched in the late 1950s, both of which provided valuable lessons for future collaborative efforts in both the military and civilian spheres. The first of these, the Bréguet 1150 Atlantic ASW (Anti-Submarine Warfare) Patrol Aircraft, began its less-than-happy existence as a cooperative project among NATO allies to replace the aging Lockheed Neptune. In the pressurized atmosphere of competition between U.S. and French industry (Lockheed vs. Dassault) for the lucrative contract to replace Germany's fighter aircraft with new models, in October 1958 Bréguet's entry in the design competition was selected to fulfill the NATO ASW requirement. But despite the rhetoric among the allies concerning the need for a common approach to weapons development—rationalization, standardization and interoperability (RSI)—Canada, Norway, Italy and Great Britain all refused to contribute to joint funding.

With a national firm the winner, the French government financed the first phase of development on its own while struggling to keep Belgium, Holland and Germany involved. An organization was created to manage the project, with Réné Bloch of the French Defense Ministry given control of the governmental aspects while Henry Ziegler of Bréguet (later the first managing director of Airbus Industrie) was to oversee industrial arrangements.[36] A prototype emerged from these efforts, but difficulty in financing additional test aircraft and initial production tooling plagued Phase II in 1960; besides, only the French navy had placed orders for it. Although the German government eventually did order 20 in 1963 and the first 1150 Atlantics were delivered to the French in 1965 only a few months behind schedule, the plane competed for sales with the Lockheed P-3A Orion, developed for the U.S. Navy (despite the fact that the U.S. government had provided about one-third of the Atlantic's development costs!). Small Dutch and Italian orders kept the project alive until 1974, but, from the French perspective, it clearly never lived up to its initial promise in either industrial or financial terms.

Whatever its shortcomings, however, French politicians and industrialists alike learned important lessons from the Bréguet 1150 Atlantic experience, the earliest and most important of these being that the NATO framework was ill-suited to furthering French aeronautical interests. Intra-European national rivalry was surely a problem to be overcome, but in the French view this was overshadowed by U.S. attempts to turn NATO RSI into a means to sell American arms in Europe. Henceforth, the French saw the newly created Western European Union (WEU) as a forum to facilitate European cooperation in arms manufacture and sought to initiate another collaborative aircraft project on this basis.

A group linking Italian, German and French interests in codeveloping a replacement for the Nord Noratlas troop transport was formed in January 1958. Called the Transall C-160, the program experienced difficulties from the outset because political considerations and industrial rivalries affected both the definition of the aircraft and the organizational structure created to produce it. First, design specifications were difficult to reconcile: Because of the Algerian situation, the demands of the North African climate and terrain were the most important French considerations, while the Germans were more concerned with conditions in the central European theater. Thus the French wanted a longer range and higher payload, while the Germans preferred a short takeoff and landing capability. Although agreement finally was reached in January 1959, "what seems clear from the joint requirements arrived at is that neither side's requirements were entirely satisfied; however it appears that the Germans did most of the compromising."[37]

More problematic still was the wholly bilateral organizational structure created; no final authority for decisions was given to any single group or person. Work sharing arrangements reflected this lack of central authority and construction was uneconomically dispersed over three production sites. Predictably, the project experienced substantial cost and schedule slippage, made all the more damaging by the fact that the Transall was in direct competition for sales abroad with the Lockheed C-130 Hercules, a cheaper and more effective aircraft.[38] In fact, the Americans pressed hard even into 1963 and quite nearly succeeded in getting the Germans to abandon the Transall in favor of the C-130A.

But although the Transall project was inordinately politicized and lacked a coherent and unified management structure, it did provide valuable lessons to its participants. Unlike the Bréguet Atlantic 1150, which really had been a French project with German and other subcontractors, "the venture was the first genuine codevelopment aircraft project."[39] The attempt, flawed as it was, brought to the fore many of the problems inherent in international collaborative ventures: shared definition of characteristics and specifications, juste retour and worksharing arrangements, and the tendency of political considerations to overshadow technical and commercial factors. But perhaps most important, the Transall "sustained and furthered Franco-German large-aircraft design and production capabilities in anticipation of the most dramatic European collaborative assault to date on U.S. aerospace hegemony, the A-300B Airbus program."[40]

## CONCLUSION: THE FRUITS OF CONCERTED EFFORT

As described in chapter 2, throughout the 1960s and 1970s Great Britain remained fundamentally divided between the Atlanticist and European orientations of its aerospace industry. As we will see in chapter 5, British ambivalence, especially the "double game" played by Rolls-Royce in pursuing the Lockheed L1011 and A300 contracts simultaneously, initially would have a negative impact on the Airbus project. But despite British vacillation, the French remained completely committed to the project and were bent upon using it as the primary vehicle for strengthening their commercial aerospace sector. Following British withdrawal, a new agreement was quickly signed with the Germans 29 May 1969 that specified financial and worksharing arrangements for the industrial partners and the respective governments. Even as the modified aircraft was undergoing design specification, negotiations among the remaining partners continued until 18 December 1970 when Airbus Industrie was formed under French law as the Groupement d'Intérêt Économique (GIE) to build and market the Airbus A300B.

Although sales prospects for any aircraft, especially one from an untested manufacturing organization, were very dim during the early 1970s (especially because of the impact on air travel and fuel prices of the first OPEC oil shock), neither the French industrial partners nor the French government would falter in their support for the project during this crucial and difficult phase. Indeed, in France the Airbus project would become a focal point for both major national companies, Aérospatiale and SNECMA, involved in manufacturing products for civil aviation. Aérospatiale enhanced the status of Toulouse as a new "technopole" in southern France through its success in locating the final assembly of the Airbus there. For its part, SNECMA signed a collaborative arrangement with General Electric to produce derivatives of the CF6 turbofan, which now was to power both versions of the new A300B.

The central role of both firms (especially Aérospatiale) in the early stages of the Airbus project can be seen as the manifestation of a long-term and consistently pursued strategy on the part of the French state to strengthen the national aerospace industry and thus improve the international position of France politically and economically. As in other collaborative efforts, French participation in Airbus was seen as not only conferring national advantage but also as assuring a prominent position for France in a revitalized and consolidated European industry capable of holding its own against both the established Americans and the emerging Japanese challenge as well. Again in contrast to the British experience, a relatively coherent political and industrial elite in France saw clearly the convergence, indeed the inseparability, of national interest and industrial collaboration on a West European scale.

# GERMAN ECONOMIC, INDUSTRIAL AND AEROSPACE POLICY, 1945–1975

*Compared to the difficulties* faced by Great Britain and France in adjusting to the new economic and political environment of Cold War super-power conflict, Germany confronted challenges of even greater severity. Defeat, occupation and territorial division of the Third Reich required the complete reconstruction of domestic economic, political and legal in-stitutions, along with a thorough recasting of Germany's relations with its former allies and enemies alike. The new German political economy also would have to adapt to international competition for markets in Europe and abroad, with the most intense pressures coming from the country most responsible for both its military defeat and postwar resurrection, the United States. While the German response to the American challenge re-flects its unique situation and capabilities, it also shows that Germany shared much with its former adversaries, Great Britain and France, in confronting the end of the European era.

The military defeat of the Nazi regime in 1945 was total, and the entire country suffered from physical destruction, the dissolution of political order and the complete disruption of economic activity. Material hardships were compounded by fear and uncertainty bordering on psychological and moral collapse. The physical presence of occupation forces and the division of Germany into military zones of administration were made much more problematic as the Soviets' postwar means and goals began to diverge markedly from those of their ostensible Western allies.

While this deepening confrontation became the focal point of Cold War tensions, paradoxically the conflict was a blessing for the Allied zones, which became the new Federal Republic of Germany (FRG) in 1949. The impact of the Soviet threat was effectively to thwart plans to "deindustrialize" and anently weaken Germany and to give new urgency to efforts to construct able indigenous political institutions and an economic capacity capable of esisting both overt military pressures and Communist "fifth columns." Indeed, it has been argued that in Germany "the establishment of a liberal capitalist system after the fall of fascism was largely predetermined by the front lines of the Cold War."[1]

Both the former occupiers and the new leaders of an increasingly autonomous (if not completely independent) FRG realized that the legitimacy of new regime would rely on the acceptance of democratic institutions and economic prosperity. The 1949 Basic Law, or Grundgesetz, underpinned both by instituting the rule of law in political and civic life and providing the framework for a new economic order as well. Legally guaranteed competition and the relatively free (but not unrestrained) operation of markets would underpin the new "social market economy" (Sozialmarktwirtschaft) and reknit the German social fabric. The Christian Democratic brand of liberalism was informed by the economic and social theories of Franz Bohm, Walter Eucken and Alfred Muller-Armack of the neoliberal Freiburg School. Under Ludwig Erhard (economics minister under the first chancellor of the FRG, Konrad Adenauer, and later chancellor himself from 1963 to 1966), the state would play a leading role in creating and maintaining a competitive order in which private initiative and the price mechanism would drive economic activity.[2]

For the new leadership, the watchword was constancy, and a stable means of exchange and accumulation was at the core of macroeconomic policy. Not only did the Currency Reform Act of June 1948 instigate the decisive break between the Soviets and the Allies in Germany (as evidenced in the Berlin crisis and airlift), "inflationary pressures and black markets began to disappear and the foundation for an economic policy based on neo-liberal principles was laid."[3] Also crucial to the establishment of prosperity and stability in the FRG was the opening of the German economy to international trade and capital flows. Price controls were lifted and tariffs reduced on most items, thus allowing Germany to participate in the general boom in consumption of capital and consumer goods sweeping Western Europe and the United States, especially during the Korean War. Exports became the motor of the German industrial and economic resurgence that undergirded its political stability and social cohesion: "More so than other advanced industrialized countries in the postwar period, the FRG has relied on expanding international markets to regulate both its political and economic development."[4]

So on the bedrock of the deutschemark, the postwar political leadership erected two pillars of German economic success and social cohesion: the "social market economy" and an export-led strategy of industrial expansion.[5] But perhaps as important as the policies of the Christian Democrats to what would become known during the 1960s as the German economic miracle[6] was that the socialist opposition, the Sozial Partei Demokratic (SPD), also accepted the basic features of the new regime.[7] The liberal (in a more classical sense) Frei Demokratic Partei (FDP) also played a crucial balancing role in providing governmental stability.

## FROM ORDNUNGSPOLITIK TO STRUKTURPOLTIK

Under the neoliberal regime in early postwar Germany, the role of the state was to provide the framework allowing competition and market forces to shape economic activity, while addressing excesses and market failures and performing a general steering function (Ordnungspolitik). Capabilities for state intervention were most developed in the macroeconomic sphere, with monetary policy taking precedence over fiscal tools, especially in the relatively decentralized and federalized German system. Though there were specific and quantified objectives within certain difficult sectors (Schwerpunkte) such as housing, roads, and agriculture, "there was never any overall growth target toward which the planners attempted to guide the economy by means of specific interventions."[8]

Although never embracing economic *dirigisme* à la française, German politicians and industrialists alike became increasingly willing to see the state move beyond demand management and play a more active role in creating a so-called enlightened market economy. Under the Grand Coalition (CDU-SPD) government from 1966 to 1969 with Karl Schiller as economics minister, and especially following the June 1967 Law Promoting Growth and Stability, "no other national government could pride itself on a similarly comprehensive set of Keynesian policy instruments at the time."[9]

By the mid-1960s neoliberal views of the market, competition and the state were clearly changing, and successive German governments endorsed sectorally oriented policies of state assistance to address perceived "structural" weaknesses in the German economy that had been exposed by international competition. Gradually declining growth rates in successive economic cycles intensified pressures to create more efficient economic units. Politicians sought to reconcile and indeed combine demand management, structural industrial policies and competition legislation in maintaining the bases of prosperity.[10] The oil shock of the early 1970s only added impetus to this interventionist trend; already some of the younger and more technocratic of the Socialists (still in power in coalition with the FDP after 1969) had pressed for and established the Ministry of Research and Technology (BMFT). This was important because the BMFT became, "through its ability to allocate credit to specific firms, the main institutional focus of sectoral industrial policy in Germany."[11]

## THE REGULATION OF ECONOMIC POWER IN GERMANY

Beyond implementing a conservative monetary policy based on a solid (if somewhat undervalued) deutschemark, opening the German economy to the world and taking an increasing number of structural initiatives, the leaders of the postwar Germany also addressed the problem of concentration of industrial and financial power there. The prevalence of legally sanctioned syndicates and cartels had been a prominent feature of German capitalism since industrialization in the nineteenth century, but many in the post-Nazi era identified their continued influence with autocracy and even fascism. On the other hand, many socialists "looked upon concentration and cartels as forerunners of rational socialist planning,"[12] so that to neoliberals, the promulgation of a viable competition policy was crucial to finding "an economic and political alternative to the corporate and the socialist society."[13]

The American and British authorities in Germany during the postwar occupation were eager to create a legal and regulatory environment insuring that the Kombinat were not simply re-created and pressed the Germans to draft and implement legislation to this effect. The ensuing debate revealed the conceptual and practical difficulties that defining and regulating restraints on trade presented to German politicians and industrialists. Indeed, the legislation of 27 July 1957 (Gesetz gegen Wettbewerbsbeschrankungen, or GWB) and its subsequent amendments exposed, yet failed to resolve, the fundamental tension existing between the two pillars of German postwar prosperity. On the one hand, the neoliberal social market was built around competition and the price mechanism, while, on the other, export-led growth ultimately depended on German firms with productive scale and market power sufficient for success in the global arena.[14] Industrialists argued (and continue to complain today) that a "general prohibition of cartels would discriminate against German firms in international competition" and could even have the unintentional and perverse effect of driving smaller firms out of business by denying them the ability to engage in rational market sharing arrangements.[15]

So while the creation of a Cartel Office (Bundeskartelamt) to oversee industrial competition and regulate collusive behavior was an important symbolic step, pervasive "exemptions" meant that "the prohibitive essence often slipped through the numerous holes."[16] The complexity of real-world financial and industrial arrangements among German firms, especially situations of "complex monopoly," oligopoly, and "partial mergers," showed clearly that in designing and implementing competition and merger policy, "the problematic aspect is to clarify what constitutes market dominance and to define its abuse."[17] Amendments to the law in 1965 and especially in 1973, which also created the Monopolies Commission, tried to address these complexities, but the latter act also included provisions to allow "Agreements and decisions whose object is the rationalization of economic activities,"[18] so long as these arrangements did not impair competition substantially. This shift in policy emphasis was reflected in the wave of mergers that swept Germany in the late 1960s (as in Britain and France): "Government and industry saw in the promotion of concentration an effective instrument of adaption to the international situation."[19] Similarly, the 1973 legislation sought for the first time to regulate merger activity, but it (and the 1980 amendment) also contain so-called balancing clauses. These recognized explicitly that the negative effects of concentration in market power within Germany might be offset by the enhanced competitiveness of firms in the international arena.

## STRATEGIC SECTORS AND NATIONAL CHAMPIONS

While "compared with most European countries, the creation of public enterprises, or the nationalisation of private firms has not been a major tool of industrial policy in the federal Republic,"[20] selected sectors received various forms of state support. These measures included research and development contracts, large orders for products and parts, substantial tax concessions or outright grants. Consistent with German merger and competition policy more generally, especially under Schiller's tenure as economics minister, the mid-1960s "saw an active policy of concentration in sectors heavily subsidized by the government or dependent on the state as a major buyer (e.g. coal, aeronautics, computers, nuclear energy)."[21]

But it is important to recognize that, as in Great Britain and especially France, the primary motives behind governmental efforts to increase the scale of industrial units were the economic and technological pressures originating in the international environment. Cold War competition and the scale of the American market had combined to give U.S. firms substantial leads in crucial industries. So, "acting under the stimulus of the technology gap and recognizing that other governments were giving extensive support to their advanced technology industries, the German government began consciously to develop national champions in these industries as well."[22]

This is not to say that all German industrial policies were designed to encourage rationalization and increase the scale and efficiency of industry. As in other European states, Germany also practiced "negative" industrial policies that were expensive and often produced poor results. Indeed, Michael Streit claims that "it can be safely stated that, on balance, subsidies were given predominately to protect weak sectors against structural change and income losses."[23] But the point is that despite its neoliberal ideology, the German state took a very proactive role in some sectors, with quite significant results for Germany, Europe and the world.

## THE REBIRTH AND CONSOLIDATION
## OF THE GERMAN AEROSPACE INDUSTRY

As in France and Great Britain, most of the aviation firms that eventually would combine into the larger companies of today had long histories, some of excellence, in aircraft design, development and production. Germany had been a leader in powered flight even before World War I; the daring exploits of its pilots and their machines, especially on the Western Front, remain legendary. Although ostensibly prohibited by the Versailles agreements from resuming work in aviation, German firms of the Weimar era produced for civil and military applications alike.[24] Far from being a creation of Adolf Hitler's aggressiveness, in the early 1930s the Luftwaffe was already an impressive force. "By the time the Nazis took power, the plans were drawn, the equipment was in the hands of some units, and the administrative machinery was in place for massive aerial rearmament. The only thing needed was the pretext and the will to act."[25]

Still, Nazi policy would irrevocably affect the German aerospace industry. Taking to heart the observations of the Italian military theorist Giulio Douhet on the importance of offensive air power, Hitler and Hermann Goering (the Nazi leader given primary responsibility for developing Nazi air power) sought to rationalize aeronautics capabilities by grouping subcontractors around major firms such as Junkers (itself nationalized in 1935), which became the flagship of the German industry. As Nazi efforts to attain economic independence (if not autarky) intensified throughout the 1930s, the fascist government exerted increasingly direct control over even nominally independent suppliers until "the division between state and private functions became indistinguishable."[26] Goering's lavishing of resources on the high-profile industry created overcapacity, and even with employment and overall production rising rapidly, jealous and mutually suspicious firms competed for the spoils of an accelerating preparation for war.[27]

Designers and engineers in these well-heeled firms turned their talents to civilian products as well. Despite its almost complete dependence on military contracts, upon entering World War II the German aerospace industry was Europe's largest exporter of aviation products. The pace of German innovation in wing design, jet engines and rocketry accelerated even during the conflict: "Whatever the motives, the productivity of German research during the war must have been higher than that of almost any research conducted anywhere."[28] Wartime production was impressive considering the constant damage done to factories by Allied raids. But neither heroic exertion nor technical excellence could change the ultimate outcome of the war, and valuable German aeronautic research and expertise fell into the hands of the victors, especially the United States. For ten years after 1945, Germany had scant opportunity to engage in such activity.

Consistent with the economic and industrial situation more generally, the aeronautics sector in the FRG began its rise from the ashes as a result of the Cold War division of Europe and Germany itself and the proximity of the Soviet threat. As the Korean conflict stretched American military and aeronautics capabilities to the limit, U.S. leaders turned increasingly to their European allies not only to provide ground troops but also to produce on license military equipment, including aircraft, for use by NATO forces. The sale by Lockheed of the F-104 Starfighter to the Luftwaffe in 1958 (see chapter 1) was of particular importance; even more so than in France, "the West German aerospace industry experienced its resurgence at first with the help of the licensing principle."[29]

In comparison to France and Great Britain, in Germany the process of consolidation in the aeronautics sector began relatively late, yet ultimately it resulted in an even greater degree of industrial concentration. Even well into the mid-1960s, the German aerospace industry remained small in absolute size, broken into numerous competing enterprises and divided regionally. In the north of the country, the major firms were Blohm-Voss and its affiliate Hamburger Flugzebau (HFB), and Vereinigte Flugtechnische Werke (VFW) in Bremen, the latter a product of the 1964 merger of Weser Flugzebau, Heinkel and Focke-Wulf. In the south, Dornier, Siebel, Messerschmitt and the Boelkow group of Munich were the major players. The process of consolidation was given impetus by the German state when on 5 April 1968 the Federal parliament took a formal decision to use public contracts and aid "to induce the enterprises to combine into larger, and thus competitive units."[30] In the south, the results were the merger of Messerschmitt and Boelkow in October of that year, and in May 1969 they were joined by the Blohm-HFB interests to form Messerschmitt-Boelkow-Blohm (MBB) and bring total employment in the new group to around 17,000. In the north, VFW extended its reach westward into the Netherlands in the spring of 1969 by merging with Fokker of Amsterdam to create VFW-Fokker, employing about 20,000, two-thirds of whom were in Germany.[31]

## INTERNATIONAL COLLABORATION AND THE RESTRUCTURING OF THE GERMAN AEROSPACE INDUSTRY

Though regional divisions persisted and firms such as Dornier remained jealously independent, by the early 1970s the German aerospace industry had undergone significant consolidation. But even more so than in Great Britain or even France, international industrial cooperation was used in Germany as a means of regaining both the technical competence and political respectability of the aerospace sector. As described in chapters 2 and 3, German aircraft firms were involved in numerous European collaborative efforts, mostly in the military field. The first of these, the Bréguet 1150 Atlantic ASW Patrol Aircraft, initially was intended to introduce commonality in NATO equipment definition and purchasing, but it fell far short of expectations in this regard.[32]

The Atlantic project was driven almost entirely by the French firm Bréguet, with Henri Ziegler, its managing director, playing a crucial role. For the Germans, the Atlantic provided an opportunity for a few firms to gain technical experience through subcontracting; Dornier and Siebel both worked on the fuselage and tail, while MAN (Maschinenfabrik Augsburg-Nurnberg) received a share of the Rolls-Royce Tyne turboprop engine.[33] But given the leading positions of both Bréguet and the French government, the German role in the Atlantic program was decidedly secondary.

Another collaborative program with the French, the Transall military transport program, provided more opportunity for German industry. Building the French Nord Noratlas troop transport on license had already "occupied nearly the entire capacities of the German northern industrial group" during the mid-1950s, and they were understandably interested in what might replace it.[34] The follow-on Transall program linked Weser and Hamburger with Nord of France, with Weser being granted project leadership.[35] As the Germans were projected to purchase 110 aircraft, a relatively large number, work also was given to both Messerschmitt and Seibel, and all firms involved gained valuable experience from the project.

But doing so entailed substantial and costly trade-offs, the main one being that the aircraft came nowhere near meeting the operational requirements of the Luftwaffe. As described in chapter 3, the design specifications of the French and German air forces for a troop transport were barely compatible, and the Germans had made most of the compromises. Moreover, while the allocation of work shares (decided 24 September 1964) gave German firms a large percentage of total project value, the industrial arrangements made little sense from either a logistical or financial standpoint: "For the purposes of expanding its aerospace capabilities, Germany insisted on a final assembly line at both the two major German firms facilities."[36] With the French not about to allow all production to take place only in Germany, three separate assembly lines were established to produce only 178 aircraft. But while less than optimal, the "political value of the Transall program far outweighed its utility as an efficient and effective acquisition strategy."[37] Both nations, especially Germany, gained valuable industrial experience while furthering the cause of Franco-German cooperation in a crucial sector. The Transall project clearly "demonstrates that the key economic considerations at stake were employment and national aerospace capabilities rather than the exploitation of relative economic advantage or the rational pooling of R&D capabilities."[38] For both the French and the Germans, collaboration, however imperfect in form or content, played a central role in these distinct yet ultimately convergent national strategies.

## CONCLUSION: THE BENEFITS OF CONSTANCY

The German firms involved in the Atlantic and Transall programs were interested in extending their hard-won gains into the civil sphere. Following with interest the Anglo-French discussions for the proposed Airbus, on 23 December 1966 five German companies (Messerschmitt, VFW, Siebel,

Hamburger and Dornier) formed the Arbeitsgemeinschaft Airbus, each having a 20 percent interest of the German share in the design study. Their industrial links were formalized after the signing of the initial Memorandum of Understanding (MoU) between the three nations 27 September 1967, as the five firms formed Deutsche Airbus GmbH, a consortium within the still-informal structure of the Airbus project. As will be seen in chapter 5, the dispute between the British and their prospective Airbus partners concerning the Rolls-Royce RB-207 engine led directly to a much more prominent role for the Germans in the project. Having initially been given only a 25 percent share in the airframe and 12.5 percent of the engine work, following the withdrawal of Great Britain and the signing of the new MoU between France and Germany on 29 May 1969, Deutsche Airbus found itself with a 50 percent stake in a project carrying severe withdrawal penalties. Recognizing both opportunity and danger in the new arrangements, the Germans would pursue two tactics, both designed to prevent complete French dominance of the program.[39] The first would be to help HSA (despite the refusal of British government support) in its effort to remain part of the Airbus project, and the second would be to press for the creation of a collaborative framework that would serve the collective interests of all involved.

Both tactics should be understood as elements of a basic strategy that used international cooperation to realize national industrial and political goals. Later developments would attest to its effectiveness, as the military and civil sectors of the German aerospace industry would continue to consolidate around European programs such as the Tornado and Airbus.[40] And, as we shall see, in serving their own interests, German politicians and industrialists would change the very structure of the European and world aeronautics business.

# 5

## Reconciling National Interests and Commercial Imperatives

*This chapter serves* two purposes: to summarize the preceding analysis and to frame what is to follow; specifically, a detailed examination of the structure and operation of the Airbus Industrie (AI) consortium. The discussion so far has provided background essential to understanding the forces behind both European cooperation in civil aerospace and the creation of Airbus Industrie as the preferred mechanism for industrial collaboration. It has analyzed developments that produced the nearly complete American dominance of the aeronautics industry in the post–World War II period, and outlined the implications of that imbalance for the former Great Powers of Western Europe.

Specifically, it has argued that the dominance of U.S. firms in the postwar market for civil aircraft has its roots in the geopolitics of the era. While the United States fought the Cold War on a number of fronts, from the time of the Berlin Airlift until the fall of the Berlin Wall, an unparalleled aeronautical capacity was at the core of the U.S. response to the Soviet threat. But the nature of aeronautical technologies and industrial processes insured that the massive resources devoted to the sector through the U.S. government's de facto industrial policy would necessarily have an important commercial impact as well. While companies such as Douglas and especially Boeing did indeed take significant commercial risks in creating the jet airliners that have so thoroughly revolutionized modern society, ultimately these firms owed their technological leadership and commanding market position to government funding.

Second, we have seen that European statesmen and industrialists alike perceived the dominance of American firms in aerospace as a threat to political and economic autonomy. But while the inadequate scale of local resources and markets was recognized as the root of European competitive disadvantage, national responses to these facts varied in ways that would be important to both the form and content of future collaborative efforts. We have thus far examined (regarding each eventual major partner country in AI) the historical and institutional factors that shaped the general character of postwar relations between state and industry and showed how these were manifested in the restructuring of the respective aerospace industries in Great Britain, France and Germany. A brief recapitulation of each of these arguments follows.

## GREAT BRITAIN

Postwar economic, industrial and aerospace policies in Great Britain reflected the influence of both historical development and more recent experience. Long the bastion of classical political and economic liberalism, British elites saw inherent virtue in separating the competencies of government and private enterprise, and thus were unwilling to countenance overt and sustained state involvement in the economy. Moreover, victory in World War II, however nominal, further convinced the political and industrial leadership of the essential solidity of British institutions and practices and blinded them to the erosion of Great Britain's position in the global economic and political systems. Finally, Britain was fundamentally ambivalent in its foreign policy orientation and indeed today remains divided on whether to rely on its "special relationship" with the United States or to pursue a "European vocation."

These factors combined to produce British policies inappropriate to the new economic imperatives of the Cold War era. The Treasury's fixation on balance-of-payments equilibrium and maintaining the value of sterling served only to exacerbate the deterioration in relative productivity that was at the root of the persistent British economic and industrial malaise. The ill effects of continued reliance on the "invisible hand" of market forces were compounded by governmental action too erratic and unsystematic to be effective in reshaping the industrial base.

These same trends were quite evident in British aerospace policy, as government contracts were spread over too many projects and too many firms for either to be viable in a now-global competition. The timid and convulsive pattern of consolidation within the industry yielded corporate agglomeration rather than true merger; "rationalization" thus was slow to produce meaningful benefits of scale. Despite the recommendations of the 1965

Plowden Report, collaboration with other European nations foundered on the designs of pet firms such as British Airways and Rolls-Royce, especially the latter, which disdained European projects in seeking the grail of American contracts.

All of these shortcomings would become strikingly evident in the British attitude and behavior toward the Airbus project. A lack of clear government policy toward industrial consolidation and European collaboration alike would allow Rolls-Royce to hold the entire A300 program hostage, precipitating British withdrawal and leaving firms such as Hawker-Siddeley (HSA) to negotiate their own terms with their European counterparts. Only the humiliating financial collapse in 1971 of Europe's premier aero-engine builder would reveal the fundamental bankruptcy of British postwar aerospace policy and begin in earnest the (as yet incomplete) focusing of financial and industrial assets on the real promise of a European solution to the problems of British industry.

## FRANCE

Postwar British policies stand in contrast to those in France, where military defeat and political collapse had provided leaders with an unambiguous mandate to restructure government institutions and economic and industrial practices. But despite the novel means used in creating the *économie concertée*, Jean Monnet's technocrats drew on a deep *dirigiste* tradition in recasting the French economy on a modernized industrial base. Though despising the inherent weakness of the Fourth Republic's political institutions, de Gaulle gladly used the fruits of its economic and technological legacy to assert the independence and grandeur of the France under the Fifth Republic. A reconstructed industrial base underpinned the creation of "national champions" that would represent France in global competition, primarily against American pretensions to economic and political hegemony.

As exemplified in the *force de frappe*, a tightly knit military-industrial complex reliant on exports to lower procurement costs was a crucial element of French resurgence. Aerospace received particular attention, as both Dassault's planes and personage were a major source of prestige and political influence, both within France and abroad. But civil aviation was not neglected, as Dassault's monopoly position in fighter aircraft (after its merger with Bréguet in 1967) eventually was mirrored in commercial ventures, as the numerous French aerospace firms surviving World War II gradually were consolidated through the selective use of government research and procurement funds. With its creation in 1970, Aérospatiale became the only French builder of military transports and helicopters and, following Dassault's brief but disruptive attempt to return to the civil market in the early 1970s, the sole French firm in civil airframe design and production. Already SNECMA had been designated the national instrument in military engine research and construction, and was encouraged in the late 1960s to extend its expertise into civil engine technology.

In addition to an effective policy of state-led industrial rationalization, French aerospace firms, both private and nationalized, had long been involved in collaborative efforts as a means of strengthening national assets and lowering costs. Although reluctant to share combat aircraft development, government-directed participation in troop transport and civil projects was an integral part of efforts to enhance national aerospace capabilities. While Nord had played the leading role in the NorAtlas and Transall collaborative programs, Sud Aviation gradually emerged as the favored French representative in major collaborative efforts such as the Concorde.

Following the 1970 merger of Nord with Sud, Aérospatiale inherited all collaborative obligations, including participation in A300 project. Consistent with the French role in earlier such efforts, Aérospatiale would play a leading role in establishing the consortium. Successfully negotiating that final assembly and flight testing of Airbus aircraft be located in Toulouse, the French would use their participation in AI to make the Haute-Garonne region into a major "technopole," drawing firms from all over France, Europe and the world to service the burgeoning industry. Political and industrial leaders viewed collaboration in European civil aerospace, including France's central role in Airbus Industrie, as an important component of a larger strategy of national resurgence.

## GERMANY

German economic, industrial and aerospace policies share features with their eventual partners in collaboration yet also have characteristics peculiar to the unique situation of Germany in the postwar era. Having, like its counterparts, been a leader in the theory and practice of powered flight, after the defeat of the Third Reich Germany found itself prohibited from having an indigenous aviation capability. Although the ban was later lifted as the increasing scope and intensity of the Cold War necessitated West German rearmament, the aeronautics industry remained fragmented and starved of resources well into the 1950s.

Lacking a base of domestic programs, Germany depended heavily on both licensed production and international collaboration to rebuild its national aeronautical capacities, often accepting a subordinate role because of both political and industrial disabilities. While the Americans, by virtue of their uniquely influential position relative to German political and especially military behavior, supplied most of the early work for German aeronautics firms, cooperation with the French was also a means to demonstrate European credentials and gain expertise. The Noratlas and Transall troop transport projects were the most important of the early Franco-German efforts, but Germany also has played a major political and industrial role in the Tornado fighter aircraft project with the Italians and British, even if the fate of its successor (EFA, or now Eurofighter 2000) is at best uncertain.

Perhaps as important, participation in collaborative efforts drew German firms into closer working relations with one another, thus providing impetus to the gradual yet ultimately quite thorough process of industrial consolidation in aerospace. While quite unlike the dirigiste rationalization across the Rhine, neither was German industrial consolidation in aerospace hampered by British-style reservations concerning the active encouragement of mergers really effective in creating benefits of scale. Rather than direct government intervention, the state used the uniquely German attitudes and practices regarding the regulation of competition and economic concentration to direct the gradual process of grouping major aerospace assets into progressively larger and more efficient units.

Yet in the early 1960s the German aerospace industry was still fragmented into jealously competitive companies and riven by regional divisions. Significantly, it was the firms that cooperated in licensed work and coproduction with the French which would coalesce into larger units that formed VFW, based in Bremen and later linked for a time to the Dutch firm Fokker. Their major competitor, MBB (based in Munich and finally consolidated in 1972), was an amalgamation of companies that also had collaborated formerly. And it was the firms that had participated in the Transall project with Nord of France which formed first the study group and then the working coalition that would become Deutsche Airbus and manage German participation in its largest civil aeronautics project to date. Thus for the Germans, industrial collaboration in general and the Airbus program in particular promised to serve as a ticket of entry into the big leagues of world aviation.

## DISTINCTIVE NATIONAL RATIONALES
## FOR INTERNATIONAL COLLABORATION

Thus, while the eventual national participants in the Airbus project faced fundamentally similar challenges in aeronautics, each brought to a prospective collective European effort in civil aircraft production a distinctive set of political priorities and industrial abilities. For British governments and aerospace firms alike, collaboration with their Continental counterparts had little intrinsic merit to recommend it, especially given their unhappy experience with the Concorde project. Lacking a clear policy regarding industrial restructuring and ambivalent in overall foreign policy orientation, the Heath administration would ignore the findings of the 1965 Plowden Report and enter into the Airbus negotiations with grave reservations concerning their inherent economic or political value. Without a firm commitment or a clear sense of long-term British interests in the venture, the government thus would be easily swung around to the position of by far the most powerful industrial interest involved, Rolls-Royce. Having in 1966 absorbed its only rival in the British aero engine sector, BSE, and able effectively to disregard the views of the as-yet unconsolidated airframers, Rolls-Royce could afford to demand control over engine development for the A300. After assuming what it saw as its rightful position in the European aeronautical hierarchy, Rolls-Royce then would subordinate the project to its more important and pressing transatlantic interests. As we shall see, the result was to create tensions within the collaborative venture that would prove irreconcilable with the continued participation of the British government or Rolls-Royce, leaving the airframer HSA to negotiate its own terms for a role in the Airbus. As a result, for ten years Great Britain would find itself officially distanced from the only European project in civil aeronautics that stood even a remote chance of challenging American mastery of the industry.

For the French, the Airbus program was seen as a vehicle through which to realize complementary objectives of further strengthening national aeronautics capacities while initiating a project that could provide a means for challenging American hegemony in civil aerospace. The necessity of conceding leadership to the British and Rolls-Royce on the A300 engine could be justified on the basis of juste retour that would confer to Sud Aviation control of the airframe and cockpit and thus influence over much of the major subcontracting decisions. In addition to the industrial benefits, support for the collaborative project was seen as solidifying the French position as the driving force behind European technological and economic integration. Therefore, participation in the Airbus program served to realize both French domestic and larger foreign policy interests, and would enjoy consistent support across the political spectrum and especially within the coherent and technocratic administrative elite.

Barely a decade after being fully reintegrated into the Western economic and political systems, the German aerospace industry saw in the Airbus program a chance to take part in a program that could resurrect moribund capacities in the civil sector while allowing the nation's political leadership to further establish its European credentials. Fully cognizant of lingering industrial and political disabilities, neither the German firms nor the government would press for a leading role in the project, remaining content with a subordinate status that would lead eventually to influence in future cooperative programs more accurately reflecting Germany's economic and industrial weight in Europe. Also, the German state would use collaboration through the AI project to further the as-yet incomplete industrial consolidation in the national aerospace sector.

But unlike the French, the German partners in the Airbus program would see not only opportunity but danger in the withdrawal of official British support for the project. While these developments would allow German firms greater industrial participation in the design and production of the aircraft, British participation also had provided an important counterweight to French influence of other collective efforts. In seeking to retain a critical element of industrial and political balance in the Airbus program, therefore, the German state would see the wisdom in supporting financially the efforts of HSA to remain in the program despite the lack of its own government's backing. In this way, Germany would defer short-term industrial and technological gains in hopes of assuring the viability of a truly European collective effort in which its own national political and industrial goals could be effectively realized over the long term.

But while each nation looked to industrial cooperation for its own reasons, a viable collaborative effort would be required not only to reconcile these distinctive national interests and attributes with one another but also to produce an effective response to the technical and commercial challenges posed by American industrial leadership in civil aerospace. With this dynamic as the central focus, the rest of this chapter will examine in detail the early stages of the efforts by the respective national governments and aerospace firms to cooperate in the definition and design of the so-called Airbus. It will highlight the political tensions and industrial rivalries that were so manifestly detrimental to this key phase in the development of the European civil aerospace sector but also show that the failure of the first Airbus project inspired an innovative attempt to reconcile these same tensions and rivalries. Even so, their continued presence would be clearly reflected in the organizational structure and operational procedures of the revamped collaborative effort that emerged at the end of 1970 as Airbus Industrie.

In bringing the analysis up to the point at which Airbus Industrie was created as a legally incorporated entity to manage the collaborative program, we will have identified the main forces and relationships that would condition the consortium's future development. Yet the precise path to be taken from this point forward was far from predetermined, and the process of engaging in effective industrial collaboration would generate unforeseen consequences for everyone involved, most of all for the industrial partners. Indeed, given the inherent unpredictability of the civil aviation industry and the uncertainties inherent in the collaborative process, only over the course of several years would it become apparent that the creation of AI represented a truly novel and effective means of transforming the tensions among the various national interests and daunting commercial imperatives into a potent and creative force.

## RECONCILING NATIONAL INTERESTS AND COMMERCIAL IMPERATIVES: REDEFINING THE AIRBUS

In Europe since the early 1960s there had been ongoing discussion of the need for and possible configuration of a so-called Airbus: a craft that would provide air transportation for large numbers of people (200-300) over short to medium hauls (800-1,200 nautical miles). Design studies were conducted with the relatively short distances between the urban populations of Europe in mind, and the whole concept evoked moving masses of people at low cost with few frills.[1]

The French and British governments had set up a joint committee in early 1965 to evaluate the commercial prospects of such an aircraft, but it established no design specifications or formalized working procedures. French and British aviation firms also took an active interest in these discussions of configuration, range and cost, and produced a number of interesting if not completely practical designs, both separately and in conjunction with one another.[2] Parallel with the industrialists, in October 1965 the major European airlines also had conferred on these requirements, and their proposals converged around the jumbo-twin, an aircraft having two engines and two aisles, an as-yet untried configuration.[3] These early Anglo-French discussions also drew the interest of the Germans; at the Paris air show in July of 1965, seven firms formed Studiengruppe Airbus to discuss design specifications with their French counterparts.[4] On 23 December 1965 it was converted into Arbeitsgemeinschaft (Arge) Airbus, which became the German partner in the A300 project.[5]

Eventually the discussions among airlines and the aeronautics industry became serious enough for the respective governments to become directly involved by selecting national firms to participate in formal negotiations. The most important aspect of this involvement was that the selection of firms for collaboration on the proposed Airbus "obeyed, in each country, strictly national considerations."[6] In fact, the French and British choices of representatives almost seemed calculated to disrupt existing cross-border working relationships. Specifically, in May 1966 HSA found itself paired with Sud, although the British firm already had been working with both Bréguet and Nord in designing the HBN-100, a design that closely resembled the eventual Airbus A300.[7] For its part, Sud was already the French partner in the Concorde project along with British Aircraft Corporation (BAC), and now it had to establish working relations with a completely new partner during 1966.[8]

September 1966 saw the first meeting at the board level for the companies selected, and on 15 October they presented a formal request for funds to the three national governments, along with the first brochure describing the A300. On 9 May 1967, the first meeting at the ministerial level took place,[9] at which research and development costs were estimated and work shares discussed. A follow-up meeting on 25 July (with French transport minister Jean Chamant taking Andre Bettencourt's place) became the basis for the formal Memorandum of Understanding (MoU) signed 26 September 1967. Although the MoU "did not authorize a final go-ahead for an A300 development program," it did stipulate that a final design of the A300 be specified by July 1968, after which a prototype phase could begin.[10]

The MoU specified how work was to be shared among the member countries, and the division of labor and responsibility reflected a predictable and well-worn approach to such collaborative projects. Since HSA would work entirely on the wing of the aircraft, the British were effectively conceding to the French the leading role on the fuselage and cockpit, with these latter responsibilities providing especially important work in overall systems integration. In return, the British would have almost complete control of the engine project. Specifically, on the airframe the MoU designated: Great Britain, 37.5 percent; France, 37.5 percent; and Germany, 25 percent. On the engine Rolls-

Royce would have 75 percent of the work and subcontract about 12.5 percent each to the French and German partners, SNECMA and MAN.

Again, this arrangement was typical of past collaborative efforts. The French almost always had sought control of the airframe, and "when a cooperative project was envisaged, the primary concern of the British representatives seemed to be assuring leadership for Rolls-Royce on the engine."[11] Also consistent with past practice, in both facets of the program the Germans were left with only a supporting role. While unable reasonably to expect more, the members of Arge Airbus nonetheless used the impetus of the negotiations to further formalize their working relationship, and formed Deutsche Airbus GmbH in 1967.[12]

Reflecting the divergence in national priorities, division between the British and their partners concerning the choice of engines for the aircraft was already evident by the time the initial MoU was signed. Since the early stages of project definition, both the French and Germans had argued that the A300 should be powered by Pratt and Whitney (P&W) JT9D engines, developed for and recently ordered by Boeing for its new 747. For the French, having SNECMA, which was already partly owned by and tooled to P&W specifications, build the JT9D on license would provide valuable engineering expertise, while the Germans wanted the A300 to have engine commonality with Lufthansa's substantial fleet of Boeings. Typically, the British were far from agreement, even among themselves; the "other" British engine builder, Bristol-Siddeley Engines (BSE), hoped to act as an important subcontractor to P&W and SNECMA on the JT9D. But Rolls-Royce successfully resisted these proposals and, in a bold move, bought out BSE in September 1966, thus removing any domestic industrial resistance to its plan to be the prime engine contractor on the Airbus.[13] So despite the concerns of the other partners, "the RB-207 was chosen for the Airbus not because it was the best choice economically, commercially, or technologically, but because its choice had become prerequisite to British participation."[14]

Allowing Rolls-Royce to offer an as-yet untested engine for the A300 added substantial risk to the project. The technical obstacles raised were compounded by Rolls-Royce's desire—especially keen since its RB-178 was rejected as the power plant for the 747—to penetrate the American market with a new engine designed to fit the proposed tri-jets, even while retaining control of the European project as well. Realizing that the RB-207 (proposed for A300) would be too large for the American application, Rolls-Royce approached the British government for launch aid on a smaller and even more experimental model, the

RB-211. Contingent on an American order, a figure of £40 million was agreed upon. Rolls-Royce spared no effort in competition with the established U.S. builders and shocked the aviation world by eventually signing with Lockheed in March 1968 to place the RB-211 on the L-1011.[15]

The transatlantic ambitions of Rolls-Royce were to prove an insurmountable obstacle to maintaining British participation in the A300. Rolls-Royce now had two new engines to develop, and it soon became clear where its priorities lay; "almost overnight David Huddie and his team at Derby pushed the European Airbus into their No 2 spot."[16] But Rolls-Royce would encounter no political resistance in doing so, since "the British government so valued Rolls-Royce as a national technological and economic asset that it quickly adopted the company's technological and financial goals as its own."[17]

Further alienating British governmental support for the Airbus project was the fact that over the months since its first definition, the aircraft had "grown" substantially in projected size and capacity, while Rolls-Royce blithely continued to promise whatever thrust necessary. The aircraft's commercial viability was now seriously in question: "Because industrial and political considerations had played a more important role in shaping the A300 than airline requirements, most European carriers were dissatisfied with the proposed aircraft's specifications."[18] As a result, the A300 was fast approaching the "go, no-go" decision date of July 1968 without a single firm order, and it looked as if Rolls-Royce and the British government might be spared the hard choice between their American and European vocations.

## Redefining the Airbus: From the A300 to the A300B

Thus there was by mid-1968 deep and mutual suspicion on the part of the A300's airframe designers and engine builder alike concerning each partner's ability to deliver its portion of the aircraft as promised.[19] The resulting impasse proved a crucial turning point in the history of the collaborative program, because it marked the beginning of the gradual ascendance of technical and commercial criteria in the development of what had been heretofore primarily a political aircraft. Realizing that the entire project was in real danger of collapsing, Henri Ziegler, appointed head of Sud in July 1968,[20] convinced the French government to grant the A300 program a three-month window of time within which to render itself commercially credible.[21] Around Roger Beteille and Felix Kracht (a German aerospace engineer who spent most of his career at Nord Aviation in France), Ziegler gathered a small team to secretly redesign the aircraft.[22]

What emerged in December of 1968 was a 250-seat plane with a smaller fuselage, weighing much less than its predecessor, and now called the A300B.[23] But the most important feature of the new plane was that the Rolls-Royce RB-207 no longer would be the sole engine offered; the A300B really was designed around existing American engines: P&W's JT9D and General Electric's CF6. This was the first clear instance of commercial considerations holding sway over national industrial interests in the definition of the Airbus.

The program managers' initiatives placed the British government in an awkward position. On the one hand, the design changes actually addressed two of its primary complaints about the aircraft: rising costs (due in large part to the development of a new engine) and a lack of marketability. But since both the RB-207 and the RB-211 were experiencing serious performance problems and big cost overruns, the British position in the European project was now increasingly untenable if not fatally compromised. Clearly, an American engine would power the aircraft if it were to have any hope of flying by 1972 as promised. "The alternative was thus between pursuit of the program while renouncing the exclusivity of Rolls-Royce, or retreat pure and simple."[24]

The likelihood of a British decision to withdraw from the project had been increased by recent events in both the diplomatic and industrial arena. The French already had unilaterally and summarily pulled out of from the Anglo-French AFVG project in June 1967, while the infamous Concorde continued to produce nothing but red ink and ridicule. Adding insult to injury, at the end of that same year de Gaulle had for a second time rejected Britain's application for membership in the EEC, a move that provoked ire in political and industrial quarters throughout Britain. So while not a foregone conclusion, few were surprised when Prime Minister Wilson's Labour government chose to interpret the proposed design changes to the Airbus A300 as an abrogation of the original 1967 MoU. Despite representations at the highest political level to resolve the issue—FRG Chancellor Kurt Kiesinger and Wilson met in Bonn February 1969—Great Britain officially pulled out of the A300 program 10 April 1969.

## THE A300B: A DEMONSTRATION
### OF FRANCO-GERMAN RESOLVE

At this point it was widely assumed that the Airbus program would simply collapse; there were no orders for the aircraft, and one of the two leading governmental partners had just withdrawn its political and financial support. But even while seeking constantly to retain full British participation, the French and Germans already had determined to press on together. Time was of the essence,[25] however, and a new agreement was negotiated in less than two months. At the opening of the Paris air show on 29 May 1969, ministers Chamant and Schiller signed for their respective governments a new MoU, "for the first time taking them into the great and exciting area of big money and real risk."[26]

The new MoU agreed that the governments would allow the industrial partners to identify solutions to technical problems without undue interference, while the project engineers were to employ designs and components providing maximum congruity with airline preferences, thus minimizing costs and development delays. This meant the use of standard technology and proven off-the-shelf systems where possible, and numerous American components were used for speed and simplicity. The most important of these components was of course the GE-CF6 engine, but the A300B also shared numerous other systems with its competitors.[27] So, beyond defining a more modest project, "the new document represented a fundamental change in approach in that it stressed cost, commercial, and market factors above other considerations."[28]

In view of the difficulties and uncertainties created by the recent British withdrawal, the MoU bound both governments to fund the project to completion, even should the industrial partners default. The agreement also formalized working relations, both between the governments and among the firms, but stopped far short of creating a single entity to manage the project. Rather, an intergovernmental committee was to approve proposals and arbitrate disputes at the industrial level, while an executive committee would implement its findings through existing governmental channels. While foreseeing the eventual establishment of a genuinely mutual decisionmaking structure, the French partner was assigned the leading industrial role: "The Executive Agency would place contracts with Sud, which in turn would contract with Deutsche Airbus."[29]

The Germans could accept the new situation because they recognized that the A300B still provided them with "a unique chance to reestablish a foothold in civil aviation."[30] But neither German firms nor government was prepared to concede the removal of what both considered a vital British role in the project. For the German industrial partners, the withdrawal of British political support for the Airbus was a mixed blessing: It offered a chance to increase their share of the A300B project while removing an important counterweight to traditional French leadership, indeed domination, of such cooperative ventures.

Well aware of HSA's bitter reluctance to accept the British pull-out, "the German government decided—and this is a measure of its will to push the project through—to share in the expenses of the development of the wing, thus substituting itself for the British government."[31] In this way the Germans maintained valuable British engineering and industrial contact with the Airbus while they hoped for an eventual reconsideration by the British government. While no such reconsideration was forthcoming, as a measure of its own commitment to the A300B, Hawker-Siddeley agreed (at the same 1969 Paris air show) to provide about $30 million of its own funds to act as a private subcontractor in providing wing-boxes for the prototype aircraft and to continue work on wing development.[32]

Therefore, while the signing of the accords 29 May 1969 brought together industrialists from three European nations—Henri Ziegler for Sud of France, Bernhardt Weinhardt of Deutsche Airbus, and Sir Arnold Hall (with Sir John Lidbury) from Britain's HSA—only two of the national governments remained committed. This situation, while seemingly anomalous, actually reflected quite accurately the distinctive positions of the national governments and industrial partners relative to European industrial collaboration in general and to the Airbus project in particular.[33] Britain's posture manifested, as little else could, its fundamental ambivalence toward its Atlanticist versus European vocations. With government support, Rolls-Royce had been encouraged to pursue both American and European business simultaneously and had finally proved unable to deliver on either. While the difficulties of Rolls-Royce and the withdrawal of official participation were arguably of ultimate benefit to the Airbus project, British inconstancy (or duplicity) had at least temporarily placed it in serious jeopardy. Absent HSA's commitment and the backing of the German government, development of the all-important wing for the A300B certainly would have been delayed if not completely grounded.

In contrast, consistent French political support for and industrial commitment to a truly European response to the American challenge in civil aerospace was translated into project leadership on the Airbus A300B. Through this role, the technocratic French elite planned to use cooperation as a means for strengthening the position of the nation's aerospace industry relative not only to its superpower rival but to its European collaborators as well. In this light, the failed gambit of Rolls-Royce was a boon because it allowed France to retain leadership on the airframe, even as SNECMA could now gain valuable expertise through its own collaboration with the U.S. engine builder General Electric (GE).

The German role in the new Airbus program of 1969 reflected both its national political and industrial objectives in aerospace at the time and substantial disabilities that still thwarted their attainment in full. Seeking a means through which to gain technical expertise for domestic firms while enhancing its own reputation as a responsible and committed European, the German state proved itself willing to do much more than its fair share in the Airbus project. By financially supporting the participation of HSA, its valuable engineering expertise was retained and at least a partial British role in the A300B was in addition preserved; this support also provided an important counterweight to possible (or likely) French dominance of the program. Indeed, the Germans would seek to build further protection against this possibility into the very structure of the collaborative arrangements.

## DEFINING AIRBUS INDUSTRIE:
## THE GIE AS A COMPROMISE SOLUTION

The situation regarding international collaboration on the Airbus project had been substantially clarified, if not simplified, by the end of 1969. Although complex, the new arrangements had removed the main source of tension within the multilateral effort–the fundamental ambivalence of both the British government and that country's most important aerospace firm, Rolls-Royce, regarding the project. But while the May 1969 MoU had reaffirmed the commitment of all parties involved, it still remained for France and Germany to establish a mutually satisfactory structure to manage the collaborative effort. Existing arrangements provided simply for industrial coordination, with Sud as project leader. The only entity representing the project to the rest of the world was "Airbus International," a small organ set up in the 1969 MoU. Authorized only "to quote firm prices and delivery schedules to clients," it was "for the moment only a sales office."[34]

For the French, the existing arrangements were nearly acceptable. Given their leading position, they wanted no more than a skeletal oversight body. But as now equal partners–actually a bit more than equal in terms of their actual financial contribution–"it was clear that the Germans did not have the intention of playing a secondary role indefinitely . . . and saw a strong organ as the only means to protect their influence in the program."[35] The negotiation of these arrangements was further complicated by the advent of Dutch participation in the Airbus program. Spurred by the merger in May of 1969 of VFW and Fokker of Amsterdam, the Dutch government ultimately agreed to contribute 6.6 percent of A300B development costs in exchange for work on wing slats and flaps being transferred to Holland.[36]

Long and sometimes difficult negotiations resulted in the creation 18 December 1970 under French law of a corporate entity known as a Groupement d'Intérêt Économique (GIE), which would be called Airbus Industrie.[37] Despite British and Dutch industrial participation, its only shareholders were Aérospatiale and Deutsche Airbus (now comprised of VFW and the MBB grouping, Dornier having dropped out), with HSA and Fokker acting only as risk-sharing subcontractors.[38] The new entity was to serve three primary functions: (1) provide a single interface with clients, arranging commercial terms, payment and service; (2) assure technical and industrial coordination, including product definition and work-sharing; and (3) conduct flight-testing. Although all were important aspects, the first of these would prove especially significant. As we shall see in Part II, by delegating commercial responsibilities to the GIE, the partners had placed between themselves and the market an entity that could effectively perform its assigned responsibilities only by exercising a degree of autonomy not imagined by the partners or, indeed, by the GIE itself.

So although not yet apparent, the creation of Airbus Industrie as a GIE would insure that "the accord marked the end of a certain type of industrial collaboration, in which one of the partners would necessarily exercise leadership of the program."[39] We have seen that this transformation had already begun during the dispute over the RB-207 that resulted in a redesigned aircraft and British withdrawal from the project. The way in which the A300 was redefined—in its overall configuration and especially the choice of engines—reflected the ascendance of commercial or market considerations over political ones, or the beginning of what has been called the displacement of the "logic of the arsenal by the logic of the market."[40] In this view, the early stages of the A300 program had represented "the consecration of the logic of the arsenal, since the aircraft and engine builders were both chosen according to a rationale that was fundamentally political."[41] But the industrial partner's acceptance on 10 December 1968 of Ziegler's redesigned aircraft began the inversion of this logic and the assertion of commercial over political concerns within the nascent organization. The use of standard components, especially the GE CF6-50 engines, showed that technical and market criteria had become the litmus test for product definition.

## CONCLUSION

As described in the introduction, the point of this study is to examine not only why Airbus Industrie was launched as a collaborative European effort in civil aviation, but also to learn how it eventually became a successful challenger to American dominance of this crucial market. The preceding analysis has attempted to show that these two questions are actually quite closely linked; AI was not simply formed and then put into motion with an inherent ability to generate results that would satisfy the demands of the industrial partners, the respective national governments, or its customers, the airlines. Rather, the consortium as an effective mechanism of cooperation emerged as a response that sought to reconcile the less than congruent demands of states and industrial firms with the technical and commercial dictates of the market.

Therefore, the initial agreements, the redefinition of the aircraft, the Rolls-Royce debacle and withdrawal official British support, the creation of the GIE—all of these events can be understood as parts of an ongoing attempt to resolve the conflicts inherent in the situation confronting the Europeans. In attempting to find common ground between distinct national interests and then reconcile these with the imperatives of the market, the European partners created a mechanism of collaboration that necessarily embodied the tensions among these forces.

As the subsequent analysis will show, the attempt to achieve an effective resolution of these tensions continues today as the consortium seeks to attain goals that are not always compatible: meeting the aspirations of the industrial partners, convincing the respective national governments to continue funding projects, bringing viable products to market and responding to critics demanding greater transparency and accountability in its operations. What makes Airbus Industrie most worthy of investigation is that it has been much more effective in doing so than other international cooperative efforts and that its success has altered the very structure of an industry crucial to the economic and military dimensions of national security.

# Part II

THE STRUCTURE AND OPERATION OF
AIRBUS INDUSTRIE

# 6

## THE FORMATION OF AIRBUS INDUSTRIE
## AND THE A300B (1970–1978)

*The first part* of this study concluded that the partners in the Airbus venture would have to be innovative on two fronts: first in offering a commercially attractive product and also in building a mechanism of industrial collaboration that would effectively combine the talents of the members while achieving their separate industrial objectives. No cooperative European effort in civil aviation had yet been able to effectively blend market imperatives and distinctive national interests, and the formation and subsequent development of Airbus Industrie was a unique experiment in integrating the two.

This part will describe and analyze the technological, organizational and commercial innovations undertaken by the Airbus partners that have proven effective in gaining market share while providing economic benefits to both the participating firms and member governments. The discussion will examine the most relevant aspects (product development, sales patterns, changes in membership or organizational structure) of AI's activities during specified periods. It will be broken into four chapters, each dealing with an important phase in the history of the consortium and emphasizing throughout how the interaction of commercial necessity and the interests of the partners continues to manifest itself in the structure, operation and market strategy of the consortium. The conclusion, chapter 9, addresses the theoretical and policy implications of Airbus Industrie as an example of international collaboration in a high-technology, strategic global industry.

This chapter will examine the process by which the partners in the Airbus project undertook the closely related tasks of developing their first product and creating the organizational structure that would assure its technical and commercial viability. It will cover the eventful period from 1970 to 1978, which saw the successful development, testing and certification of the A300B, intensive but quite disappointing early efforts to market the new plane, important commercial success (even in the tough American market) and British re-entry into the Airbus Industrie consortium on the A310 program.

In bringing its first product from the drawing board to the tarmac, the partners in the A300B project would adopt a strategy that was technologically conservative yet quite innovative from both an organizational and commercial standpoint. The technical conservatism stemmed from two related concerns. First, Roger Beteille, Felix Kracht and others close to the real problems of aircraft design and production recognized that the use of standard components, especially complex and expensive ones such as engines, nacelles and auxiliary power units (APUs), would greatly reduce the complexity of the task before them. By keeping the aircraft relatively simple, its designers and builders stood a much better chance of actually bringing a viable product to market within a reasonable time at an acceptable cost. Second, it was recognized that airlines would be much more likely to adopt the products of an untested manufacturer if the aircraft shared important characteristics with existing ones, some of which might be in their own fleets.

In contrast to these compelling rationales for pursuing a conservative technical strategy were features inherent in the situation facing the Airbus partners that also required important innovations be undertaken. First, there could be little hope of penetrating the market for large civil aircraft if the new product offered nothing whatever to distinguish it from what was already available. Clearly, to be commercially attractive a new aircraft would have to promise prospective operators some economic advantage. Second, delivering what was offered to customers would be even more problematic since no mechanism for collaboration yet existed that could be guaranteed to produce an aircraft on time and at cost. Nor could an airline be expected to purchase such a major capital good from a business concern that could not credibly promise to stand behind its product for many years to come. Such an organization would have to be created and maintained for a novel commercial strategy to bear fruit.

## CREATING AIRBUS INDUSTRIE

It was widely expected in European aeronautical and industrial circles that British withdrawal in April 1969 from the A300 program would mean the collapse of the entire Airbus enterprise. But the remaining industrial participants, along with the French and German governments, realized that "abandoning the project would have marked the end of European pretensions of remaining in the first rank of aircraft manufacturers."[1] Still, the real difficulties lay ahead, for the firms and governments had to translate technical expertise and political will into a marketable product supported by a viable industrial and commercial organization, something no European collaborative project in civil aeronautics had come close to achieving.

The 29 May 1969 agreement[2] took important steps toward establishing a much more explicit and systematic set of arrangements than had been envisioned at the outset of the Airbus project; "the cooperation accords signed at the interstate level were much more elaborated than those signed in the preceding era with England."[3] The interfirm agreements also were much more formal and specific, yet they left important and difficult work undone. The partners still had to agree on a collective management structure for the project. In so doing, the national governments and partner firms would be venturing beyond mere cooperation in developing and producing an aircraft. Rather, they would be entering the realm of true collaboration, which "also entails joint financing, marketing and work sharing arrangements and thus the creation of some form of transnational decision-making and administrative structure."[4]

Both its scale and degree of development would set this new structure apart from prior collaborative efforts, even those heretofore governing the A300 and A300B projects. For example, management of the Concorde project had been completely bilateral, with no organization beyond that required to coordinate what remained essentially two distinct national programs.[5] Similarly, the 1967 arrangements for the A300 designated separate project leaders on the engine (Rolls-Royce) and airframe (Sud) portions of the program, with no provision for overall management. And even the May 1969 A300B accords stopped short of creating a truly autonomous entity for program management; the emphasis still was on the coordination of complementary efforts. The main difference was that the 1969 accord granted Sud temporary project leadership, but stipulated that this "would be transferred as quickly as possible to a common organ to be created by Sud-Aviation and Deutsche Airbus."[6]

Since the task of defining precisely this new mechanism of collaboration involved reconciling the divergent objectives, capabilities and characteristics of the actors involved, the process was protracted and difficult. Beyond delineating interfirm relationships and responsibilities, the organization also would have to present a credible face to potential customers understandably wary of entering into expensive and long-term business relations with an unfamiliar entity. Thus, the heart of the problem was for the partners to define their mutual rights and responsibilities in such a way as to inspire confidence; they spent the 18 months following the signing of the May 1969 agreement in determining the exact nature of their obligations toward one another as well as toward third parties. During the negotiations, it became quite apparent that these issues actually were quite closely linked. The most immediate problem to be resolved by the members "was the extent of the financial responsibility of the future organization vis-à-vis the client airlines and the private credit institutions who would be called upon to finance the production of the A300B."[7] Defining the precise form of interfirm relationships was crucial in this regard, and the ensuing debate reflected the divergence in the background and very nature of the two industrial partners. For their part, the German firms comprising Deutsche Airbus envisaged endowing the new entity with capital of around DM100 million and limiting their collective liability to that sum. In contrast, Aérospatiale insisted that both the German and French members be liable up to the entirety of their resources, in order to demonstrate that the new entity "was resolutely engaged in realizing the project."[8]

This contrast in perspectives stemmed from the differences in fundamental characteristics of the partners themselves, differences that in turn were rooted in the divergent experiences of the two national aeronautics sectors in the postwar period. Deutsche Airbus was a grouping of independent firms that, although recipients of governmental support, were still for the most part privately owned and thus reliant upon bank lending and equity markets for financial resources. Having agreed to cooperate on the Airbus project, they now were faced with the prospect of risking their futures on an uncertain technical and commercial bet.[9] On the other hand, Aérospatiale had been forged by the French state by merging already nationalized firms into a true national champion ready to represent the nation in the global arena. It was owned by the French government and thus could rely on the full backing of the state in its undertakings.

Given the important disparities in the stature of the respective national industries and partner firms, it is not surprising that the legal and financial attributes of the new organization created to manage the A300B project were closer to the French view than the German. Indeed, Airbus Industrie was formed under French law as a Groupement d'Intérêt Économique (GIE),[10] a form of business organization that "permits participating firms to integrate their activities in certain domains while preserving their individual identities, and without resorting to such an extreme process as merger."[11] In this sense, a GIE is an unlimited partnership in which the partners are corporations. But even though the partners remain separate corporate entities, they are responsible both individually and collectively regarding obligations incurred through their shared business venture. This is because the GIE formulation specifies (as the French had required) that all partners are jointly and severally liable, up to the full extent of their resources and worth, to third parties with whom the GIE becomes contractually obligated.

Besides the unlimited liability incurred by distinct corporate entities that are combining their resources for a specific and delimited purposes, as a form of business organization the GIE has several other features that bear directly upon its relationship to the partners in performing its assigned task. First, a GIE might have no proprietary capital of its own; in such cases its creation "thus does not entail the immobilization of partner's funds."[12] Also, a GIE does not itself incur tax liability; costs, revenues, losses and profits flow through to the members, and any taxable consequences are borne by them under the laws of the state in which they themselves are incorporated. Moreover, the industrial and financial results of GIE activity are considered as an integral part of partners' overall business activities and need not be accounted for or reported separately. These flexible arrangements are well suited to international ventures in which firms not interested in merger wish to coordinate activities with others while avoiding the sunk costs and tax consequences of an incorporated joint venture.

The statutes and internal regulations governing the formation on 18 December 1970 of Airbus Industrie as a GIE[13] specified that it was created to undertake the development, production, sales and support of the A300B. With its seat in Paris, AI would be owned in equal parts by the two partners, Aérospatiale and Deutsche Airbus, and have no capital of its own. Each partner assumed unlimited liability relative to the project, and neither could withdraw unilaterally prior to its complete realization.[14] While the GIE could accept new members, they would be admitted only with the express consent of both partners.

The December 1970 accords also established an organizational structure for AI intended to provide effective oversight of all phases of the project. At the same time, it would deal directly and exclusively with third parties, such as customers and major subcontractors. In addition, not only would the new organization have to sell aircraft, it also had to be able to provide pilot and crew training, insure the availability of spare parts and develop maintenance procedures and literature—in short, it was responsible for all aspects of product support. Yet beyond addressing commercial concerns, in its very structure the new entity also would have to defer to political reality by guaranteeing to each of the national partners important positions whose authority was to an important extent independent of the other's. In this way, both market imperatives and political considerations would find institutional expression in the collaborative arrangements.

Atop the hierarchy of AI was the Assembly of Members (see Article 15 of the statutes), consisting of at most two representatives from each industrial partner, and its vote was required on important matters such as modifications of the statutes of the GIE, the admission of new members or the anticipated liquidation of the venture. But more important for the actual functioning of the consortium was the creation of the Supervisory Council (see articles 19 to 21 of the statutes), consisting of five members from each of the two partners, appointed for five years each. Also, because of their importance as subcontractors, representatives of Hawker-Siddeley and Fokker were allowed to participate in meetings, but only with consultative, nonvoting voices. The council would appoint a president and vice-president, each for five-year periods, but the Germans were in effect given the dominant role since the first president of the Supervisory Council was Franz Joseph Strauss, a towering figure in Bavarian and national politics and patron of the aerospace industry in Germany, a position he held until his death in 1987.

But the Supervisory Council was created to do precisely that, supervise, and thus was given no means of achieving its objectives or implementing its decisions. Therefore, the Assembly of Members also appointed for a period of five years a managing director, who was "to have the powers necessary" to carry out the objectives of the GIE effectively (Article 19, Item 1). He was to attend the meetings of the Supervisory Council and then take measures to see that its directives were realized. In order to insure that the director's powers flowed directly from the partners and not from the Supervisory Council itself, two important provisions were included. First, the statutes expressly provided for his removal by the Assembly of Members in extremis (Article 18, Item 3), and they also stated that the director could not be a member of the Supervisory Council (Article 19, Item 3).

In addition to giving the managing director an important measure of autonomy relative to the Supervisory Council, the statutes also insured that his authority would extend directly into the internal workings of the consortium. In discharging his executive functions, he was to have under his authority the four major functional areas of operation: technical, production, administration and finances, and marketing and after-sales service. Directors for each area of responsibility were designated (with the approval of the Supervisory Council), and one of these would be charged with coordinating their efforts.[15] Then, in further codifying a balance of national power within Airbus Industrie, the internal regulations[16] specified that the managing director was to be a representative of Aérospatiale. Henri Ziegler (formerly of Bréguet and then Sud) was elected by the Assembly of Members to the post in December 1970.

In creating this elaborate organizational structure to oversee their collaborative effort, the partners had hoped to set up a system whereby their technological and industrial objectives could be realized through success in the commercial realm. Therefore, a new entity had been created that would go beyond mere bilateral coordination of complementary but distinct national efforts and would be instead a mechanism of true collaboration. But this structure also had to reflect the importance of national concerns and sensibilities and to insure that the effective authority created was shared between the partners. Thus, power was divided between the Supervisory Council and the managing director, making each reliant on the other for its actual exercise. "The advantage of such a system is that it institutes real cooperation; the inconvenience, paralysis of the GIE in the case of disagreement between the managing director and supervisory council."[17]

Anticipating the potential for gridlock inherent in any situation in which authority is so divided, the statutes and internal regulations also included explicit provisions for resolving differences among the partners (Article 25). Not only were specific procedures and timetables for their implementation laid out, the statutes also foresaw the appointment of an outside arbitrator if the parties failed to reach agreement after a specified period. The findings of this arbitrator would be taken as final and binding upon the partners. These provisions, especially taken together with the other organizational aspects just outlined, reflect the care taken by the partners to define relations among themselves and with third parties so as to establish the commercial credibility of the consortium. The governments and member firms alike sought to establish AI as a viable new player in a hotly contested strategic game; therefore, "the importance attached to the continuity of the program is one of the principal characteristics of the Statutes and Internal Regulations."[18] But proof of the new organization's real capability and significance would ultimately be measured in the technical and commercial success of its product, which had not yet seen the light of day.

## CREATING THE AIRBUS

Even as negotiations among the governments and partners concerning the formation of AI as a GIE were making their slow progress, the project engineers were continuing to define the A300B and to develop a system for its testing and production. British withdrawal had greatly simplified these matters and accelerated the pace at which commercial considerations began to take clear precedence over political ones in designing the aircraft. Definition proceeded rapidly on the basis of the December 1968 proposals made by Beteille and his cadre of engineers. From a technical standpoint, there was an "unquestionably beneficial result of British withdrawal at the government level: it eliminated British Ministry influence on the design."[19]

So after the French and Germans agreed to press on in December 1970, the newly formed consortium could concern itself with developing and marketing the A300B, and actually it adhered quite closely to the schedule laid out in the original 1967 MoU. Although as many as nine variants of the A300B were considered, two basic designs, the B2 and the B4, were settled on by 1971. Though differing slightly in their dimensions and carrying capacity, both versions of the wide-body, twin-aisle aircraft could carry 260 to 290 passengers over about 1,200 nautical miles.[20] Prototype development and flight testing went forward with the GE CF6 engines.[21]

As major subcontractors, HSA was given responsibility for the wing-box, while Fokker-VFW[22] took the wing's moving surfaces, with the wings then being assembled and outfitted by MBB (by then the other major firm in Deutsche Airbus) in Germany. Deutsche Airbus also was given most of the work on the forward and rear fuselage, including fitting out the interior of the cabin, along with the vertical tailfin and its rudder. CASA of Spain[23] took the horizontal tailplane, the forward passenger doors and the landing-gear doors. Aérospatiale was given responsibility for the nose and cockpit, the section of the center fuselage above the wing and the engine pylons, and would handle final assembly of the aircraft.

The first A300B fuselage was assembled in September 1971, and in November the first pair of wings was shipped from Britain to Toulouse.[24] The landing gear was attached in January 1972, the engines hung in April, and systems testing progressed throughout the year. First rollout of the A300B was on 28 September 1972 (face-to-face with a Concorde at Toulouse),[25] and the first flight was one month later, on 28 October 1972. Additional airframes were constructed for both static and flight testing, with the first two production-type aircraft being flown in June and November 1973, respectively. Completion of the 1,580-hour test program culminated in French and German airworthiness certification on 15 March 1974. United States Federal Aviation Administration (FAA) approval followed on 30 May 1974, with Air France having already flown its first A300 service on the Paris-London route on 23 May 1974. "The technical bet was thus won. Airbus Industrie had proven the industrial and technical feasibility of the program."[26]

The remarkable smoothness of the aircraft definition, flight testing and certification process was ample evidence of the technical ability of the engineers and flight crews. But it also showed that commercial imperatives had been incorporated not only into the design of the aircraft itself,[27] but built into the very structure and operation of the collaborative effort. Indeed, the high-profile political turmoil during the early stages of the project had masked ongoing developments of real significance at the organizational level, where Roger Beteille and Felix Kracht had painstakingly been using marketlike incentives to elicit "on-time and on-cost" performance from the partners. For Beteille and Kracht, "the principal idea from the beginning and which remains the basis of the industrial organization is that each participant is completely responsible for the element they must construct. . . ."[28] Their system was (and remains) based on the integration of large subassemblies that are worked to near completion by each partner and then transported to Toulouse in huge transport aircraft for final assembly.[29] "Stuffing" the components as fully as possible with the necessary wiring, tubing and other parts before sending them on to the next phase of production minimizes shipping costs and insures that final assembly represents only 4 percent of the total man-hours involved in building the aircraft.[30]

The practical effect of adopting such a system has been to place the same firms that own Airbus Industrie in the paradoxical position of being subcontractors to an organization of their own creation. Within the limits of the rather broad work shares just described, each firm is required to specify the precise content of its portion and to quote prices and delivery schedules for those components. As will be explained in greater detail later, arriving at these specifications is a matter for prolonged and intensive deliberation among the partners, as each seeks to define and price its share of the work in a way most favorable to itself.

In this system, Airbus Industrie (the GIE) acts as moderator and sometimes as arbitrator; the end result is a detailed set of agreements among the partners and AI that are promises by each to fulfill their specific obligations related to the development, production and sale of the aircraft in exchange for a designated compensation. In effect, the GIE acts as general contractor and "buys" components from the members with the proceeds of sales: "The 'prices' charged by the partners provide the basis of an invoicing system linking Airbus Industrie to its contractor-owners."[31] AI keeps a meticulous set of accounts for itself and each of the partners, which track the delivery of components and the disbursal of funds. Invoices are reconciled every ten days, and monies then are either allocated to or requested from the partners. Approximately 70 percent of all revenues flow through to the partners, with the balance going to the purchase of large items sourced from outside (such as engines and nacelles, auxiliary power units) and any overhead expenses. "At the end of the financial year, Airbus Industrie divides a profit or loss according to the member's share of Airbus Industrie."[32]

It is important to remember, however, that the partners producing the subassemblies "are not subsidiaries or divisions of an integrated company to be cut or expanded according to demand, but remain discrete components of an international consortium."[33] While having a collective interest in controlling overall program costs, they are concerned primarily with their own profitability. An obvious flaw inherent in such a system is that "a company has little incentive to reveal its increased efficiency if this subsequently led to a reduction in the price of its part of the program."[34] And not only are members not obliged to pass along savings to the other partners or AI itself, they also may be reluctant to invest in new cost-cutting technologies or processes that might require large capital outlays.

## Paying for the Airbus: Funding and Governmental Oversight

While subsequent discussion will analyze in greater detail the commercial and political implications of this system of international industrial collaboration, some mention should be made here of the funding arrangements. There are three major elements: (1) AI's routine payments, (2) nonrecurring development costs and (3) production funding. The first is provided by the members based on a budget proposed by AI and approved by the Supervisory Board. As described earlier, it provides for the purchase of major equipment items (engines, etc.) and overhead expenses.[35] The other two categories of expense are borne by the partners. In its role as a subcontractor responsible for a specified portion of the work, each partner also is required to finance the research, development and production of those components. Given the scale and complexity of the tasks in question, the industrial firms involved in Airbus program have looked to their respective national governments to provide this money, usually in the form of loans (on relatively attractive terms) that are to be repaid from the proceeds of sales.

Understandably, playing the crucial role of paymaster has given the governments in question an enduring interest in making sure that the entire project is managed efficiently. This oversight function is carried out through several levels of authority. The first of these is the interstate, or diplomatic, level, manifested in the Memoranda of Understanding that commit the states in question to the project in its most broadly conceived sense. While not consisting of treaties binding under international law (as did the ill-starred Concorde project), these enduring political commitments provide the context within which successive governments can negotiate specific agreements regarding the realization of the general objectives outlined in the MoU.

On a level immediately beneath the diplomatic accords are the intergovernmental agreements, "which govern the contribution each state makes to project development."[36] While themselves not comprising binding promises to fund a given aircraft program, they do "provide the basis for the guarantees provided by each government to its partners."[37] Still, each firm must negotiate with its respective national government both the amount and precise form of financing, including a schedule for repayment.

Clearly, such arrangements provide the national governments with potentially decisive influence over the fate of any proposed project within the Airbus framework. Without loans and other forms of launch aid, the A300B (or any subsequent aircraft) would never get off the ground. Certainly, the national governments thus would have a direct interest in the commercial feasibility of these projects and also would be vitally concerned with the technological and employment effects they might generate. But, as we shall see throughout the rest of this study, what makes the Airbus program different from other cooperative efforts in civil aerospace is that the governments have chosen to allow the firms to determine both the technical characteristics of the aircraft and the division of labor best suited to produce and market it. While staying in close and constant contact with a program for which they have ultimate financial responsibility, the governments have adopted an arm's-length approach. Thus "most Airbus activity and associated decision-making has become routinely a matter for Airbus Industrie and the industrial partners."[38]

## SELLING THE AIRBUS:
## THROUGH THE SALES DESERT AND BEYOND

We have seen that the partners in the Airbus consortium took pains to create an organization that would be credible in the eyes of potential customers. The formation of Airbus Industrie as a GIE committed the member firms to develop and produce components for an aircraft that would be marketed by an entity having no capital of its own, but that was backed by the full resources of the firms involved and ultimately by the national governments providing the funding. Few observers, however, including those within the consortium, anticipated that Airbus Industrie (the GIE) would gradually emerge as an entity exercising an influence in the global civil aeronautics industry that was substantially autonomous of the firms making up the consortium.

The necessity of actually selling airplanes was the main factor behind this development. Beyond having to explain the concept of a GIE and convince potential buyers both of the aircraft's merits and AI's ability to provide product support, the sales force had to reassure customers "whose greatest fear was having to deal with several interlocutors who would toss the ball amongst themselves."[39] Careful attention thus was given to cultivating a perception of AI as the sole entity competent in all aspects of the A300B. Significantly, in sales negotiations the real owners of the consortium's productive assets were referred to more and more frequently as "divisions" or "principal subcontractors" rather than "partners" or any other term implying a division of interest or authority.[40]

In practice, identifying the GIE as the sole point of contact between the airlines and the member firms meant that the importance of the partners, both individually and collectively, was diminished while the influence of those in charge of overall program management increased. The growing autonomy of AI was perceived as a capitulation by the principals at Aérospatiale in Toulouse, who recognized that the traditional French leadership role in European aerospace collaboration was at stake here. As an example, flight testing of the A300B became an early bone of contention, with the French insisting that their pilots, engineers, certification rules and terminology be used in this prestigious phase of aircraft development. The Germans had quietly argued that this crucial function be performed by a multinational group under the auspices of the GIE. Even more galling to the French than their loss of sole control over flight testing was that Airbus teams insisted upon using an Anglo-American vernacular ("Boeing slang") as the working language of the consortium, again in deference to the reality of the technical and commercial situation in world aviation. So even though the French and Aérospatiale remained very influential within the consortium, at this early stage "the umbilical cord between Aérospatiale and the GIE began to be severed."[41]

In asserting its autonomy, the GIE had relied on its role as the single interface with both suppliers and customers, making success in the sales arena crucial to its continued independence. But the A300B came on the market during the economic upheaval precipitated by the 1973 oil shock, which, through the combined effects of recession and large increases in fuel prices, had seriously cut into air travel demand and airline profitability. In this inhospitable environment, sales of the first product from a newly created manufacturer were predictably slow; the national airlines of the two major partners were the first to announce their intention to purchase the A300B (Air France in November 1971 and Lufthansa in May 1973).

However, the economic difficulties created in the West by the oil embargo of the Organization of Petroleum Exporting Countries (OPEC) also worked to the advantage of the Airbus consortium. Though technically conservative in many respects, the A300B was quite innovative in that it was the world's first large-capacity aircraft with only two engines. As the price of aviation fuel suddenly became a much more significant factor in determining direct operating costs (DOC) for airlines, the advantages of a wide-body twin became apparent, especially on frequently flown, high-traffic routes. In addition, the A300 was introduced at a time when its competitors either had just launched a major new venture (Boeing 747) or were fighting among themselves for the same market niche (Douglas DC-10 vs. Lockheed L-1011). The attention of the U.S. builders also remained concentrated on the still massive American market just when commercial aviation was becoming internationalized rapidly.[42]

Therefore, many of the A300B's early sales battles would be fought in countries where the Europeans had historical influence and where market requirements were more closely met by the specific capabilities of the new plane–Asia, the Middle East and the Third World. Recognizing opportunity, Bernard de Lathière (who succeeded Henri Ziegler as managing director of AI in 1975) "concentrated his efforts on the consolidation of the external image of Airbus through direct contacts with the leaders of the major airline companies."[43] Even before the aircraft had been certified to fly passengers for revenue, Lathière launched a series of ambitious and publicity-making overseas sales tours. The first, to the Americas, began on 18 September 1973 and covered 21,000 nautical miles, allowing guests (including airline officials and pilots) to see the aircraft in action. The A300B was displayed to interested crowds in Sao Paulo, Caracas, Miami, New York, Boston, St. Louis, Chicago and elsewhere. A few days after the first tour's completion, a second was undertaken from 31 October to 8 November 1973 to Southwest Asia and the Indian subcontinent, including stops in Athens, Tehran, Karachi, Delhi and Bombay.[44] Soon after came a quick run through Africa, with the special objective being the South African market. In the spring of 1974, an extensive tour was made of the Middle and Far East, including stops in Singapore, Hong Kong, Sydney, Jakarta, Bangkok, Manila and Seoul.

Not only did these tours generate commercial interest and some important sales,[45] they were especially important for Airbus Industrie (the GIE) in that they "cemented the team . . ." which self-consciously "began to exist as a professional community."[46] But despite the persistence of Lathière's sales efforts and some significant successes on the European and international markets, only two aircraft were sold from December 1975 to April 1977, one being the conversion of an already existing option.[47] Times were tough for the partners and the GIE alike, and the latter found the basis of its newfound influence being undermined.

Especially frustrating was the fact that, despite intense efforts and some disappointing near misses, penetration of the lucrative American market continued to elude Lathière and his team.[48] The first real break came on 4 May 1977 when Frank Borman of Eastern Airlines agreed to lease four A300B4s. He then proceeded to put them through severe tests of performance and reliability on the airline's busy New York (LaGuardia)–Boston shuttle. Duly impressed, Borman followed through on 6 April 1978 with a firm order for 23 of the aircraft (with options on nine more), along with an order for 25 of the planned A310s, a smaller version of the A300B.[49] Given Borman's reputation as a savvy buyer and Eastern's as an efficient operator of aircraft, the sale conferred credibility upon AI no promotional efforts could ever match.[50]

## THE BATTLE OF BRITAIN

The sales team at Airbus Industrie redoubled its efforts after the successful deal with Eastern Airlines, and continued to sign contracts and fill the order book.[51] But the optimism flowing from these accomplishments was accompanied by trepidation and even division among the partners. Success in the market had raised new questions about the direction the consortium should take in building on the technical and commercial foundation of the A300B, while also drawing the attention of AI's major American rivals. Much of 1977 and all of 1978 would be spent in determining the configuration of AI's next product, and these deliberations also would lead to decisions that would have a direct impact on the very structure of the world civil aviation industry.

As had been the case ten years earlier, the focal point in 1978 of both intra-European and transatlantic discussions in civil aeronautics was Great Britain. Specifically, the question was: Would the Europeans or the Americans claim the allegiance of the British government, airframers, engine builders and airlines in launching their next product? And, since British policymakers and industrialists alike remained (as in the past) fundamentally divided on where the interests of the industry and the nation lay, no decisive response was forthcoming. However, it was clear that the British decisions (plural because there would not nor could there be a single response) would likely shift the balance in what was becoming an increasingly complicated and high-stakes strategic contest between the American and European manufacturers. Whoever could count on British technological skill, industrial assets and financial support would possess an important advantage in the upcoming rounds of international competition.

Having survived the grueling trip across the "marketing desert" of 1975 and 1976, the members of the Airbus consortium turned their attention to extending the product line.[52] It had long been recognized within AI and among the partners that the basis for Boeing's success lay in its ability to offer airlines a full range of aircraft. Commonality among designs reduced customers' training and maintenance costs while allowing the manufacturer to transfer knowledge, embodied in both tooling and skills, among design and production programs. Having paid the high cost of the "entry ticket" into the large civil airframe business, Airbus Industrie was ready to capitalize on the steep learning curves and economies of scope and scale inherent in the technology and production process.

The French were inclined to go after what they saw as a market segment that would emerge as airlines recognized a need to replace their noisy, fuel-thirsty 727s, 737s and DC-9s with more modern and efficient aircraft in the 130- to 180-seat range. From the French perspective, building the next-generation single-aisle also would have the beneficial side effect of creating a plane on which the new CFM-56 engine could be attached, it being the first offering by a 50/50 joint venture of GE and SNECMA.[53] For their part, the German partners were inclined toward a more conservative strategy that would involve introducing a smaller variant of the A300B, a design in which both

Lufthansa and SwissAir had expressed preliminary interest.[54] The apparent solidity of market prospects for the A310, as manifested in the express interest of two such important European airlines, tipped the balance in the Germans' favor. Debate within the consortium now shifted to how much the proposed aircraft would retain in common with its predecessor, and factions formed around two basic alternatives.

The focal point of the debate was the aircraft wing. The simplest and least expensive route, called the minimum-change option, would be merely to shorten the fuselage of the A300B while keeping the wing as it was, giving operators a smaller-capacity, medium-range aircraft with twin-engine efficiency. But there were disadvantages inherent in such a solution, the main one being that the wing really would be too big for the new aircraft, which would impose penalties in fuel consumption and thus in direct operating costs (most simply conceived as cost per seat/mile).[55] The other option was to design an entirely new wing expressly for the new configuration, thus optimizing the relationships among range, payload and fuel consumption and maximizing the DOC advantages to potential operators.[56]

Given the uncertainty of the economic environment (especially regarding future fuel costs) and the stated preference of Lufthansa, the engineers at AI opted for the latter choice and determined to design the A310 around a new wing.[57] Already early in 1977, HSA engineers at Hatfield had begun work on a new wing for the B10, as the proposed aircraft was still called then. But the future of HSA's participation in the Airbus program was clouded by ongoing negotiations with the Labour government and BAC concerning the merger of the two firms into a true British national champion, British Aerospace (BAe).[58] The uncertainty and delays associated with these developments had led to the emergence of a direct threat to British control over this vital part of the project: "Contingency plans were already being made for the Germans to assume responsibility for Airbus wing design and production."[59]

The consortium's principle rival, Boeing, was an even more immediate source of uncertainty within the aerospace community during 1977 and 1978 concerning continued British participation in Airbus Industrie. At first dismissive of the upstart but then stung by AI's success (especially the sale to Eastern Airlines) in its own market, Boeing "tried to prevent the return of the British to Airbus and draw in the British airframer and engine builder in constructing the 757."[60] At first labeled the 7N7, the single-aisle 757 program was attractive to all three of the major firms in British civil aerospace: BAe could play major subcontractor to the world's leading airframer, Rolls-

Royce perhaps could supply the launch engines for the aircraft, and British Airways (BA) could gain favorable terms on refitting its single-aisle fleet by being an important launch customer for the new aircraft. But for BAe, the choice was particularly difficult; Boeing would clearly assume a dominant position in any partnership and thus might permanently reduce the British to second class citizens in the world civil airframe business. A formal offer came from Boeing in February 1978 for BAe to develop the 757 wing, consisting essentially of a "fixed-price contract determined by estimates based on Boeing's in-house costs."[61] For the BAe leadership, the risks seemed high and the payoff uncertain: "After weighing up the options, BAe became convinced that its future lay with Europe."[62]

For its part, the British government, under the leadership of Prime Minister James Callaghan, seemed indifferent regarding the proper course of action for any of the national firms.[63] Having pledged explicitly not to interfere in the decisions of the newly created and government-owned BAe, the Labour government faced pressure both from the BAe board and the governments of France and Germany to accept Airbus Industrie's proposals to rejoin the consortium, albeit under certain conditions.[64] These included provisions that BAe contribute to AI for the sunk costs incurred with the development of the A300B, a capital contribution adequate to finance BAe's portion of the A310 program, and an order by BA for either the A300B or the A310. With the official launch of the A310 on 6 July 1978, the French and German partners thus confronted the British with a stark choice.

Events reached their climax during the late summer of 1978, as the British seemed determined to extract maximum benefit from their inherently ambiguous position. In August it was announced that BA would become the proud owner of 19 757s and that these would be equipped with Rolls-Royce RB211-535 engines. But at the same time, BAe would be allowed to rejoin AI, bringing with it an entry fee of £25 million sterling and loan capital for its portion of the A310. Now it was the French who were faced with a choice: to continue insisting that BA buy Airbus aircraft, or to relent and accept British participation through BAe as it stood. The issue was set aside if not finally resolved by a timely order from Sir Freddie Laker for 10 A300B4s for his low-price transatlantic "Skytrain" service, which allowed the French to save face with an order from a British carrier, even if it wasn't BA.

On 24 October 1978 the governments of France, Germany and Great Britain officially announced new agreements making BAe a full partner in Airbus Industrie from 1 January 1979. BAe would take a 20 percent stake in the consortium, reducing the holdings of Aérospatiale and Deutsche Airbus each by 10 percent to 37.9 percent and leaving CASA's share at 4.2 percent (see figure A.4). It was further decided that existing industrial and financial arrangements governing the A300B program would remain in force. Also, other concessions limited the voting power of BAe until the sale of 150 A310s or until BA placed an order for either version of the Airbus. Most important, BAe was to be given responsibility for the wing, a move that gave the A310 project additional credibility and allowed it to proceed on schedule.[65]

## AIRBUS INDUSTRIE: A EUROPEAN COLLABORATIVE EFFORT

With the return of the British to full participation in the Airbus Industrie consortium, "at last all three major industries were partners in a permanent commercial organisation whose aim was the development not of a single project, but of a family of aircraft."[66] The decision of BAe and the government were important ones for the future of the British, European and world civil aeronautics industries,[67] but also were clear evidence of the extent to which the very structure of the industry had been changed by the emergence of the consortium. In less than 15 years since the initial 1967 MoU, and less than ten years after the formation of the GIE in December 1970, the designers and builders of the Airbus seemed poised to consolidate their success by penetrating an important market niche in a rapidly globalizing industry. This commercial success would bring new challenges as well, however, for now the American competition had been aroused, and in the 1980s a real technological, economic and political battle would be joined.

Not that the route had been an easy one for the industrial partners and national governments involved in the Airbus project. The early disagreement concerning British participation and RB-207 affair was a near debacle, survived only with the strong commitment of the French and German governments to a technically sound aircraft with promising commercial prospects. But sales were slow to materialize, making the period from 1975 to 1978 one of maximum uncertainty for the partners, governments, and the consortium alike. Even the French began to look as far afield as the United States for possible collaboration, while many of the industrial partners in AI cast about for other collaborative opportunities within Europe itself. First had come the so-called Group of Six (later seven when Dassault had joined) European aerospace firms whose studies of numerous design concepts had culminated in Dassault's Mercure 200 program. Later, in 1977, another European civil aircraft design group, called the Joint European Transport (JET) consortium, was formed to study possible single-aisle configurations.[68]

All of these developments represented potential threats to Airbus Industrie's position as the emerging focal point of European civil aviation. Each ultimately foundered, at least in part, on problems inherent in international industrial collaboration: the difficulties of collectively defining a viable product and attaining agreement on a division of labor that would serve the interests of all parties. But these abortive attempts all faced the prior existence of a collaborative project involving the firms and governments of the leading powers in Europe, the Airbus program. The A300B and the organization that had defined, produced, sold and supported it was a fait accompli that, by the mid-1970s, had begun to shape the calculations of those around it. This was especially true for the British firms seeking a viable long-term source of work: "The French and German governments were so deeply committed to Airbus Industrie as the focal point for European civil aerospace that in practice, prospects for Britain in any new European civil project soon hinged upon a relationship with Airbus Industrie."[69]

So when contemplating its American vs. European options in 1978, because of the existence of Airbus Industrie, the choice for Britain was a much different one from ten years before. Not that BAe's joining AI resolved the fundamental ambiguity in British policy; indeed, with government aid British firms were able to benefit by playing both sides of the Atlantic at once. For example, Rolls-Royce supplied the launch engine for Boeing's 757 and the RB-211 would be the core of its global business for the future. But while the British did not make a wholehearted choice for Europe, their return to AI with governmental support was an important step that had been made much easier by the existence of a truly viable European option.

# 7

## TECHNOLOGICAL INNOVATION AND
## COMMERCIAL STRATEGY (1979–1986)

*This chapter will discuss* and analyze what is arguably the most important phase in the development of Airbus Industrie. With the commitment of British capital and political support to the collaborative European project, during the early 1980s the consortium undertook important new programs in an attempt to alter permanently the competitive balance in the world commercial airframe industry. In the space of only seven years, the Europeans found themselves engaged directly in a global confrontation with the American leaders in not one but two of the industry's three major markets. AI's success, especially in penetrating the crucial single-aisle segment, served notice that the Europeans had devised an effective means of combining their technological, industrial, commercial and political assets in a strategy clearly aimed at sharing leadership in the era's most vital industrial sector.

In seeking an explanation for the success of this strategy, the chapter will describe the way in which AI brought to market two new aircraft, the A310 and the A320, and in so doing emphasize how technological, commercial and political factors interacted in producing these quite significant additions to the world's fleet of commercial airliners. Particular attention will be paid to the configuration and operational attributes of these aircraft, not only because in some cases these features marked important technical developments in the history of powered flight but also because of the significance of these attributes in shaping the evolving pattern of competition within the industry. In discussing the specific aspects of the equipment developed for commercial passenger use during this time, we shall see how Airbus Industrie was able to combine technical skill and commercial necessity with the political will of the national governments not only to expand its product line but also to alter the competitive dynamic of the industry.

## THE A310

In chapter 6 we saw that Airbus Industrie, in less than ten years since its inception, had been able to gain a foothold in the world civil airframe market with the twin-engine, wide-body A300. The consortium had survived crossing the sales desert of 1975 to 1978 and, with the April 1978 Eastern Airlines deal, established the technical and operational capabilities of the aircraft as well as the credibility of the marketing and product support organization.[1] (See figure A.5 showing the cumulative pattern of growth in AI's order book. Figure A.6 depicts the pattern of deliveries in a similar manner.) AI's stature, both industrially and politically, also had been greatly enhanced by the official admission of Great Britain as a full participant, with its newly formed national aerospace champion, British Aerospace, becoming a 20 percent partner on 1 January 1979. AI was now clearly better positioned than any previous European venture in civil aerospace to engage its American competitors in a serious contest for market share.

At this juncture, the next major element of AI's bid to challenge the commanding positions of McDonnell Douglas and especially Boeing was a new wide-bodied, twin-engine aircraft. As discussed in chapter 6, the A300-B10, or more simply the A310, was a shortened version of the A300, with a fuselage of the same diameter and a projected capacity of about 220 passengers.[2] More significant both technically and commercially was that the A310 was designed around a completely new wing, which, with the definite entry of BAe into the consortium, was to be built in Bristol.[3] AI was careful to consult closely with potential customers in designing the A310; both Lufthansa and SwissAir had been especially influential, and these two prestigious airlines served as its launch customers in early 1979.[4]

With BAe joining the consortium for the launch of its second aircraft, Airbus Industrie began to draw attention from all quarters, not only Europe's premier airlines. In the spring of 1979, a consortium of Belgian companies along with the Walloon development authority formed Belairbus to produce slats and tracks for the A310 wing, plus a major wing/body fairing. Although Belairbus did not become a full risk-sharing partner in the consortium or take direct responsibility for product design, its participation provided needed work in Belgian facilities.[5] Also, the successful launch of the A310 and the growing order book for the A300/A310 line spurred both aero engine builders that had heretofore ignored Airbus, Rolls-Royce and Pratt and Whitney (P&W), to seek actively to have their engines offered on the new aircraft. Rolls-Royce went as far as signing an MoU with AI in June 1979; although it would not bear fruit for some time, its purpose was to seek mutually satisfactory ways to have the RB211 hung on Airbuses.[6] For its part, P&W made an all-out effort during 1979 to have Air France select for its A310s a new version of its P&W JT9D, but GE's advantage as the incumbent whose engines had launched the entire Airbus program proved too strong to overcome.[7] P&W did later succeed, however, in convincing influential airlines such as SAS and SwissAir to place "dependable engines" on their A310s, thus beginning a long relationship between AI and P&W.

Although a derivative of the A300, the A310 included several innovations that would affect not only its immediate sales prospects but also serve as important features of future Airbuses as well as on competing aircraft. The most revolutionary of these innovations, the forward-facing cockpit crew (FFCC) flight-deck design, instigated a showdown with pilots associations in Europe and elsewhere. Based on new computer and information-processing technology that allowed a marked simplification of cockpit instrumentation, the FFCC concept eliminated the need for the flight engineer, who traditionally occupied a sideways-facing seat to the rear of the pilot and copilot. If adopted as the industry standard, such a change would reduce from three to two the number of pilots needed to fly airliners. Although this labor-reducing technology was welcomed by the carriers as cost reducing, pilots understandably felt threatened.[8] The controversy became so serious that threats of pilot strikes forced leading European airlines such as Air France and Lufthansa to order their A310s with the traditional side-facing cockpit crew (SFCC). In fact, it was Garuda Indonesian who first put the new FFCC system into service in December 1981, albeit with traditional instrumentation rather than the new cathode ray tube displays—the so-called glass cockpit.[9]

Another innovation by AI on the A310 was to incorporate a fuel storage tank into the horizontal tailplane, both increasing range and making it possible to adjust the aircraft's center of gravity during flight, thus increasing fuel efficiency by improving trim and reducing drag. Although this modification too was the subject of controversy and even ridicule in the industry, it proved quite successful both technically and commercially, and was later emulated by other manufacturers, including the industry leader Boeing.[10] A third addition to the A310 was the introduction of so-called wing-tip fences, small, delta-shape attachments on the ends of the wings designed to diminish the powerful vortices generated as air swirls from the aircraft. These vortices not only increase drag but are potentially dangerous to other aircraft following behind, a special concern on landing. As a result of this seemingly minor change, Airbus was able to improve fuel efficiency on the A310 and other aircraft at cruising speeds by over 1 percent, not an insignificant difference when the total distance flown by an aircraft over its lifetime is taken into account.

By introducing these design changes with the A310, Airbus Industrie had adopted an approach to product development that, while fundamentally conservative in that it relied on a derivative aircraft, also was commercially innovative in that it differentiated the new Airbus from its competitors in important respects. While the wide-body, twin-engine configuration offered airlines a unique combination of range and payload (both passenger and freight), the technical advances also provided substantial performance and thus cost advantages to operators. This tactic of blending continuity and innovation allowed AI to continue its exploitation of a neglected market niche while also establishing its reputation as a force capable of shaping industry standards and practices.

So while "the launch of the A310 took Airbus Industrie beyond the single-product formula, and represented the first step towards a family of aircraft," because of the substantial design changes, AI could offer to airlines both commonality and enhanced performance in what was to be the first head-to-head competition with its principle rival, Boeing.[11] As we have seen, open competition between AI and Boeing had already begun in the spring of 1978, as the market leader invested substantial time and energy in courting the British government and aeronautics firms concerning participation in its proposed new 757 and 767 projects. Boeing's aim was to prevent British capital and expertise from being incorporated into any new Airbus aircraft, yet France and Germany pressed on regardless and "had already announced 6 July 1978 the launch of the A310 program, without knowing if Great Britain in the end would participate or not."[12] Thus failing in its bid to disrupt the A310 program, Boeing resolved to challenge the interloper European directly in its own market niche; only days later, on 14 July 1978, it launched the twin-engine, twin-aisle 767.[13]

So while Boeing was partially successful in its British strategy, in that British Airways and Rolls-Royce became active players in the single-aisle 757 program, the joining of BAe with AI on the A310 was a blow both to Boeing's pride and to its hopes of nipping the upstart's designs in the bud. Therefore, both sides spent the next several months in conducting "no-holds-barred" sales campaigns for their respective aircraft. The years 1978 and 1979 were very good ones in which to be selling aircraft, since growth rates in air traffic were high and orders for aircraft at record levels.[14] All of the airframe manufacturers did well, especially Airbus, recording 69 orders in 1978 and 130 in 1979, which allowed the European consortium to take over from McDonnell Douglas second place in the world rankings with 20 percent of the orders placed that year.[15]

These halcyon days ended abruptly with the second oil crisis of 1979-1980: "if the first oil shock was 'destabilizing,' for the airline companies, the second was 'ravaging.'"[16] Pinched between the forces of slowing traffic growth and rapidly rising fuel prices, beginning in 1980 the world's airlines began to lose money quickly and massively, eating up profits made in previous years. The airlines' financial problems were compounded by dramatic changes in U.S. laws governing competition in the industry. President Jimmy Carter's signing of the Airline Deregulation Act in October 1978 "ended 40 years of American air transport regulation and threw it into indescribable chaos, which would aggravate the effects of the second oil shock."[17] By lifting restrictions on the number of airlines that could fly given routes and the prices they could charge, the new legislation precipitated vicious fare wars among the new companies that sprang up to challenge the established carriers, which vowed not to cede market share at any cost.[18]

The impact of the airlines' financial crisis upon the aircraft manufacturers was predictable; orders for new airplanes fell dramatically and existing contracts came under pressure for renegotiation. Moreover, the effects of deregulation in the United States were especially hard on Airbus. Active only in the wide-body segment of the market,[19] the European manufacturer lacked a product with which to meet changes in the demand for aircraft created by deregulation. Specifically, with the introduction of the "hub-and-spoke" system, U.S. airlines sought smaller aircraft that would be used to feed passengers into a few central locations for connections onto more heavily traveled routes. Feeling the combined effects of recession and deregulation, Airbus had especially hard times in 1981 and 1982; in the latter year, the consortium received a grand total of two orders. Able to offer a complete line of aircraft, Boeing fared better. Its established single-aisle product line continued to generate business, while the 747 continued to enjoy its monopoly position in the long-range, high-capacity segment of the market.

Although not the most promising of times in the commercial airframe business, both AI and Boeing continued with their respective product development and certification schedules, with the 767 first flying in September 1981 and the A310 following suit at the Farnborough air show in April 1982. Already quite comparable in terms of both configuration and performance, the competition between the A310 and the 767 became as complex as it was intense, as each manufacturer continually offered potential customers improved versions of the basic configuration. Mainly because of a significant augmentation during the course of their development in the power ratings of the engines offered with the new aircraft, both airframers could market extended-range variants, in some cases doubling that projected for the original plane, thus bringing them close to the status of true long-range aircraft.[20]

Although the American market for commercial airliners remained by far the largest and most lucrative in the world, the sales battle between the 767 and the A310 was a global one in which everything from personalities to international politics played a role in the outcome.[21] Having failed to break Boeing's hold in the United States, AI turned its attention to traditional Boeing customers elsewhere.[22] The competition for sales in the Middle East was especially heated, as the Europeans were not slow to take advantage of negative perceptions of the United States that had been perpetuated in the region by the Iranian hostage crisis and particularly by U.S. support at the United Nations for Israeli policies in the occupied territories.[23] Airbus used the opening to garner orders from Egyptair, Kuwait Airways, Middle East Airways of Lebanon (MEA) and Saudia; the latter served as the launch customer for the A300-600.[24] John Newhouse has assessed the sales competition in the Middle East, clearly showing how political and commercial factors combined in shaping the outcome in favor of AI. He observes that once the politically influenced Kuwaiti decision in favor of the A310 had been made, MEA factored this new commercial reality into its comparison of the 767 and the A310, paying particular attention to the fact that no other carriers in the region were likely to purchase the Boeing aircraft. For MEA, buying the 767 thus "would mean no commonality—no spares to be traded back and forth in the remote airports, where carriers tend to rely on one another in that way."[25]

Following AI's sweep in the Middle Eastern market, Nigeria and Australia were also areas of direct competition between the rival aircraft, with Airbus winning in the former and splitting a decision in the latter. But whatever their outcome, all of the campaigns were fought with a vigor and indeed a viciousness that remains nearly legendary.[26] Each side repeatedly accused the other of using unfair sales tactics, including the linking of aircraft sales to other political and commercial concerns, and of spreading disinformation about the competition and its products. And while the number of planes to be ordered in any one of the smaller markets paled in comparison to the stakes in the United States, as evidenced in the Middle East, individual situations took on added significance because of the impact each might have on other negotiations.

This marketing momentum was a function not only of perceptions (which are obviously crucial factors in any sales competition) but also very real in a technological and economic sense. Because of the zero-sum nature of these sales contests, an order for one meant blocking the other out of potential business. This strategic aspect was important for both manufacturers, but especially so for Airbus, because each contract meant the chance to build additional aircraft and thus to proceed farther along the lengthy and initially quite steep learning curve associated with aeronautical technology and aircraft production processes. Thus, every sales campaign was imbued with a sense of urgency, because of the contribution each commercial success would make to placing the consortium on a more solid technological and industrial footing. By the end of 1980, with total deliveries of A300s having exceeded 100 and its order book for them and for A310s at well over 300 units, Airbus Industrie seemed to have crossed a threshold and was well on its way to becoming a major player in the global commercial airliner business. The next challenge was to find the most effective way to build on this success.

## THE A320

As Airbus and Boeing struggled for the lion's share of the wide-body, twin-engine market, developments were unfolding quickly in the short-range, single-aisle segment, undeniably still the most important portion of the commercial airframe market in terms of potential sales. First the province of the Douglas DC-8 and Boeing 707 in the late 1950s and early 1960s, both of the American manufacturers had introduced improved derivatives of these pioneers, the DC-9 and Boeing 727 and 737 models, which had formed the bulk of the world's airline fleet up to the mid-1980s. (See Table A.1 for aircraft deliveries by year and type, 1958-1984.) In 1980, the replacement market for these now-aging, noisy and inefficient aircraft was estimated at around 3,000 units by the year 2000, for total sales of $50 to $70 billion.[27] Without a product to offer in this crucial segment, Airbus would in effect concede to the Americans continued mastery of the world airline business.

The significance of the single-aisle market was lost on neither the partners nor the managers of Airbus Industrie, yet disagreement remained over whether the consortium's limited resources would be best used in entering an entirely new segment. Without an aircraft for which tooling and skills already existed, such a move would require massive investments in design and production facilities. Not only was the scale of the resource outlay daunting, the lengthy development time involved meant increased risk that market conditions would change and render any investment unprofitable. Indeed, under the best of conditions, over 15 years would elapse between the decision to launch the new product and the point at which cumulative sales could reasonably be expected to yield substantial return.

Within the AI consortium, there had been for some time two main lines of thinking on the most effective strategy of product development, and, as discussed earlier, the divergence between them became evident soon after the consortium's first aircraft had been introduced. Along with the A300, in the early 1970s the consortium had studied a number of possible variants of its basic big-twin, and the Germans in particular saw the further extension of this configuration as the most prudent course.[28] This logic had prevailed in the launch of the A310 in 1978 and again in offering the A300-600 in 1980, and debate had centered around the extent to which the new models should vary from the basic pattern established by their predecessor, the A300. The French, on the other hand, had consistently argued that if Airbus Industrie wanted to become a permanent and influential factor in the civil airframe business, eventually it would have to challenge the Americans in the single-aisle segment. While the logic was compelling, the difficulty lay in convincing the other partners and the national governments that doing so would have sufficient commercial merit to serve their larger political and industrial interests.

As far back as 1977, and thus even before the A300 had realized any commercial success, French politicians and industrialists alike had sought to generate interest in producing a new European single-aisle aircraft.[29] Intrigued by both the sales potential and the engineering challenge, in that same year the companies involved in Airbus Industrie (including BAe, although it was not yet officially a member) set up a team to study possible designs under the auspices of a group called Joint European Transport (JET). Various fuselage lengths were considered, and consensus gradually formed around a 160-seat plane, with two turbofans (although propfan engines were evaluated) hung under the wings. Discussions also were held with Fokker on its proposed F-29, but AI recognized that little was to be gained by admitting to the family a new member and then immediately placing it so close to the head of the table.[30] Thus, after assessing the market potential, the GIE would decide in June 1981 to adopt the single-aisle project (from that point designated the A320) as its own and "make itself the champion of that which would be in greatest demand by the carriers."[31] Yet despite such promising indications, concerns over financing and especially the glaring lack of an engine adequate to power the A320 would delay the official launch for another two full years, giving the American competition the chance to play its own cards in "what resembles a high-stakes poker game as much as anything else."[32]

Close observers of market trends and of the indecision in Europe, both Boeing and McDonnell Douglas were anxious to accomplish two ends at once: to garner as quickly as possible a large portion of the huge sales potential latent in the DC-9 and 727/737 replacement business while deterring others, most especially Airbus, from entering the market. Both ends dictated quick action, and McDonnell Douglas wasted no time in capitalizing on its reputation and the spectacular success of its DC-9 by offering a derivative series of aircraft, the MD-80. The DC-9 Super 80 had flown first in 1979, and based on slightly modified fuselage and wing, with modern avionics and new engines, five versions of the MD-80 eventually would be built.[33] Although the aircraft itself was far from truly innovative, the sales financing tactics of McDonnell Douglas surely were. In late 1982, the firm convinced American Airlines to forgo the purchase of 30 Boeing 757s and take instead MD-82s on very attractive leasing terms, which included a controversial "walk-away" provision that permitted the carrier to return the aircraft without penalty on short notice. The gamble paid off, and by the time Airbus Industrie was prepared to give the official go-ahead for its single-aisle, McDonnell had sold 230 of the modified DC-9s.[34] Not to be outmaneuvered by either of its challengers, Boeing joined the single-aisle fray with a modified version of its tried and true 737, and on 26 March 1981 had launched the 737-300. With upgraded avionics and CFM56-3 engines, the new aircraft provided improved fuel economy and delivery with ready availability. In addition, the market leader informed prospective customers of its intention to develop an entirely new aircraft, the 7J7, which would effect a generational leap over existing products by using a radical new engine technology.

With Boeing and McDonnell Douglas now offering derivative aircraft, "Airbus Industrie decided it had to attack this market with a new, advanced technology A320."[35] But while the conversion of the AI management to the idea of designing and building a completely new single-aisle aircraft would prove an important and indeed necessary factor in moving the program forward, the consortium had to convince reluctant national governments of the A320's financial merits. Prospects seemed promising, as Air France announced at the Le Bourget air show in the summer of 1981 its readiness to order 50 A320s, on the condition that the aircraft was officially launched by March 1982. Even more temptingly, the major U.S. carriers—Delta, United and Eastern Airlines—also expressed their interest in a new 150-seater as well and their willingness to place huge orders for an aircraft meeting their specifications.[36]

But what of the European governments whose role in financing both prior Airbus projects had been absolutely essential? Any uncertainties concerning the new French Socialist government's support for Airbus Industrie in general and the A320 program in particular had been quickly dispelled,[37] and the government declared itself ready to see the aircraft launched with a new variant of the CFM56 engine.[38] Yet the governments of Margaret Thatcher in Britain and Helmut Kohl in Germany remained unconvinced and indeed feared that the French were seeking their support merely to insure that SNECMA and CFM finally would have an airframe on which to hang their engine. Also, airlines were well known to assert their need for marvelous new aircraft and then be unable to come up with the necessary funds to buy them; London and Bonn wanted to see more firm orders. Already heavily and recently committed to expanding the wide-body branch of the family, "the British and German governments held fast to the position that the A320 had first to prove its commercial viability."[39]

Despite the stated interest of numerous prestigious airlines in an all-new 150-seater and the orders being won by the derivative American aircraft, in early 1982 it still looked as if the Airbus A320 might not see the light of day. A sort of self-reinforcing stalemate had been reached, with AI and the French government eager to push forward but confronting technical, financial and commercial circumstances that seemed to conspire in delaying the program. For their part, the airlines wanted the vastly improved cost-per-seat/mile that a completely new generation aircraft promised, yet these advantages depended primarily on the availability of a modern and fuel-efficient engine, which at the time did not exist. While the CFM56 series was designed for precisely such an application, the engine-builder had been several years ahead of the market with its earliest versions, and even the CFM56-3 selected by Boeing for the 737-300 could not meet the demanding expectations of AI and its potential customers. So while AI had settled on a basic aircraft configuration acceptable to a number of airlines, it still had to convince one or more of the engine-builders to take the major risk of developing a new or dramatically enhanced power plant.

For both technical and commercial reasons, the lack of a suitable engine perpetuated the reluctance of the British and German governments to fund the program. Predictably, until the issue of a viable engine for the A320 could be settled, many airlines would express their interest but stop short of making the kind of firm commitments the governments were waiting for. Yet neither CFM nor any of the other engine firms were ready to stake their time, money and reputation on developing a new engine without solid indications that there would be an aircraft to hang it on. The logjam was decisively broken in May 1982 with the formation of International Aero Engines (IAE), which joined Pratt and Whitney, Rolls-Royce, Fiat, MTU and a consortium of three Japanese firms (Japanese Aero Engine Corporation, or JAEC) to compete with CFM for the "ten-tonne," single-aisle segment of the market.[40] This was clearly a boon to the A320 program; not only would the participation of Rolls-Royce "reinforce the chances of British government support for the A320 program," the spur of competition would remove any remaining uncertainties on the part of GE and SNECMA on the need for CFM to come forward with a new engine.[41] Pressing this new opening, at the end of 1982 a somewhat exasperated Charles Fiterman convened a meeting of "the principal protagonists in the imbroglio" over whom he as French transport minister had direct influence.[42] These included Aérospatiale, Airbus, Air France and SNECMA; the former three all expressed their interest in moving forward quickly on the new aircraft, and the latter came away convinced of the wisdom of developing an advanced version of the CFM engine.

With the design of the aircraft specified and the prospect of not one but two new power plants to hang under its wing, all that stood in the way of an official launch of the A320 was for AI to gain the financial support of the British and German governments by obtaining firm and credible orders from airlines. While quite sizable, the commitment of Air France to purchase up to 50 aircraft was not wholly convincing in this regard, even after Air Inter also expressed its interest in ten A320s. What the program needed to demonstrate its commercial viability was an order from a important carrier outside France, and for a time it seemed that none less than British Airways actually might play this crucial role. But while BA predictably opted to lease several Boeing 737-300s, it was the other quite prestigious British airline, British Caledonian, that announced its need in October 1983 for seven A320s, with options on ten more. While Caledonian "was the first A320 customer outside France, and took total orders and options to 80," more important, its reputation as an astute and careful evaluator of aircraft was especially important to the British government.[43]

These orders, along with BAe's willingness to sink its own capital into the project, appeared to place the A320 on a commercially sound foundation. Yet the British purse strings remained firmly drawn, and it was the Germans who first relented, at least partially, in November 1983, by agreeing to advance credits for development work on the A320. In Germany, domestic and international political forces had been converging for some time around the A320. On the one hand, the president of Airbus Industrie, F. J. Strauss, publicly argued that the A320 was crucial to the future of AI and thus also to the fate of the German aerospace industry. Coming from the self-styled "king" of Bavaria, where much of the German aerospace assets were located and much of the CDU/CSU coalition's political support resided, Strauss could not be ignored even if he exaggerated the industrial impact of the Airbus programs in Germany. On the other hand, the president of France, François Mitterrand, continued to advocate the program personally as well, and the A320 was on the agenda in early 1984 summit meetings between the three heads of state. Thus, Chancellor Kohl was pressed from both sides and "if not swayed by the economic arguments, regarded the Airbus as a symbol of Franco-German cooperation and supported the A320 for diplomatic reasons."[44] As the combined result of the project's improved commercial prospects and growing political expectations, on 22 February 1984 the German government agreement to finance 90 percent of MBB's share in the A320 program. For their part, the British put together a package involving government funds with BAe's own resources and outside private venture capital: the British government was to provide £250 million sterling in "upfront" launch aid, with the remaining £400 million coming from BAe's internally generated resources and financing from "the City."[45]

With government financing officially arranged, Airbus Industrie announced the formal launch of the A320 on 12 March 1984, with total non-recurring costs estimated at over £2 billion. While the French had provided sustained political impetus to the program, the A320 saga showed also that Airbus Industrie was "a force to be reckoned with in European aerospace policy."[46] Not only had the consortium designed and developed a technically sound and commercially viable product, it also "had played a significant role in the industrial and political lobbying surrounding the A320 launch, helping to maintain pressure on its more reluctant government sponsors."[47] Also, because of its nascent commercial success as well as its promise for the future, the entire Airbus program had become perceived "as vital to the health of major industrial assets in France, Britain and Germany, and as a result stimulated considerable political support."[48]

Despite its leading role in the launch of the A320 and the international sales successes of the A300/A310 line, Airbus Industrie faced pressing difficulties. While the Americans were providing customers with scores of modified DC-9s and 737s, the A320 would not be ready for delivery until 1987. Meanwhile, the Boeing 767 offered AI direct and stiff competition in the twin-engine, twin-aisle segment that it had carved out so laboriously. Indeed, the early 1980s were a throwback to the dark days of 1976 to 1978, as Airbus Industrie found itself faced with falling sales and pressure to cut production rates as "white-tails" again appeared on the tarmac at Toulouse.[49] But as it turned out, this unforeseen and unwelcome presence of unsold aircraft would be quickly converted into commercial opportunity.

As in 1978, it was a major American airline that came to the consortium's rescue in a complex and controversial deal that demonstrated clearly the close connection between political and commercial factors in the civil airframe business, especially regarding Airbus Industrie. Eager to be rid of old and inefficient 727s and L-1011's, Pan Am airlines sought to upgrade its fleet for both its internal routes in Europe and also on the vacation flights to the Caribbean that had made the carrier so popular.[50] With aircraft available for practically immediate delivery, AI was both willing and able to offer singularly flexible contractual terms. But attractive business arrangements alone were not enough to convince Edward Acker, Pan Am's chief executive officer, to take such a long-term commitment with the European consortium. Therefore, before signing anything Acker insisted that he receive direct and personal assurances from responsible figures in the governments of France and Germany that public support for Airbus would continue and thus guarantee the consortium's viability.[51] Acker's concerns apparently were addressed adequately, and a letter of intent was signed in Paris on 11 September 1984 between AI and Pan Am. In it Pan Am agreed to lease 12 A300B4s and four A310-200s, thus relieving AI of two-thirds of the 24 "white-tails" that were the cause of so much controversy in France and Europe. In addition, Pan Am agreed to purchase 12 A310-300s and 16 A320s, yielding a contract for a total of 44 aircraft with a value of $1 billion. This second phase also included options on an additional 13 A310-300s and 34 more A320s, "bringing the total to 91, representing a total investment by the airline of close to $2 billion, discounting support costs."[52] And all this from the airline so instrumental in inaugurating the jet age and mass air travel—Pan Am had served as the launch customer for both the Boeing 707 and the 747. Eager to please its important new customer, AI quickly painted up four "white-tails" in Pan Am livery and delivered the first A300B4s in December 1984.

Predictably, the Pan Am contract had an immediate influence on the commercial and technical decisions of other airlines. Not only did it seem to unleash a veritable flood of orders for Airbus Industrie, especially for the A320, the contest over who would provide engines for the new single-aisle was affected as well. In June of 1985 Lufthansa ordered 15 A320s with options for 25 more and selected the same engine as had Pan Am, the IAE V-2500; the latter had launched the new consortium's first offering to the world's airlines. For AI, the order book continued to grow; in early 1986 Continental Airlines strengthened AI's position in the U.S. market, with an order for six A300B4s. Alia of Jordan ordered six A310-300s and six A320s, followed by CAAC of China and Finnair, who both became wide-body customers. Despite the competition from Boeing, by 1986 AI was firmly anchored in the wide-body, twin-engine segment: "By 30 June 1986 AI had delivered 350 aircraft to 54 operators, this total comprising 263 A300s and 87 A310s."[53]

Even more impressive were developments in the single-aisle market. Most notable was the Northwest Airlines order in October 1986 for 100 A320s, which was important not only for its massive size but also because "NWA is the chief airline of the northwest part of the United States, and the No 1 operator through Seattle, home of Boeing."[54] Technically astute and commercially savvy, the Northwest contract represented not only a vote of confidence in the A320 and in Airbus as an organization but also dealt a blow to Boeing's attempt to convince airlines to wait for its promised new-generation aircraft based on unducted fan (UDF) technology.[55]

The sales success of the A320 in the two and one-half years since its launch had surpassed even the expectations of its more optimistic advocates. By the time of its spectacular rollout in Toulouse on 14 February 1987[56] and its first flight eight days later, the A320 had broken records for prelaunch sales not only for Airbus products but for those of its competition as well, thus making the A320 the fastest selling commercial airliner in history. "By mid-1987, 15 airlines and three leasing companies had signed for 287 A320s, plus 160 on option, a total of 447."[57]

## CONCLUSION: TECHNOLOGICAL
## INNOVATION AND COMMERCIAL STRATEGY

What accounts for the enormous commercial success of the A320?[58] How was the European manufacturer able to penetrate a new market segment with such apparent ease, even after having the entry of its product delayed while government financing was secured? The answers to these questions lie in the close connection that exists between technological innovation and commercial strategy in the civil airframe industry, especially regarding the AI consortium. For Airbus Industrie, developing the A320 entailed more than garnering a substantial percentage of sales in the largest segment of the commercial airframe market. Competing in the single-aisle segment meant challenging established players in a business that they themselves had created and subsequently defined with their products, and doing so without the benefit of a proprietary offering that might confer customer loyalty or credibility. But AI turned these seeming liabilities into advantages and made a virtue of necessity by introducing a product whose technical and operational characteristics distinguished it markedly from existing aircraft. Such tactics inverted those used with the A300B, in which a technological conservatism was combined with the commercial innovation in the twin-engine, twin-aisle configuration that allowed AI to gain initial entry to the world market for large civil airframes. On the other hand, with the A320 AI took substantial risk in employing new concepts and practices to create a truly novel aircraft and thus penetrate an existing sector already occupied by entrenched rivals. But even more important, in the process of applying technological prowess to create commercial opportunity, Airbus Industrie was able to seize the competitive initiative and redefine industry standards.

As described earlier, Airbus Industrie had set the configuration of the A320 in October 1981, offering two basic models that differed only in the amount of fuel each could hold and therefore in the distances each could fly nonstop.[59] Having the same fuselage, each could carry between 140 and 160 passengers, depending on the exact cabin layout, over approximately 2,500 to 4,000 nautical miles. Other than the fact that the fuselage was somewhat wider than that of the competition, the A320 looked like a conventional single-aisle aircraft. Appearances can be deceiving, however, especially during periods of rapid and fundamental change to the materials, processes and systems that make up so complex a product as a modern airliner. While the A320 retained convention in that it is not inherently aerodynamically unstable, as are many of today's most modern fighter aircraft, actuation of the moving surfaces that control the aircraft is accomplished through electronic signals rather than mechanical or hydraulic devices. These so-called fly-by-wire controls are integrated into an electronic centralized aircraft monitor (ECAM) system, which includes navigational, flight control and communications capabilities. This allows the pilot to receive and respond to information about the aircraft in flight using a group of only six display screens in the cockpit, which are managed by three com-

puters, "and any one computer can handle the entire flow of information."[60]
Also, rather than the traditional "yoke," or wheel, in front of the pilot to guide
the aircraft, the A320 instead employs small "side-stick controls" (SSCs) beside
each cockpit seat, either of which can assume complete control of the flight in
case one of the pilots is incapacitated.[61] With the A320, therefore, the cockpit
is the real innovation, particularly in "the interfaces between the pilots and the
controls and, above all, in the new digital computer capacity to fly the aircraft
better than humans can."[62]

Ironically, the performance of the A320 and thus its appeal to customers
was arguably enhanced significantly by the delays surrounding its launch,
because the engines that power it also are the beneficiaries of recent advances
in computer technology. Both the V2500 and the CFM56-5 are equipped with
fully authorized digital engine control (FADEC) systems that optimize the
thrust and fuel consumption rates of the power plant in response to the
demands placed on it by the aircraft throughout its flight domain. For example, if the plane encounters substantial wind shear upon approach, the aircraft
computers calculate the air speed and ground speed required for safe landing,
and any deviation from these "automatically triggers a change in engine power
to maintain the correct speed."[63] So while not removing critical decisionmaking responsibility from the crew, the A320 flight control system combines
human knowledge and experience with new electronic and data management
capabilities to produce an integrated man-machine unit able to respond
quickly and predictably to the environment around it.

Since it changes dramatically the relationship between man and machine
in powered flight, "the A320 could be considered as the precursor to new
race of aircraft."[64] Yet our analysis shows that the conceptual and technological breakthroughs realized in the A320 were not achieved quickly or
suddenly; rather, they were the product of gradual and consistent experi-
mentation and innovation. While the A300B utilized standard, mostly
American-made components, with the A310 Airbus Industrie introduced a
number of important changes in aircraft design, such as cathode-ray cockpit
displays and especially the FFCC. The A300-600 incorporated these
advances as well and also introduced even more flexible and interactive types
of instrumentation that would receive fuller application in the A320. And like
its predecessors, the A320 made use of advances in construction techniques
and the use of composite materials, including carbon fiber and exotic metal
alloys, to reduce the weight of the aircraft while increasing its strength and
resistance to corrosion.

In addition to innovations introduced on production aircraft, AI engineers employed test beds and flight simulators to evaluate new concepts and designs. But Airbus Industrie did not carry out this perpetual and sometimes radical process of innovation in product design and development merely for its own sake, as many argued had been the case in former European aircraft projects, most notably the Concorde. In order for technological skill to be translated into commercial success, the customer must benefit in terms of realizing lower operating costs over the life of the aircraft. Thus AI had to convince both the airlines that would buy it and the governments that would pay for its development that the A320 did in fact embody commercially significant technological changes. Having done so, AI was able to enter a new market segment successfully, and further alter the competitive balance in the commercial airframe industry. So rather than manifesting an obsession with gadgetry, in the case of Airbus Industrie and its series of aircraft, especially the A320, "technological innovation is integrated into a strategy for reconquering the market."[65] As we shall see in the next chapter, Airbus Industrie would not relent in its efforts to combine the technological prowess of the industrial partners with the political will of the national governments in a commercial strategy designed to reestablish a permanent and significant European presence in a highly competitive and global commercial airframe industry.

# 8

## ADAPTING TO THE POLITICAL CONSEQUENCES OF COMMERCIAL SUCCESS (1987–1994)

*In the last chapter* we saw that the Airbus Industrie consortium had followed the initial market penetration of the A300/A310 with further technological and commercial breakthroughs with the single-aisle A320.[1] Not willing to rest upon its laurels and eager to challenge Boeing in the long-range, wide-body segment of the market, on 5 June 1987 AI announced the launch of the A330/A340 models. By basing two new aircraft of different payload and range on the same basic fuselage, wing and cockpit while incorporating much of the A320's avionics and flight control technology, AI planned to extend its product line while minimizing cost and risk.

The A330/A340 program was to be the culmination of a long-range strategy. It had been recognized early on within the Airbus consortium and throughout the commercial aviation industry that the ability of an airframe manufacturer to offer potential customers a "family" of aircraft carried substantial advantages. On the demand side of the market, airlines could realize lower training and maintenance costs by purchasing over time a fleet of planes having substantial commonality across types. On the supply side, the producer could realize significant economies due to the powerful learning effects associated with aircraft design, construction and after-sales support. Therefore, having already established a market presence and having put into place an elaborate but effective industrial system, with the A330/A340 AI and its members were ready to emulate the market leader, Boeing, in being propelled along a steep learning curve by the motor of follow-on sales.

This chapter will show, however, that the efforts undertaken to realize these commercial objectives brought to the fore two distinct but related sets of problems for AI and its members. On the international front was the intensification of political conflict with the United States, as both its air-framers and government showed an increasing intolerance of the subsidies paid to the industrial partners of AI by their respective governments. Thus, with the A330/A340 program, the consortium earned itself center stage in a dispute over "unfair competition" in civil aviation that, while simmering throughout the 1970s and early 1980s, became one of the most contentious issues in transatlantic relations by the end of the decade and remains so to this day.

In Europe, extending the Airbus family generated powerful pressures within the consortium for reform of both its structure and operation. Of primary concern for the participants was refashioning an organization that had grown unwieldy with the addition of new members and expansion of the product line. Timely decisionmaking, all the more important in the increasingly competitive environment, was hampered by both the size and number of meetings required to resolve problems or take new initiatives. But an even more fundamental challenge emerged; as the product line continued to grow, the partners began to question seriously the existing division of labor among them. By the late 1980s the British and especially the German members were asking with increasing insistence for a share of the high value-added systems integration work such as cockpit design and final assembly, both of which were still the exclusive responsibilities of Aérospatiale. Paradoxically, therefore, it was the attempt to capitalize on past success that would impel the partners to question the very structure that had made their collaboration commercially viable. Ironically, the attempt to realize new market opportunities would make manifest the tensions built into the consortium: those between a commercially oriented system of program management based on elaborate division of labor, and the divergent industrial and technological aims of the partners themselves.

While each of these issues—the subsidy dispute and internal reform—would be played out in its own venue, they were closely linked in an important way. Critics from both outside and inside Airbus Industrie were united by misgivings about a lack of transparency and accountability within the consortium. It was widely perceived that the Airbus system prevented competitors and participants alike from gaining a complete and accurate view of the actual costs and benefits of its programs. AI thus was faced with building and converging pressures from both without and within to transform itself into a more "rational" form of industrial and commercial organization. During the late 1980s and early 1990s, therefore, the AI consortium faced twin challenges stemming from its own past success: to follow up on prior accomplishments while retaining (and perhaps improving) the political and industrial system that had made these accomplishments possible, even as the very success of the system was generating these same challenges.

## THE INTERNAL REFORM OF AIRBUS INDUSTRIE

The growing tensions in transatlantic relations associated with Airbus Industrie and its place in the world civil airframe market were accompanied by significant upheaval within the consortium as well, and this connection was no mere coincidence. Both debates stemmed ultimately from the commercial success experienced by AI, and both were directly attributable to stated plans to build on this momentum by extending the product line. By following so quickly the success of the A320 with the launch of an entirely new line of aircraft, Airbus Industrie was certain to exacerbate the tensions and reveal the fault lines that had been built into the very structure of the consortium.[2] Moreover, the issues of subsidy and internal reform were linked explicitly in that AI's unconventional structure made it easier for critics to claim that the participants were deliberately obscuring the financial links between the member firms and the national governments by hiding them within the GIE configuration. Thus, external political pressure had led to "the growing acceptance that unless there were changes in the system, there was a European flank that would remain vulnerable."[3]

Therefore, in the summer of 1987, the governments of the four national backers of AI appointed an expert commission to conduct a review of the consortium's administrative structure and issue a set of recommendations for its improvement.[4] Each government selected a figure prominent in industry, politics or both. "For their nominee, the French found it natural to go to the heart of their aeronautical establishment"; the choice was Jacques Bechinou.[5] At that time president of the peak industry group representing French aerospace companies, the Groupement des Industries Français Aéronautiques et Spatiales (GIFAS), Bechinou had run the firm of Messier-Hispano-Bugatti in the 1970s and since 1982 had been head of SNECMA, the state-owned engine manufacturer. The German representative was Peter Pfeiffer, who had been director of Bayerische Vereinsbank for 25 years and by virtue of that position had served on the supervisory boards of both MBB and Deutsche Airbus. The Spanish sent an aeronautical engineer and former banker who had served on the board of Iberia, the Spanish airline. Emilio Gonzalez Garcia also was a member of the team that negotiated Spanish entry into Airbus Industrie and had served as chairman of CASA and later as a member of the Airbus Supervisory Board. The British sent Sir Jeffrey Sterling, chairman of Peninsular and Oriental Steam Navigation Company, with broad experience in both finance and government yet none specifically in aerospace.

They began work in January 1988 and in April issued a report that "in spite of its even tone was as devastating as it was brief."[6] While congratulating the consortium on its technical and commercial success, they identified several areas relating to its structure and operation requiring immediate attention. First, they observed that the administrative body was too large and followed decision rules that made timely and effective action difficult. Second, the report noted the absence of a consolidated balance sheet showing the financial status of the consortium's entire operations and urged that a financial officer be appointed to create and manage a more rational accounting system. The third criticism was closely related to the second; in the opinion of the "wise men," there existed an effective divorce between the marketing and production functions of the consortium and therefore no effective means of overall cost control. On the one hand, the sales force was negotiating deals without an accurate picture of input prices, while on the other "the four partners 'fix or impose their prices on Airbus Industrie and make known neither amongst themselves nor to Airbus Industrie their effective costs.'"[7]

On the basis of these criticisms, "les sages" included in the report some concrete recommendations for reform. They agreed that, in the long run, the best solution would be to create from the existing arrangements a fully integrated European civil aerospace company, perhaps even a public limited company (PLC), but they also felt that the obstacles were too great for the time being. So they proposed, in a seemingly contradictory manner, that the GIE be strengthened, even while giving the partners more control over its operations. This would be accomplished by making the management structure more efficient and at the same time by giving the partners direct oversight over day-to-day operations.

Regarding the streamlining of the decisionmaking structure, their focus was on the Supervisory Board, which, in their view, should "become the main instrument of policy of the consortium as a whole."[8] Rather than merely ratifying decisions taken either above it at the political level or below it among the partners, instead the board should be fashioned into a coherent body responsible for defining the consortium's strategic direction. In particular, they recommended that the Supervisory Board be slimmed down drastically from 20 members to five, and that both its president and other members be willing and able to devote their full attention to the affairs of the consortium.

Next, they sought to strengthen the partner's hand in calling for the creation of an Executive Board, a true board of directors with real authority to exert effective control over Airbus programs. Its decisions should be binding and taken by majority vote whenever possible, with the prevailing unanimity requirement being invoked only when the partners' direct financial interests were affected. The proposed board was to have seven members, one each from the partners, plus three others: the managing director, a commercial director and a financial director. The managing director would chair the Executive Board and thus be the main point of contact between the owners and the actual aircraft programs. The proposed commercial director would look after marketing and after-sales support. The post of financial director was to be especially important to the overall package of reforms, since he would be responsible for instituting a comprehensive system of cost accounting and control and thus would be given access to the partners' records concerning the prices charged to AI for their portion of the work.

Further, the report recommended AI take over more of the subcontracting with outside firms, a responsibility that currently lay almost completely with the partners. The "wise men" felt that AI might be more aggressive in seeking the lowest possible price and the best possible terms, as in the direct tender procedure used for major items such as engines, nacelles and APUs. It also asked that AI hire more of its personnel directly rather than having them "seconded" from the partners, so as to avoid any conflicts of interest or division of loyalty. The report also wished to see an end to the practice of reserving certain key positions within the consortium for individuals of specific nationality; hiring and promotion, especially of high-level executives, should be based on merit only. Predictably, these findings did not meet with universal acclamation among the partners or at the GIE, and it would be nearly one year before any of the reforms were implemented.

Debate within the consortium over the proposed reforms was interrupted in October 1988 by the death of Franz-Josef Strauss, chairman of the Supervisory Board of Airbus Industrie and prominent Bavarian politician; it was said that "Strauss left as big a hole in Airbus as he did in German politics. . . ."[9] Attention was thus turned to the immediate task of finding a successor, and while some consideration was given to recommendation of the "wise men" that key positions not automatically go to individuals of a particular nationality, noone was really surprised when Hans Friderichs, a German politician and banker, was chosen for the slot.[10] His first challenge was to decide precisely which of the findings of "les sages" were to be adopted and how they would be implemented.

## THE REORGANIZATION OF AIRBUS INDUSTRIE

In March of 1989 the management reorganization plan was finally approved, and the new arrangements took force 1 April 1989. Not all of the report's recommendations were carried out, but important and lasting changes were made. (Figures A.8 and A.9 depict the corporate structure of Airbus Industrie after the reorganization). One of the more drastic steps was to reduce membership on the Supervisory Board to only five members. It would henceforth be comprised of the highest officials of each of the four partner firms and be presided over by the Airbus Industrie chairman.[11] As spelled out in the report, the purpose was to provide for a more streamlined and rapid decisionmaking process regarding the consortium's overall strategy. Second, direct control over day-to-day operations was to be enhanced through the creation of a seven-member Executive Board, although not of the precise composition recommended by the "wise men." Jean Pierson, the (then and current) president and CEO of Airbus Industrie, was named managing director, and was joined by the heads of the partners' respective aircraft divisions. The two remaining slots were filled by a chief operating officer and the financial director (See figure A.8 for the current composition of the Executive Board.)[12] Beneath the Executive Board in the organizational hierarchy was a tier of senior vice-presidents in charge of various functions, such as commercial, engineering and technology.

While Airbus Industrie was to remain a GIE, and thus not move quickly to become a more "normal," PLC-type company, perhaps the most controversial organizational change was the creation of the position of finance director. Invested with considerable oversight authority, at least on paper, the position was given to Robert Smith, who had held an analogous position at Royal Ordnance, since 1987 a division of BAe. His job was to institute a single and comprehensive cost-accounting system for the entire organization. Doing so would serve a dual purpose: to quiet critics both inside and outside the consortium who argued that Airbus aircraft were being sold at commercially unrealistic prices. As it stood, nobody within AI could refute these charges conclusively, because noone knew the actual costs of producing the planes.

Success in this endeavor obviously would depend on the new appointee having access to the partners' books, but this issue would make Smith's stay in Toulouse a short and tumultuous one. Sent to Airbus headquarters in March of 1989, Smith set out to identify the partners' costs on the components delivered to AI but found them decidedly unwilling to divulge this information. He quickly found out that not everyone involved was eager to make the consortium more like an Anglo-Saxon-style PLC, especially if this might eventually entail converting the partners' design and production facilities into divisions of a single corporation. Objections were especially strong at Aérospatiale, where even before Smith had been appointed to the new post, the chairman, Henri Martre, had expressed his fears that the resulting entity would be too small and weak to compete with Boeing. Its status would be especially problematic since the new AI would lack the backing of military contracts so crucial to the financial health of all civil airframe manufacturing firms.[13]

Moreover, for the French partner, creating the position of financial director and investing it with the wide-ranging authority envisaged by the "wise men" was anathema. For his part, Martre was quite willing to continue with the current system in which the members acted essentially as major subcontractors to AI without revealing their costs to AI or to one another.[14] Regarding opening the books, it was felt that his having full access to the partners' books would confer too much power upon the financial director: "I have never come across a company where the financial director has authority over everybody else. That would make him managing director, not financial director."[15] This view was shared by Jean Pierson, the chairman of the Executive Board and managing director of Airbus Industrie, who let it be known that if the issue was pressed too far, his own resignation was not out of the question. For Martre, therefore, the idea of full transparency was "a completely artificial idea."[16] Confronting such attitudes, a frustrated Smith "ran into such resistance and secrecy that he quit in early December."[17] But rather than representing a personal failing of the appointee, the incident was "revelatory of the difficulties associated with moving from a system of cooperation toward a more integrated one."[18] Submitting the details of their costs to examination by an official of the consortium would have entailed a dramatic change in the character of the relationship between the partners and the GIE.

Difficulties within the consortium also were encountered because of changes to the process of allocating work to the partners on the various sections of the aircraft. The "wise men" had recommended that future work shares be determined more through competitive bidding among the partners rather than simply being distributed according to past practice. Such a procedure was adopted for the new components, including the fuselage plugs and wing flaps that would be required for the A321, a "stretched" version of the A320.[19] The unexpected result was that BAe won the right to produce the new fuselage sections, a responsibility that traditionally had been MBB's. For its part, MBB got the work on the wing flaps.

These changes in procedure still failed to resolve a more important issue, the eventual location of the final assembly line for the A321. For several months both MBB and the German government had been pressing within AI for an A320 assembly line in Hamburg. Aérospatiale resisted these proposals, and the 24 November 1989 launch of the A321 only added to the clamor. Unable to reach a decision, the AI management appointed a working group (composed of one member from each partner, along with a representative of AI) to study the issue.[20] Further complicating matters for the consortium during this time—especially for production of the A320—was the strike at BAe's manufacturing facilities, which was an evident source of tension between Pierson and the BAe management.[21] But sales of the A321 continued so strongly that the working group was able to recommend that a separate assembly line be established for it in Hamburg, and this decision was endorsed by the Supervisory Board on 26 January 1990.[22] This location of the A321 assembly line led to a further reshuffling of work shares within the consortium. While assembly and final cabin outfitting of the A321 would take place at Hamburg, cabin outfitting for A330/A340 aircraft now would be handled by Aérospatiale in Toulouse. Although each partner would have to invest substantial sums in order to handle the new work, it was believed that important savings would be realized.[23] These savings would be sorely needed, as the heady environment of a boom market was about to undergo a drastic change.

## GULF WAR AND RECESSION: A DEPRESSED MARKET FOR CIVIL AIRCRAFT

Despite the intensifying political conflict with the United States and upheaval or internal reorganization, things had gone especially well on the sales front for AI in the late 1980s, both in the United States and elsewhere. The year 1989 had been especially good; in the United States Northwest Airlines had ordered ten of the proposed new A330 model in addition to its previously announced commitment to 20 A340s, and Trans World Airlines (TWA) followed with a request for 40 A330s (20 on firm order and 20 on option).[24] In the Far East, prestigious Cathay Pacific of Hong Kong had asked for ten A330s to replace its aging and fuel-thirsty L-1011s.[25] AI's other products also had sold well. In the wide-body twin segment the recently introduced A300-600R was gaining interest, and the A310 continued to draw customers worldwide.[26] Even the Soviet airline Aeroflot signed a letter of intent to buy five A310-300s and had taken options on five more.[27] In the single-aisle segment, at the Paris air show that summer, Northwest took delivery of the first of 25 (later 50) A320s it had ordered; total orders for the A320 now stood in excess of 500.[28] Overall, by the end of 1989, AI had booked 421 firm orders to create a backlog valued at an estimated $34 billion. That year the consortium delivered 105 aircraft to produce revenues of about $5 billion.[29] (Figures A.5 and A.6 show the cumulative buildup of Airbus orders and deliveries, and Figure A.7 depicts the Airbus share of all aircraft orders placed).

With the strike at BAe finally brought to an end in March 1990,[30] production of the A320 soon began to accelerate to fill the backlog of unfilled orders. Construction of Aérospatiale's huge new assembly facilities at Toulouse for the A330/A340 was well under way, as was the tooling and lining up of subcontractors for the new aircraft.[31] Although there were disturbing incidents, such as the crash on 14 February 1990 near Bangalore of an Indian Airlines A320 that killed 90 people,[32] clearly the consortium was "riding the crest of the buying surge" that swept the airlines in the late 1980s.[33]

The buying spree was not to last. All of the optimistic projections of traffic and revenue growth were thrown into disarray by Iraq's invasion of Kuwait on 2 August 1990. Although the military phase of the United Nation's response was essentially completed within six months, the political and commercial effects of the conflict linger even today. The Gulf War had two complementary and negative effects upon the world's airlines and thus upon the builders of commercial airframes. The first was to raise the price of aviation fuel, while the second and more damaging effect was to cause a dramatic drop in passenger air traffic because of a fear of terrorist action against citizens of Western nations.

Coincidental with the Gulf War and reinforcing to its economic impact on the airlines was the onset in 1990 of a general recession among the industrialized countries. Demand for air travel proved especially sensitive to the downturn, and in 1991 airlines saw for the first time since the advent of jet travel an actual decrease of 3 percent in the number of revenue passenger miles (RPM) flown. While 1992 registered a slight revival in RPMs, the damage to airline balance sheets was already mounting and was exacerbated by the ensuing cut-throat competition among the airlines for fares. The effects upon the air-framers were as predictable as they were disastrous. As the world's airlines began to bleed red ink, along with other cost-cutting measures they began to reconsider recent decisions to expand capacity.[34] At best, this meant the delaying of delivery schedules or the cancellation of options taken for aircraft; at worst, the reduction or even outright cancellation of firm orders.

While all three of the manufacturers of large commercial airliners confronted a bleak economic environment during 1991 and 1992, for AI in particular it was crucial to limit the impact on the consortium's current and future prospects. Along with the delicate process of negotiating with valued customers concerning the deferral or cancellation of orders, AI also had to begin adjusting production schedules to reflect the new reality. The numbers were clear;[35] while 1991 had seen a 70 percent increase in Airbus deliveries (from 95 in 1990 to 163 in 1991) and a corresponding increase in revenues (from $4.6 billion in 1990 to $7.6 billion in 1991), new orders had fallen precipitously (from 404 in 1990 to 101 in 1991). Moreover, 24 of these were cancelled during the year, leaving net firm orders at only 77 for the year.

While the certification schedule for new A330/A340 was not affected,[36] 1992 would see both a slowing of production rates for the A320 and a delay in the launch of its newest planned derivative, the A319.[37] Especially problematic was the fact that A320 production had been deliberately accelerated during 1990 to make up for the 31 aircraft not built during the strike at BAe; now it had to be geared down in late 1991 and into 1992.[38] While new, large and controversial orders continued to be won,[39] much of the news was bad, especially from Northwest Airlines, Airbus Industrie's largest customer in the vital North American market. First requesting in September 1992 to defer delivery of 16 A330s, in December 1992 Northwest dropped a "bombshell" on AI by announcing the cancellation of its order for 24 A340s and 50 A320s.[40] Particularly disturbing and quite symptomatic of the airline industry's predicament during this time were the troubles of Guiness Peat Aviation (GPA), the world's largest aircraft leasing firm and Airbus Industrie's second largest customer at that time. Caught between falling demand for leased aircraft and a very highly leveraged capital structure, the position of the Shannon-based firm became increasingly untenable. When repeated attempts to raise new capital failed in 1992, GPA was forced to turn to creditors and aircraft suppliers alike for a complete renegotiation of its commitments.[41]

## THE TRANSATLANTIC DISPUTE OVER SUBSIDES

The difficulties posed by the internal reorganization in conjunction with the dramatic expansion of the Airbus product line, coupled with the abrupt yet protracted collapse in aircraft demand following the Gulf War, form an appropriate backdrop to analysis of the other major challenge facing the Airbus consortium during this period: the subsidy dispute with the United States. As discussed earlier, AI's international sales successes and especially its breakthrough into the American market with the A300/A310 in 1978 had finally drawn the attention of U.S. airframers. BAe's decision that same year to reject the subcontracting relationship proposed by Boeing and to rejoin AI as a 20 percent partner had made the European consortium an even more formidable opponent. Boeing's decision to launch the 767 and thus take on AI directly in the wide-body market had led to a bruising international sales competition between the two. Each accused of the other of unfair pricing and sales tactics, including the alleged use of high-level political arm-twisting to influence airline buying decisions.

As the 1980s progressed and AI continued to gain market share, even penetrating a lucrative new segment with the A320, the protests from the U.S. side were increasingly focused on the various forms of subsidization received by the AI partner firms in developing and producing its aircraft. Specifically, both Boeing and McDonnell Douglas argued that none of the Airbus programs up to that point had even begun to approach profitability and that the proposed A330/A340 program would not be viable when measured by normal commercial standards.

Political pressure from the U.S. airframers and frustration within the U.S. government mounted to the point that a high-level negotiating team was dispatched to Europe in March 1986 to discuss with European Community officials what was fast becoming a major bone of transatlantic contention.[42] While this first round of talks was a "lengthy, frank and honest"[43] attempt to find common ground, no really substantial progress on reaching a common definition of either subsidies or unfair political "inducements" to buy aircraft materialized.[44] Also, the U.S. administration had met with only thinly veiled advice from its counterparts in Europe to mind its own business concerning the commercial rationality of launching the A330/A340.[45] After an even less satisfactory second European excursion by officials of the United States Trade Representative (USTR) and the

Department of Commerce (DoC) in February 1987, the U.S. administration was ready to consider other options seriously.

The United States adopted a two-pronged approach. The first element was to commission a private research firm, Gellman Research Associates (GRA), to conduct a thorough study documenting European government support of AI and assessing the commercial viability of its past and planned programs. The second element of the U.S. strategy was to raise the public profile of the issue by requesting a special meeting of the General Agreement on Tariffs and Trade (GATT) Aircraft Committee. But both of these measures would take time to bear fruit, and the immediate result was only to initiate a new round of meetings, with the promise of some agreement by July 1987. The atmosphere surrounding the transatlantic negotiations was poisoned by the official launch by Airbus Industrie of the A330/A340 on 5 June 1987 and was worsened further by the opening U.S. Congressional hearings in July that were quite confrontational toward Airbus in both tone and content.[46] Although two additional high-level meetings were held in the late months of 1987, nothing encouraging was produced.[47] Even six months later, U.S. negotiators had nothing to show for their efforts, and tensions clearly were on the rise.[48]

The simmering controversy was brought to a head by events in Germany. There had been for some years in German business and political circles discussion of the possible takeover of MBB (the aerospace conglomerate and by then 100 percent owner of Deutsche Airbus) by a larger and more financially resourceful German industrial concern. In late 1988 negotiations with the automotive giant Daimler-Benz had reached an advanced stage concerning the details of its possible purchase of just over 50 percent of MBB for a price of at least DM 1.7 billion.[49] But in order to gain the consent of the Daimler-Benz board, the German government had to offer inducements that revolved directly around MBB's Airbus participation.

These inducements would take two basic forms. The first required the government to absolve Daimler-Benz of all past public indebtedness by MBB regarding the Airbus program. Also, the government was to take a 20 percent stake in a new holding company that would be created to manage MBB's Airbus interests, though it was planned that Daimler-Benz would gradually purchase the government's holding before the year 2000.[50] The second provision was even more controversial in relation to the ongoing subsidy dispute, since it required that the German government provide up to DM 2.6 billion in protection to Daimler-Benz for any losses it might incur through exchange rate (forex) movements on existing Airbus programs. It also provided reduced but similar forex protection for new programs, including the recently announced A330/A340 aircraft, as well as a possible A320 "stretch."[51]

The granting of exchange rate protection, finally approved by the German government cabinet on 7 November 1988, marked a watershed in the subsidy dispute. No longer could it be claimed that Airbus received governmental support only in the form of repayable launch aid or loans; from the U.S. perspective, the forex guarantee was an unambiguous example of government assuming commercial risk. To make matters worse, in March of 1989 the European Commission (CEC) approved the German exchange rate support program, arguing that the entire Community would benefit from having a stronger aerospace sector, an end that would be served by the forex guarantees.[52] The CEC also argued that having Daimler-Benz take a controlling interest in MBB (possible only with the forex provisions) was actually a move in the direction of privatizing the German and European aerospace sectors, something the United States had been calling for all along.[53]

The new Bush administration remained unconvinced, and decided in March 1989 to bring the dispute under the auspices of the GATT. U.S. Trade Representative (USTR) Carla Hills argued that the forex guarantees violated the Subsidies Code concluded in the Tokyo Round of GATT negotiations (1973-1979) and wanted the dispute heard before the GATT Subsidies Committee. The CEC responded that the proper forum was instead the GATT Civil Aircraft Committee; therefore negotiations continued throughout 1990 concerning not only the substance of a possible subsidies agreement but also the appropriate forum for the forex dispute resolution.[54] Disappointed with results on both fronts, on 14 February 1991 the United States initiated formal proceedings under the Subsidies Committee on the exchange rate issue, and in May 1991 formally requested consultations with the EC, under the auspices of the same committee.

By bringing what was essentially a bilateral issue before the world's largest multinational trade negotiation body, the U.S. government was making quite public its displeasure with European practices regarding civil aircraft manufacture and with the pace of negotiations. Despite the fact that the United States finally succeeded in having the Subsidy Dispute Panel hear the forex case and actually won a decision in January 1992, the multinational forum and process really were inadequate to handle a dispute between powerful adversaries with vital economic and industrial interests at stake.[55] So even while the subsidy issue made its slow progress in the GATT, both parties had been pursuing other avenues to strengthen their respective bargaining positions in what promised to be a protracted round of head-to-head negotiations.

## The Gellman Research Associates Report[56]

As mentioned earlier, the U.S. government had commissioned Gellman Research Associates (GRA) to study the extent and impact of European government subsidies to Airbus programs. The report, issued in September 1990, had as its stated purpose "to deepen understanding of the complex web of relations between the participating companies, the governments and the AI consortium."[57] But its agenda actually was much narrower than that, as the bulk of the report was devoted to showing that AI programs "have not been and will not become commercially viable in the foreseeable future . . ." and that a "privately financed firm would not have invested in any of the AI programs because none of these programs would show sufficient profits."[58]

The authors then constructed an analytical framework through which to demonstrate these points. Following a brief background section on the history and basic structure of the consortium drawn almost entirely from Keith Hayward's 1986 book, they began by defining commercial viability: "expected revenues must exceed all projected costs, including repayment of government supports, by an amount sufficient to defray the cost of the funds employed."[59] The task then was to determine the net level of governmental support given to AI programs and then calculate whether, given that support, any of the AI programs would generate a commercial rate of return.

## GRA findings and conclusions[60]

Having consulted European government budget documents and reports on funding for AI, GRA stated: "In total, the three countries through 1989 committed about $13.5 billion in support to AI aircraft programs."[61] But rather than using this nominal figure as a basis for assessing the commercial viability of AI programs, GRA adjusted this amount to reflect the estimated cost to the governments providing the funds and then also calculated what the cost would have been if the firms had been forced to raise the money themselves on the private capital markets. GRA argued that these adjustments were required in order to take into account the "opportunity costs" of the funds provided to Airbus, or the value the money would have had in another use. Their conclusion: "At the prime private sector borrowing rate in each country, the value of committed net government support by 1989 had reached almost $26 billion."[62]

The point of this analysis was to show "that AI was able to enter and remain in the commercial aircraft industry only through substantial amounts of government support."[63] But this left the job only half done, since the overall purpose of the report was to show that AI had never been and would never be a commercially viable entity. Therefore, GRA then used estimates of AI's share in narrow and wide-body segments of aircraft sales from 1990 to 2008 and of prices and costs on the various AI aircraft models to generate a quantitative assessment of the Airbus programs' commercial and financial viability. This was calculated by plugging the sales and cost estimates (all expressed in 1990 dollars) into a "cash flow model"; the results showed that all AI programs to date had generated negative nominal and cumulative cash flows.[64] Although the cash flows on all programs were projected to turn positive in approximately 1998, even with repayment of government support, the inflow would not be sufficient to recoup what had been lost up to that point.[65] And while the A330/A340 program was forecast to generate a positive cumulative cash flow over its lifetime, these figures (or any of the other projections) included no allowance for the time value of money. GRA concluded, therefore, that for the A330/A340 "revenues will exceed costs but not by an amount sufficient to earn a market rate of return."[66]

Having argued that AI's government-supported entry into the large commercial transport market was based on a product line having no prospects of commercial viability, the rest of the GRA study examined the impact this unwarranted competition would have upon the U.S. aerospace industry. First, GRA argued that the emergence of AI had changed the very character of the industry in which U.S. firms must compete: "The formation of the AI consortium has imparted significant rigidity in the structure of the civil transport aircraft manufacturing industry."[67] This reduced flexibility stemmed from the fact that, because of their participation in the consortium and their agreement not to compete with existing or projected AI programs, its members no longer were available as subcontractors or joint venture partners to other firms. Second, the GRA report asserted that AI's entry into the market for large civil aircraft had produced an undesirable form of competition. Since its products lacked commercial viability and required continued government support, AI's very presence was economically detrimental to the industry. Any damage done would be attributable directly to AI because "if the long-term profit-potential in the market is reduced to levels below the rate-of-return necessary to attract and sustain private capital in-flows to aircraft manufacturers, then the new inefficient producer may displace a more efficient incumbent in one or more aircraft market segments."[68]

Moreover, the negative effects of AI on the U.S. industry were expected to be cumulative and long term. GRA asserted that U.S. companies would see declining profits and shrinking market share, which might deter or prevent their launching new, technologically advanced products or perhaps press them to seek outside, even foreign, sources of capital. Worse, just the mere threat of AI developing the next generation supersonic aircraft "may force U.S. manufacturers to join with AI for this program."[69] And while the effect on U.S. components manufacturers had been more mixed (as the engine builders and other subsystems manufacturers have benefited), "a more disturbing trend has been the 'Europeanization' of the advanced technology avionics and control systems on AI aircraft."[70] The French and then the Germans had been successful in capturing high value-added research and production work on sophisticated components. Finally, because of the eclectic nature of aircraft design and manufacture, the effect of AI's market penetration would be felt throughout the U.S. economy as reductions in employment—in the areas of aeronautics research, development and production—rippled across a variety of industrial sectors.

But whatever the ultimate impact of Airbus Industrie on the American aerospace industry and economy might be, GRA was careful to remind its audience of the overall point of the study. AI had been able to enter the market for large commercial civil transports only with the massive and long-term support of European national governments. Moreover, since its products had no prospect of commercial viability, AI's continued presence could be assured only through continued support. Therefore, any damage to U.S. industry resulted directly from those policies:

> It is important to note that whatever the impact of any such loss to the U.S. economy, the cause for the loss can be traced to the continued subsidization of AI. It is the subsidization of AI, not its success in the market, which should be an issue for U.S. policy.[71]

The long-awaited publication of the Gellman Research Associates Report in September of 1990 clearly staked out a U.S. position that took a very dim view of Airbus and the government money supporting it.[72] In addition to this broadside, the United States also pressed on in the GATT, where in March 1991 the Subsidies Committee agreed to establish a dispute panel to hear the forex issue. The CEC responded by stating its desire to have the Civil Aircraft Agreement renegotiated. For its part, Airbus management, in the person of Jean Pierson, stated its intention to "use every legal weapon at its disposal" to defend Airbus."[73]

Political and commercial developments during the rest of 1991 did nothing to quiet the dispute. That summer Airbus won large orders from Kuwait and from Federal Express, the Memphis-based freight company; the latter was a major coup within the U.S. market. On the other side, Boeing added to AI frustrations by having British Airways order the proposed 777; again the flagship British carrier had refused the European aircraft.[74] The transatlantic temperature was raised again in December by the CEC's release of its own commissioned report, which documented the extent of government support received by the U.S. civil aerospace sector. Given its findings and the timing of its release, all that was needed was the added pressure of a U.S. presidential campaign to make negotiations between the CEC and the Bush administration in early 1992 concerning a bilateral accord on aircraft subsidies as interesting as they would be significant.

## *The Arnold and Porter Report*[75]

Not to be outdone by GRA or the U.S. government, the CEC responded by hiring the prominent Washington, D.C. law firm of Arnold and Porter (AP) to document that the U.S. government had, both directly or indirectly, provided valuable resources to the nation's aeronautics industry. In identifying its sources and estimating its extent, AP focused on three main aspects of this support: the Department of Defense (DoD), the National Aeronautics and Space Administration (NASA) and the U.S. tax code.[76] Each was evaluated in turn for its contribution to the technological, industrial and financial bases of civil aviation in the United States, with particular emphasis on the two major firms involved in airframe manufacture, Boeing and McDonnell Douglas. Looking primarily at the past 15 years, AP estimated that the combined support from the three categories totaled $18 billion to $22.05 billion in actual dollars, or $33.48 billion to $41.49 billion in current dollars. In their report, AP also included a short section on other benefits U.S. aerospace firms realized through their association with the U.S. government.

### Department of Defense support for civil aircraft programs

In first addressing the impact of DoD programs on civil aircraft manufacture in the United States, AP estimated that the department had spent approximately $50 billion in research and development between 1976 and 1990. Only a portion (15 percent) of these funds went to firms engaged in aircraft manufacture, and in turn only a fraction of that money had gone to civil programs. Regarding Boeing and McDonnell Douglas specifically, AP estimated that 25 to 50 percent of the total amount they received from DoD had commercial applicability.[77]

> This means that the $1.79 billion of aircraft-related R&D grants that Boeing received from 1979 to 1990 probably had a value to Boeing's commercial operations of between $449 million and $898 million and that the $4.55 billion of aircraft-related DoD R&D in the same period probably had a value to McDonnell Douglas of between $1.14 billion and $2.28 billion.[78]

In addition, AP also noted that these estimates of direct funding took no account of other commercial benefits accruing to manufacturers of civil aeronautics products from military R&D. These included training of personnel, defrayal of costs on basic equipment and tools, use of labs and test facilities, and experience with technological and industrial "dead-ends" that could not be pursued profitably. Moreover, military contractors engage in independent research and development (IR&D) and undertake bids and proposals (B&P) for DoD projects; AP pointed out that both types of expenditure are reimbursed by DoD in proportion to the military relevance of the spending. However, AP assert that much of this independent research, initiated as it is by the companies themselves, can be expected to have commercial applicability. As with the direct funding, AP used a range of 20 to 25 percent in estimating the commercial impact of the reimbursements: "Therefore, the approximately $5 billion of IR&D and B&P cost reimbursements that aeronautics contractors have received in the past 15 years entailed a benefit of between $1 billion and $1.25 billion to the commercial aircraft industry."[79]

In their report, AP also described DoD's Manufacturing Technology (ManTech) program, whose purpose is to bridge the gap between basic research and industrial application, thus reducing costs and risks to U.S. manufacturers. While ManTech expenditures (totaling $2 billion between 1976 and 1990) ostensibly are dedicated to technologies with clear military relevance, AP asserted the reasonableness of assuming some beneficial commercial spin-off effects from this research as well. As with DoD R&D more generally, AP assumed that 15 percent of these monies went to aeronautics during the period and reduced costs in both its military and commercial sectors.

Commercial benefits of DoD expenditures like those just outlined are supposed to be recouped by the U.S. government, and AP evaluated the laws and procedures that govern this process. They argued that it was very difficult in practice for the government to make accurate estimates of the government-funded military content of aeronautical products, such as commercial airline components, and even harder to then assess and collect the corresponding sums from the manufacturers after the sale. AP therefore asserted that "the amount of recoupment paid by the US commercial aircraft industry is much less than the benefits that the industry had derived form the tens of billions of dollars of DoD R&D funds for aeronautics in the 1976-1990 period."[80] The section of the report on the impact of DoD programs then concludes by analyzing four examples of commercial aeronautical products that benefited directly and substantially from government funding of military R&D.[81]

## *NASA support for civil aircraft programs*

The section of the AP report devoted to the impact of NASA funding on the U.S. civil aviation industry first shows that the mission of NACA (founded in 1915) and NASA (since 1958) has been to promote and preserve U.S. leadership in aviation: "NASA is the primary provider of civilian funds for the aeronautics industry."[82] NASA has four major divisions: (1) Aeronautics Exploration and Technology, (2) Space Science and Applications, (3) Space Flight and (4) Space Operations.[83] Of special importance regarding the dispute over government support for commercial aircraft programs is NASA's Aeronautics Division. It funds four major groups of programs of direct relevance to civil aviation.[84] In the period from 1976 to 1990, the NASA Aeronautics Division budget totaled $8.9 billion, and AP estimated that 90 percent (about $8 billion in actual dollars, $16.96 billion if an opportunity cost/compound interest formula is used) of this money was directly applicable to the civil aviation sector in the United States.[85] Finally, the report also includes shorter (but still substantial) analyses of other NASA programs and contracts.[86] It concludes with a section on NASA recoupment policy, which emphasizes NASA's wide discretion in assessing (or even waiving) fees on manufacturers who have benefited from funding, and laments the paucity of solid data on the recoupment process.

### The impact of tax laws on civil aircraft manufacture[87]

In their report, AP argued that benefits also accrue to U.S. firms engaged in the manufacture of civil aircraft because of specific provisions in the federal tax code. These can be broken into three major types: (1) Completed Contract Method (CCM) of accounting for long-term contracts, (2) Domestic International Sales Corporations (DISCs) and Foreign Sales Corporations (FSCs) and (3) investment tax credits. The AP report evaluates the first two of these in detail.

First, the CCM method of calculating the taxable consequences of engaging in military contract work for the U.S. government defers income calculations and federal tax liability until the project is completed. AP assert that this practice in effect gives the firms involved an interest-free loan for the period, during which income is generated but not taxed. These rules were reformed by Congress in 1986 and eliminated in 1989, and the companies have been compelled to pay back the deferred taxes. Yet the interest saved by the companies was not repaid and tax rates have fallen in the interim, meaning that the companies in question reaped substantial benefits.[88]

Next, DISCs and FSCs are special divisions set up by corporations engaged in export to take advantage of laws that allow them to defer or eliminate altogether the taxable consequences of export sales conducted through these divisions.[89] AP asserted that these provisions have substantially benefited both Boeing and McDonnell Douglas by producing tax-exempt income.[90]

### Other programs and activities

AP also discussed briefly other aspects of the benefits accruing to aeronautics firms through their relationship with the U.S. government. For example, AP asserted that U.S. aeronautics firms, including the civil airframe manufacturers, benefit from the use, either for free or at a low cost, of laboratory and testing facilities of several government agencies and divisions, including: navy, army, the Departments of Energy, Commerce and Transportation, and NASA.[91]

AP also discussed the U.S. government's order of 44 KC-10 military transport aircraft from McDonnell Douglas in 1982, which AP argued was significant to the firm's commercial fate because of the military plane's nearly complete (88 percent) commonality with the DC-10 commercial transport. Without the KC-10 order, both the military and civilian production lines were in danger of being shut down. On this basis, AP asserted that the KC-10 order "kept McDonnell Douglas in the market for large commercial aircraft long enough to develop the MD-11, a derivative of the DC-10."[92] This was seen as crucial to the company's future; "absent the ability to build the MD-11 and to thereby answer the competition provided by Boeing and Airbus, McDonnell Douglas would have had to leave the market."[93]

Though not addressed in detail in the report, AP noted that most observers of the aerospace industry, including executives of major U.S. firms engaged in civil airframe manufacture, agree that military programs subsidize civilian ones in a variety of ways.[94] This is especially significant regarding the steady stream of financing provided by military contracts, which helps to fund the long and risky development of civil products.

Finally, throughout their report AP noted that specific information on the type and extent of U.S. government aid to civil aviation is difficult to obtain, particularly in the case of DoD funds, which flow to the firms through classified programs. Even the Freedom of Information Act proved of very limited help in tracking these flows, and recoupment practices for both DoD and NASA are equally opaque. But the larger point made by the Arnold and Porter report is that the lack of transparency is neither accidental nor coincidental; rather, "it is an inevitable feature of the intimate relationship between the U.S. government and the U.S. commercial aircraft industry."[95] Furthermore, the report asserts that despite the difficulties in quantifying the amount of aid and its precise impact, "it is clear that U.S. government support has played a critical role in assuring the key technological advances made by the U.S. industry and thus, in assuring the competitive position the U.S. enjoys today in markets throughout the world."[96]

## THE JULY 1992 AGREEMENT

Despite the high-level political posturing and the publication of slick reports backing up hard-line positions, throughout the period analyzed so far the two sides in the subsidy dispute actually had been converging in their views concerning acceptable types and levels of government support for civil aircraft programs. Initially unwilling to countenance a limit on direct governmental subsidies on aircraft of less than 75 percent of program costs, the CEC gradually had moved to a position where a cap of approximately one-third might be accepted. But this significant shift had been made possible only by parallel concessions on the American side, which entailed the admission that indirect forms of subsidization (as described in the AP report) did in fact exist and were the legitimate subject of regulation as well. So, by April 1992 the USTR and officials of the CEC were able to announce that a tentative bilateral agreement had been reached in Brussels on limiting both forms of government support while establishing a mutually acceptable mechanism of dispute resolution outside the GATT.

Signed in July 1992 and thus commonly referred to as the "July Agreement,"[97] the accord between the United States and the European Community regulating government support for civil aircraft applied only to programs committed to after the signing date; projects already in progress were not affected. While dealing in specifics, the broader purpose of the July Agreement was to defuse what had become an explosive issue by removing it from the center of political controversy, thus preventing further complications in already volatile transatlantic trade relations.

Articles 4 and 5 formed the core of the agreement. Section 4.2 dealt with direct government funding and limited such support to 33 percent of the program's total cost, and this aid would be subject to repayment. Specifically, Section 4.2(a) limited direct government support for civil aircraft development to 25 percent of the program's projected cost, with provisions for reimbursement yielding full repayment of the loan within 17 years at the government's cost of borrowing. Section 4.2(b) allowed for government support of an additional 8 percent of the program cost, also to be repaid over 17 years, but at the government's cost of borrowing plus 1 percent. Section 4.3 (a,b) laid out a repayment schedule based on the pace of aircraft deliveries.

Article 5 defined and then set limits on indirect government support, making these subject to an either/or cap as defined.[98] Specifically, Section 5.2(a) stipulated that the annual value of such support should not exceed 3 percent of the annual turnover of the commercial aircraft industry within that country, while Article 5.2(b) limited indirect aid to 4 percent of the annual turnover of any single firm engaged in commercial aeronautics in that country. Indirect government aid provided for an aircraft program in excess of either limit would be deemed unacceptable.

Article 10 dealt with possible conflicts and litigation and specified that neither of the parties would initiate unilateral action under domestic trade laws as long as the agreement remained in force. Article 11 provided for regular (twice yearly) consultations, and Article 12 proposed that the parties work to have the July Agreement incorporated into the existing GATT Agreement on Trade in

Civil Aircraft. The July Agreement also included two annexes. Annex II defined the terminology contained in the agreement. More important, Annex I contained an interpretation of Article 4 of the GATT Agreement on Trade in Civil Aircraft in its relation to the issues addressed in the July Agreement. In it, the parties addressed restrictions on trade in civil aircraft other than government subsidies, such as government procurement and sub-contracting policies, and political inducements regarding aircraft sales to third countries.

While the parties' agreement to these provisions clearly represented an improvement in relations concerning government subsidies to civil aircraft manufacture, numerous "escape clauses" weakened the effectiveness and significance of the accord. For example, Article 7 states: "Equity infusions are excluded from the scope of this Agreement."[99] Given the fact that Aérospatiale remained almost entirely state-owned (as does CASA), this is an important exclusion. Further, while Article 8 in general provided for "transparency" and regular exchange of information between the parties, Section 8.12 contained an important restriction: "Nothing in this agreement shall be construed to require any contracting Party to furnish any information the disclosure of which it considers contrary to its essential security interests."[100] In a similar vein, Article 9 provided for "exceptional circumstances" under which the parties could exempt themselves from the terms of the agreement—specifically, if "the survival of a significant proportion of the civil aircraft manufacturing activities in one of the Parties and the continued financial viability of the company or the division responsible for such civil aircraft manufacture are put in jeopardy. . . ."[101] Finally, Article 13.3 provided that either of the parties could pull out of the agreement simply by submitting written notification to this effect, and the withdrawal would take effect 12 months later.

## The year 1993 and beyond: No rest for the weary

While the July Agreement of 1992 temporarily removed Airbus from the political spotlight, the subsidy dispute with the United States remained far from resolved. Many in the U.S. government and aerospace industry were left unsatisfied, feeling that the Europeans had conceded little of real substance while Airbus and the governments behind it continued to behave much as before. Dissatisfaction with the 1992 accord provided fertile ground for debate during the 1992 presidential primary and election campaigns concerning what the U.S. government should do to protect "threatened" industrial sectors such as aerospace, and Airbus remained the primary target of criticism.

In addition to political difficulties, the second half of 1992 and into 1993 saw only marginal improvement in the economics of the air travel industry. Airbus Industrie garnered only 38 orders for new aircraft in the 1993 calendar year, while delivering 138 for a 1993 turnover valued at $8.3 billion. The higher prices received for the A330/A340 aircraft account for the favorable comparison to 1992 (154 units and $7.3 billion turnover); however, the excess of deliveries over orders combined with 69 cancellations to reduce the Airbus 1993 backlog to 667 aircraft valued at $55 billion.[102] However, things would get worse before they got better, as the circumstances of the sales competition for the largest aircraft order in years showed as nothing else could that the consortium was confronting a most hostile commercial environment.

### International politics and airliner sales: The Saudia deal

The economic team assembled by the new Democratic administration quickly showed itself even more ready than its predecessors to engage in confrontation with Airbus concerning subsidies and competition for sales.[103] USTR Mickey Kantor played the role of "point man" in the carrying the political battle to the Europeans, raising the possibility that the July 1992 accord might be renegotiated or that the United States could take additional measures on the subsidy issue, either before the GATT or through domestic legislation. Soon after his inauguration, Bill Clinton himself also adopted a decidedly high-profile position on subsidies and the July 1992 accord.[104] His well-publicized visit to the Boeing facilities in Seattle on 23 February 1993 provided the occasion for the new president to make an explicit connection between job losses in the U.S. aerospace industry and competition from Airbus, and to announce a proposal that was "in all but name a national industrial policy that would use the federal government as an incubator for advanced technology."[105] In this context, he also promised strong new measures in support of the American aeronautics sector, particularly regarding the promotion of export sales.[106]

The opportunity for Clinton to make good on his promise was not long in coming, and in August 1993 the U.S. Export-Import Bank (EX-IM) announced that it would provide financing for the proposed sale of U.S. aircraft to Saudia Airlines of Saudia Arabia, commenting that the "commitment would enable Boeing to match the financing terms available to Airbus for its bid."[107] The lure of attractive financing was reinforced by a personal phone call from President Clinton to King Fahd of Saudia Arabia promoting the McDonnell Douglas and Boeing products. The administration also made use of the considerable persuasive talents of Secretary of Commerce Ron Brown by sending him both to the Paris air show and to Saudia Arabia in support of U.S. aeronautic exports. In addition, Transportation Secretary Federico Pena and a prominent FAA official, David Hinson, paid a visit to Saudia Arabia to discuss the negotiation of a new bilateral aviation agreement between the two countries. The significance of these contacts was not lost on Airbus management, of course: "There is no Mr. Europe who could do a similar job [to President Clinton's]," said an Airbus official,[108] and Airbus managing director Jean Pierson was quick to point out in a letter to EC trade commissioner Leon Brittan that Pena and Hinson could easily use the aviation agreement talks as a lever to influence the Saudia purchase decision.[109]

Further raising the ire of the Europeans was the announcement that the United States would allow the Saudia Arabian government to "restructure" $9.2 billion in debts owed for the purchase of U.S. military hardware, the bulk of which consisted of 72 F-15E fighter aircraft built by McDonnell Douglas.[110] Delivery rates were to be slowed and payment schedules stretched out for the warplanes, and the commercial implication was evident: the deal "could also clear the way for a reported plan by the Saudis to buy $6 billion in commercial airliners from Boeing and McDonnell Douglas."[111] Despite European protests and their own attempts to sway the Saudis,[112] the concerted American effort evidently was effective, as President Clinton and Prince Bandar announced in an elaborate White House ceremony the $6 billion Saudia order for a mix of 50 to 60 American aircraft, including 737s, 747s and MD-11s.[113]

Predictably, the circumstances and outcome of the Saudia sale elicited harsh responses from Airbus officials, European aerospace industry executives and politicians, with Louis Gallois of Aérospatiale seeing evidence of "real state-to-state negotiations" rather than commercial considerations as behind the deal.[114] But the Europeans were more disappointed than shocked at the Americans' tactics, as Pierson and his sales team were no strangers to the timely use of political clout to clench deals in the past. Still, the Saudia saga served notice to AI and all other interested parties that the Clinton administration shared none of its predecessor's ideological reluctance concerning the use of the full complement of political and financial leverage in support of American industry in global sales battles.

Airbus has fared better in sales competitions since the Saudia deal, even in the Americans' own backyard, as Air Canada announced on 10 June 1994 its intention to buy 25 A319s plus another ten on option, bringing total orders and options for the newest Airbus type to 44.[115] More promising in the long term is the fast-growing Asian market, where AI has obtained orders in mainland China, Hong Kong and Singapore.[116] The most important of these deals was from Singapore Airlines (SIA), which added substantially to its January 1992 order by asking for another seven Boeing 747s, along with ten more A340s. Including options and spares, the SIA order is worth $4.9 billion for Boeing and $5.4 billion for Airbus. The prestigious airline has included provisions that would allow it to substitute the latest of both airframers' "big-twin" aircraft, the Airbus A330 or the Boeing 777.[117] SIA's eventual decision, like those of its competitor Cathay Pacific of Hong Kong, certainly will shape the outcome of this latest round in the battle between Boeing and Airbus.[118] For 1994 overall, in fact, the contest went to Airbus over Boeing, as "the European consortium concluded orders with 12 airlines and leasing companies for 125 aircraft valued at $9.1 billion, up from 38 aircraft in 1993."[119] And in an apparent attempt to press its advantage in the face of a sluggish recovery in airline earnings, AI recently announced the formation of a sales financing unit, to be called Airbus Finance Company (AFC).[120]

Whatever the result of any particular sales contest or the battle for market share in any year, therefore, it is apparent that Airbus Industrie has no intention of retiring from the field.[121] The consortium continues to press forward with certification of its newest models, despite the tragic adversity experienced in conducting this difficult process.[122] On a more positive note regarding its approach to aircraft design and technology, AI recently has gained approval from the FAA for its "Cross Crew Qualification" (CCQ) program that allows pilots and flight crews to operate multiple types of Airbus aircraft by undergoing instruction in their common characteristics and then training to master any differences among the specific types. Under CCQ, airlines could use a single group of pilots and crews to operate an entire fleet of Airbus aircraft, presumably saving on overhead and raising productivity levels.[123]

Recent developments within the consortium concerning possible additions to the Airbus product line also suggest that Airbus Industrie intends to remain a major player in the global airframe industry for years to come. Regarding future product development, AI has long recognized the eventual need in the air travel market for "superjumbo" aircraft having intercontinental range and capable of transporting at least 600 people. Boeing too had identified a similar need and in late 1992 created a major stir in the industry by approaching the separate Airbus partners—Aérospatiale, BAe and DASA—concerning a possible partnership, saying the market could absorb only one such program.[124] For its part, AI management rejected Boeing's proposal as a tactic to sow dissension within the consortium and proceeded to talk with Japanese aeronautics firms about their possible role in an AI led superjumbo project. Since Boeing's initial contacts, talks between the rivals regarding the superjumbo have taken place but have produced no concrete joint proposals. In the meantime, the Europeans remain wary of American intentions while "Airbus Industrie and its partners are pursuing independent preliminary studies of the 3XX very-high-capacity transport. . . ."[125] The likelihood of transatlantic cooperation seems further diminished by Boeing's filing suit against AI and its three major partner firms over alleged patent infringement on wing parts for the A320 and its A330/A340 derivatives.[126]

In addition to continued research in the commercial field, AI soon may find itself in the business of designing and manufacturing a military aircraft. Several of Europe's airframers, including Aérospatiale, BAe, DASA and Alenia of Italy, have expressed strong interest in filling the troop and equipment transport needs of the RAF and other air forces into the next century. Unwilling to concede the field to Lockheed and its replacement for the C-130J Hercules, the European builders are actively considering using the facilities and organization of the AI consortium as a vehicle for collaboration for the Future Large Aircraft (FLA).[127]

Beyond ongoing activity in the realm of product development and sales financing, the Airbus consortium continues to seek ways to enhance the organization's image as a "normal" business enterprise. The appointment on 25 March 1994 of Edzard Reuter, formerly chairman of the board of management of Daimler-Benz AG, to succeed Hans Friedrichs as chairman of the Airbus Industrie Supervisory Board is a clear indication of the consortium's intention to become even more closely attuned to commercial and industrial demands in the manufacture and marketing of airliners in a rapidly globalizing sector.[128]

## CONCLUSION

This chapter has shown that the commercial success so long sought by Airbus Industrie and its member firms brought in its wake some of the most formidable challenges yet faced by the consortium. As the focal point of transatlantic political conflict, AI faced powerful pressures to become less reliant on public funds for product development and operations. Those in Europe impatient with the consortium's failure to achieve profitability, who asked that it become more transparent and accountable or that public support for Airbus be reduced or even ended, echoed these demands. Demands from within the organization itself that it become responsive to market forces and thus better able to respond to intensified competition reinforced these external pressures.

We have seen, however, that meeting these challenges did not produce fundamental changes in the consortium's strategy, structure or operation. The subsidy dispute was ameliorated but certainly far from resolved through an agreement that, while setting important limits in the amount of public support that could be given to future commercial aircraft programs, affirmed the European governments in their right to support AI. And while the internal reforms of 1989 were quite significant in their scope and effect, Airbus Industrie retained its basic character as a pooling of distinct entities rather than as a truly integrated enterprise. For all of the pressures and attendant adjustments, AI remained a delicate balance of separate national interests seeking to realize larger political and economic goals through collaboration in a sector of great technological and industrial salience.

Yet while confirming the AI consortium as an effective instrument of European strategy, the experience of the post–Gulf War years also has served notice to the members of Airbus Industrie that the commercial environment remains the ultimate arbiter of the consortium's success. Without customers who themselves can rely on a stream of income, no technological innovation or sales savvy can assure future sales sufficient to sustain the consortium's continued existence. In addition to reminding everyone involved in civil aeronautics that this inherently unpredictable business entails risks that include the real possibility of financial failure, the experience of the Saudia deal confirms aerospace as the most politicized of international commercial activities.

The challenges Airbus Industrie faced during the period from 1987 to 1994—political conflict with the United States concerning government subsidies, the external and internal pressures for reform of the consortium's structure and operation, the vagaries of the commercial environment—all remain closely related concerns for AI in 1995 and beyond. It seems certain that the current and future commercial environment will sorely test both the political will and the technical competence that has made the consortium successful up to this point. Perhaps national rivalries will prove too much for the AI structure; but it seems more likely that the demands of the competition will force a more complete integration of the production and commercial sides of the organization. Whatever the future holds, Airbus Industrie has redefined the terms of the strategic game that is the commercial airliner business. Chapter 9 will evaluate the significance of the consortium's accomplishments to date for both the theory and the practice of international economic relations.

# 9

## ASSESSING THE CASE OF AIRBUS INDUSTRIE: LESSONS FOR THE RELATIONSHIP BETWEEN STATE AND MARKET

*This study has traced* the evolution of Airbus Industrie from the earliest discussions among European firms and governments in the mid-1960s to its current stature as the world's second-largest producer of large commercial airliners. In doing so it has articulated several distinct but related themes that serve to place the creation and development of the consortium in proper historical and analytical context. This final chapter will draw together the main findings of the study, evaluate the consortium as a possible model for collaboration in other industries and assess the significance of Airbus Industrie for both the theory and the practice of international trade and competition.

An important theme developed in this book is that the structure and operation of Airbus Industrie embodies tensions inherent in the environment in which it was created and evolved. From its inception, the Airbus program had to balance, if not completely reconcile, the distinct national interests of its partners with the technological and commercial imperatives imposed by the world market for airliners as it had been defined by the American competition. The formation of Airbus Industrie as a GIE institutionalized the tension between these forces by separating the functions of aircraft development and production from those of marketing and after-sales support. The result has been a business organization of a hybrid or even schizophrenic character, in which the owners act as subcontractors to an entity of their own creation. And while this entity, the GIE, has used its substantial skills in aircraft sales and support to gain important influence over the partners, and even to play a prominent role in the world airline business, because of the tensions that it embodies, Airbus Industrie remains far from constituting a fully integrated corporate entity with a centralized set of product and cost controls.

This study also has argued that the success of Airbus Industrie in creating an organization capable of meeting the technical and commercial challenges of the world airframe market is the product of sustained political will as applied to the specific functional necessities imposed by American leadership in civil aeronautics. Without the substantial and consistent financial support of the respective national governments, the consortium would have had neither the credibility nor the staying power to become an important actor in the global airliner market. Backed by a steady and reliable stream of governmental funding, the Airbus consortium was able to establish the credibility of both its products and its organization, and thus begin to move along the steep learning curves that make entry into the airliner business so difficult.

Therefore, the creation of the AI consortium is understood here as a means to attaining two main ends: extracting the intermediate benefits of high-value added employment and technological spin-offs associated with aircraft design and manufacturing, while at the same time achieving the larger political goals of the governments of France, Germany and Great Britain: that of reestablishing a permanent European presence in world civil aerospace. Yet these same governments had the acumen and foresight to defer to the engineering, management and marketing expertise of the partners and the GIE and, at least after December 1968, eschewed a direct role in the definition or sale of Airbus aircraft. Moreover, government funding was promised and delivered only after the engineers and sales analysts had established that any proposed aircraft did in fact stand a reasonable chance of success on the world market. Thus it was the demands of the market that ultimately dictated the characteristics of the aircraft produced through the collaborative effort; the overriding political priority of ending American hegemony in a crucial economic sector thus was realized through technological expertise and commercial savvy.

## CREATING A STRATEGIC INDUSTRY: TRANSLATING GEOPOLITICAL PRESSURES INTO ECONOMIC FACTS

The same forces and tensions manifest within the structure and operation of the Airbus Industrie consortium—between national interest and commercial imperative, between political will and functional necessity—also are present in the larger industry in which AI is now a central player. The aeronautics industry, because of its singular background and pattern of development, also embodies contradictory imperatives: the desire on the part of governments and firms to maintain indigenous control of research and production assets versus the pressures (generated by the scope and complexity of the industry) to seek sources of technology and capital outside national borders. These tensions, present in the industry since its birth, were greatly exacerbated as the advent of jet propulsion and electronic flight control multiplied the expense and organizational capacity required to produce aircraft. The dynamics of rapid technological change and escalating costs "act as centripetal forces impelling states and corporations toward collaboration, while the industry's strategic value acts as a centrifugal force impelling protectionist policies designed to avoid perceived vulnerabilities associated with mutual dependency."[1]

Thus, the major firms active in both the military and the commercial sides of the industry, such as those involved in Airbus Industrie, have been forced to "reconcile the tension between the economic imperative for a global strategy and the political realities of national government's interest."[2] Paradoxically, however, aerospace firms and national governments face these difficulties because of the very state policies that channeled an enormous volume of public and private resources into the industry. Acting under the pressure of geopolitical competition, powerful states seeking the material means of national self-preservation created formidable capabilities in aerospace and acted as the primary provider of both research and development funding while also serving as the industry's largest customer. This stimulus to both the supply and demand sides of the aviation market has driven an extremely rapid rate of technological and organizational change, while the eclectic nature of aircraft design and construction insured that the industry would be crucial to the development of other high-technology sectors. Commercial applications proved especially important, as the combination of engine and airframe technologies that emerged from the military programs of the Cold War opened new possibilities in the speed, comfort and reliability of air travel. Therefore, the effect of massive government spending on military aeronautical capability was to create a lucrative new air travel business having global scope and impact and further increasing and perpetuating the industry's economic and political salience in industrial(izing) states.

Therefore, within the space of a mere 30 years (1940-1970), the aviation sector was transformed through government procurement policies from a marginal factor in military, economic and political international relations into an industry absolutely vital to all aspects of national security. It is, however, ironic that these same state policies also had the effect of extending the scope and scale of product design and development far beyond the capabilities of any single business unit. Under the pressure of rapid technological change, the volume of capital required to participate fully in modern aeronautics quickly exceeded that generated internally by even the largest and most successful corporations in the world, and firms that wished to enter or simply to remain active in the industry were compelled to seek supplemental resources, often outside national borders.[3] Paradoxically, therefore, the efforts of states seeking to provide the material means of national security in a highly industrialized context have created the necessity of transnational collaboration to achieve the requisite scale and scope of operations even to participate, much less to compete successfully, in the aerospace industry.

## CREATING AN OLIGOPOLISTIC INDUSTRY: GOVERNMENT SPENDING, ECONOMIES OF SCALE AND BARRIERS TO ENTRY

The technological, industrial and organizational effects of state procurement policies on the aerospace industry made its commercial airframe segment strategic in two senses. Not only would capabilities in civil air transport bear more and more directly on both the military and especially the economic dimensions of national security,[4] but because of the scale and pace of technological change in aeronautics, the manufacturing of commercial airframes inevitably had taken on an oligopolistic structure. This tendency toward oligopoly or even monopoly was driven by the same forces that were behind the industry's rapid growth in national and global salience. Massive and sustained state research and procurement funding produced the huge economies of scale and steep learning curves that now constitute barriers to industry entry and long-term participation. By the 1970s only a very few firms had proven able to acquire and maintain the requisite capital and skills to stay in the business; therefore, decisions taken by those surviving firms necessarily were salient for any and all others in the field. Rapid development, driven by government spending, had produced an industry of extreme economic and technological significance, with an inherently concentrated structure, and had created the era's most important strategic sector.

Therefore, the same set of forces that had shaped the industry more generally imposed upon the governments and aeronautics firms of France, Germany and Great Britain the necessity of industrial collaboration. In responding to the geopolitical imperatives of the Cold War, the United States government had financed the creation of an important new set of industrial and technological capabilities. Although owned and controlled by private capitalists, the U.S. aeronautics firms of the 1960s (and the commercial product line they were able to offer to the world, through which they created and then dominated an entire new industry) owed their impressive industrial capabilities and dominant market position to government funding. Indeed, the configuration of entire aeronautics industry, including its oligopolistic structure, its important firms and their productive capacity, its technology and the products based on it: All of its defining features should be understood as geopolitical imperatives that had been translated into new and very important economic, industrial and technological facts through government procurement policies.

## THE PRODUCT LINE AS FRONT LINE RATHER THAN BOTTOM LINE: TECHNOLOGY, SEGMENTATION AND MARKET ENTRY

The aerospace industry, including both the military and commercial sides of the business, embodied and powerfully reinforced American political and economic hegemony in the Cold War era. U.S. firms had, by virtue of their participation in large military contracts, developed the technology and expertise necessary to make jet airliners, and they aggressively pursued the opportunities created by their early lead. Moreover, at that time the huge U.S. market was controlled regarding pricing and fare structures and therefore, "the regulated, large domestic market provided a strong base of demand for technological innovation by the aircraft producers."[5] Boeing was especially astute in converting the KC-135 tanker into the 707, and then followed upon its success with improved derivatives that provided operators with the cost benefits of owning a common fleet of aircraft. Outmaneuvering both its European and American rivals, by the mid-1960s Boeing had become the dominant firm in a new and rapidly expanding market. "These advantages enabled Boeing to establish the industry standard of excellence in technology, manufacturing, marketing and product service."[6]

Once established, mainly because of economies of scale that raised further barriers to entry, the market power of American firms in the world civil aviation market continued to grow well into the 1970s.[7] Of special significance here concerning the creation and subsequent development of Airbus Industrie is that the products of the American manufacturers (McDonnell Douglas and especially Boeing) were the concrete representation of U.S. leadership in the aeronautics industry and thus also of American political and economic dominance in the Cold War era. The characteristics of the American commercial aircraft lines—range, payload, fuel consumption—defined the very terms in which any prospective European response to the American challenge would have to be expressed. In order to be effective, European political and economic aspirations would have to be translated into the same currency used by the Americans: a line of aircraft with credible after-sales support yet able to attract demand in a market in which the terms of competition already had been set by the leading firms.

Given the extent of American control of the world civil airframe market, the aeronautics firms and national governments of the major European states had to engage in a calculated gamble. In order to resurrect their capability in the production of commercial airliners, and thus regain the right to engage the Americans in a battle for current and future market share in a high-cost, high-risk, oligopolistic industry, the Europeans would have to devise and implement a strategy capable eventually of changing the very rules of the game. In a market in which design, production and marketing constituted the operational level of a larger strategic contest, therefore making the aircraft themselves the point of contact in an economic and industrial rivalry of much broader scope, each and every decision concerning product development would be of crucial significance. At stake was more than the benefits of high value-added employment or technological spinoffs, or even the prestige of building aircraft. Due to its strategic character and oligopolistic structure, the very configuration, and thus the future evolution of the commercial aviation sector, would be affected by the fortunes of the Airbus program.

These observations emphasize the importance of Airbus Industrie not only as a mechanism of collaboration but also as an instrument forged by the European partners in their attempt to redress a marked economic and industrial, and therefore political, imbalance in transatlantic relations. Both the form of industrial collaboration and the precise tactics used in implementing the European strategy thus became of significance not only to the industrial partners and national governments but also to customers and current and future competitors as well—indeed to all interests affected by the fate of the civil airframe business. But in order to be successful, not only would the Europeans have to accommodate the distinctive interests and capabilities of the national firms and governments, they also would have to do so in a way that translated commercial imperatives into a business strategy capable of wresting the technological and industrial initiative from the Americans.

## CHALLENGE AND RESPONSE: AIRBUSES AS TACTICS, AIRBUS INDUSTRIE AS AN INSTRUMENT OF EUROPEAN STRATEGY

As discussed in Part I, initially it seemed that the cooperative European effort would fall prey to national rivalries as each partner sought to use the Airbus program for its own political and industrial purposes.[8] The real challenge was to retain the political interest, financial support and industrial expertise of all three nations without allowing the aircraft projects themselves to be held hostage to differences among them. We have seen that the early phase, from 1968 to 1978, was not completely successful in this regard, as Great Britain was divided in its political and industrial counsel regarding participation in European collaboration in civil aerospace and remained officially outside the Airbus program. The withdrawal of official British political and financial support following the redesign of the A300 aircraft placed the Airbus program, and thus the Europeans' strategic designs, at a crossroads. Had HSA been forced to end its participation, it would have been necessary to redesign the A300B around a new wing, literally taking the entire program back to the drawing board.

Since the very configuration of the first Airbus represented the opening move in a larger strategic gambit, the support of the German government and HSA's commitment of its own resources were crucial not only for the immediate prospects of the A300B but also for the overall European objectives. Even before the formation of Airbus Industrie as a GIE, Henri Ziegler and Roger Beteille had identified what they correctly perceived to be significant and emerging demand unmet by aircraft in the product lines of either Boeing or McDonnell Douglas. Thus, with the A300, AI created an "availability advantage . . . not based on a demonstrated technological superiority, but rather on Airbus Industrie's ability to differentiate its products in terms of range and payloads."[9] By designing and producing a twin-engine, wide-body, medium-haul plane using American engines and other standard components, the AI management opted for a tactical move that was cautious yet innovative. While quite bold in terms of market segmentation, the first Airbus was technologically conservative and thus more likely to attract customers reluctant to buy the initial product of a fledgling company. The move was successful, for with the 300B, "Airbus management sought to fill a particular niche in the global market . . ." but also began the process of rebuilding the foundation for an autonomous European civil airframe sector.[10]

If the A300 and its specific range and payload configuration are correctly seen as an initial tactical move in a larger strategy, the decision to adopt the GIE formulation to manage the collaborative effort is also a crucial element of the overall European plan. Not only did this formula clarify the rights and responsibilities among the partners, the "GIE format and its emergence as a clear focus was vital in building confidence and credibility amongst airline customers."[11] Particularly important in this regard was the joint and several liability of the industrial partners, with government backing (and even outright state ownership in the case of Aérospatiale) providing the ultimate security to prospective customers. "In other words, Airbus products had the guarantee of the two powerful European nations—France and Germany—not an insignificant factor in establishing its much needed credibility."[12] The creation of an innovative framework of collaboration among its leading aeronautics firms therefore reinforced the European strategy based on a technically and commercially feasible product.

The Airbus A300, and thus European hopes to reenter the commercial airframe business, both benefited and suffered from the fact that the aircraft was introduced at a time of transition and even upheaval in the market. Entering service during the first OPEC oil shock of 1973-74, the fuel-efficient Airbus was attractive to customers, especially in a rapidly internationalizing market with route characteristics matching those for which the A300 was designed.[13] These developments dovetailed nicely with the consortium's overall view of the market and how Airbus might fit into its growth: "From the beginning, the management of Airbus recognized the need to be a global player if it was to succeed at all."[14]

However, demand for air travel also was hurt by the accompanying recession in the West. Bernard de Lathière and the AI marketing team thus had to traverse the "sales desert" of 1975 to 1977 with no assurance of success, and they were especially dismayed by the difficulties encountered in penetrating the lucrative American market. Yet despite the absence of any certainty of return on investment, the consortium's management was not deterred in its intention to establish the requisite capability to remain in the business over the long haul. With confidence in the fundamental soundness of the A300 as a tool for initial market penetration, during this period of low sales and lower hopes, "the company made a large investment to build a centrally coordinated marketing and service organization."[15]

Everyone in the commercial airline business recognized that Boeing had attained its commanding position by designing and building a whole family of aircraft, a concept that offered substantial benefits to both customer and manufacturer. As a prospective competitor to the market leader in an oligopolistic industry, AI realized that it would have to adopt similar tactics or ultimately fail in its attempt to alter the competitive balance. While the A300 did indeed exploit an existing market gap, it alone could do little to diminish the relative strength of the American producers. The consortium either had to press onward or else become a one-shot cooperative project having no real impact on the larger strategic situation in the commercial airframe market. Therefore, what was a "political decision in the 1960s to support a European civil aircraft industry by subsidizing the development of one new aircraft, the A300, has over time turned into the need to subsidize the market entry of a producer of a complete family of aircraft."[16]

Thus, the relatively safe (in technological terms) "entry ticket" of the A300 was followed by a move that reveals the skill of AI's management in using commercial tactics to achieve the larger strategic goals of the consortium and its backers. As described in chapter 6, in the mid-1970s the partners and governments of the consortium faced a crucial decision concerning how precisely to expand the AI family. The French and British partners argued for launching a product addressed to the single-aisle segment of the market and wanted to build an entirely new aircraft to replace the aging 727s and DC-8s of the world airline fleet. However, the Germans pressed for "putting the accent on further establishing the place of Airbus in its original niche . . ."[17] and building another twin-aisle, twin-engine aircraft. The German position prevailed. But once the fundamental decision to launch a derivative aircraft was taken, the question became whether simply to "shrink" the A300 with minor modifications to the basic plane or to take a more substantial technological leap. The eventual solution was a compromise that nonetheless leaned decisively toward the latter; the A310 would have a new wing, tail and landing gear, and (significantly for future product development) also incorporate recent advances in electronic flight control technology.

AI's decision to undertake significant new financial and technological risks concerning the configuration and capabilities of the A310 was not merely a response to existing market imperatives. While opting for a substantially modified version of the A300, the consortium hoped to use technological initiative to effect a change in the strategic dynamics of the industry. With the A310, "the GIE tried to regain control of the market not by launching a completely new product, but in perfecting an existing product so as to make a 'half-generation' advance."[18] Therefore, the decision to build a substantially modified aircraft, even while the consortium's first product still was far from commercially remunerative for the partners or the governments, was a second tactical move primarily based not only on an assessment of short-term financial considerations or existing market opportunities, but also on the place of the new aircraft for the consortium's longer-run strategy. "With the A310, the European consortium tried to impose upon the market its own specific rhythm of technological change in such a way as to constrain the competition. . . ."[19]

But since sales of the A300 to that point had provided nowhere near enough capital to finance the necessary investments in technology, tooling and training, at this juncture can be seen most clearly the crucial role played by the political and financial support of the national governments in the ultimate success of the European gamble in civil aviation. Not only in terms of short-term prospects, but more important for the consortium's future ability to remain in the business, government support allowed AI to overcome the market uncertainties of high costs and long product development lead times that, for private capital, would have constituted an insurmountable barrier. In "bankrolling billions of dollars, the member countries minimized that risk, enabling Airbus Industrie to design the A300 series in order to take advantage of a market gap."[20] Looking at the A300/A310 product line as a two-stage opening gambit, public resources not only allowed the first line of aircraft to remain in production despite the dearth of sales, but the sustained commitment of government finance permitted the consortium's managers to begin implementation of the next phase of the game plan.

## SUBSIDIES, PRODUCT DEVELOPMENT AND MARKET LEADERSHIP

For the U.S. civil airframe manufacturers, AI's persistence in building, marketing and even designing new aircraft despite any apparent prospects of program profitability were an anomaly. At first it had seemed safe to ignore the upstart: "Until the late 1970s, the U.S. manufacturers had dismissed Airbus as just another feeble and disappointing effort of the European commercial aerospace industry."[21] But with AI's sale to Eastern Airlines in 1978, attitudes in the U.S. industrial and political circles changed rapidly, as Americans recognized that the consortium was "committed to a fundamental goal that was different from their own."[22] From this point forward, both U.S. aerospace executives and government officials began to perceive the Airbus consortium for what it was: a means to larger ends in a strategy calculated to reestablish a permanent European presence in global civil airframe manufacturing.

In a "zero-sum" contest such as the emerging transatlantic struggle in civil airframe manufacturing, success for one player in garnering outside resources also would deny their use to the other. In the late 1970s, therefore, British financial capital and technology represented an important prize for both the Airbus partners and the American manufacturers: "Great Britain became the first battleground."[23] Seen in light of the strategic engagement, BAe's decision to join AI from 1 January 1979, even paying an entry fee for the privilege, was a major victory for the consortium. Although Rolls-Royce and British Airways remained unreconciled to the collaborative effort, once again the national governments of the three major European aeronautics powers were officially committed to the Airbus program. This commitment would prove important not only financially and industrially, especially for the new A310 program, but also in international marketing efforts in regions where British political influence remained strong.

By solidifying the financial, commercial and political prospects of the collective European effort, the official British return to the Airbus program also allowed the consortium to consider more daring options regarding its next move. As discussed in chapter 7, the next major decision point for AI regarding product development came in the early 1980s. In relation to the consortium's long-term objectives, this juncture was an especially important one: Boeing, the market leader, had just introduced two new products, the single-aisle 757 and the wide-bodied, twin-engine 767, with the latter a direct competitor of the A300/A310. At this point, the Germans argued for designing a long-range, large-capacity aircraft that would challenge Boeing in that segment of the market in which, with the famed 747, it possessed an outright monopoly. As before, the French pressed for the single-aisle option in hopes of garnering a significant share of the anticipated 727/DC-9 replacement business, thus opening a completely new market niche for Airbus products.

As we know, French opinion prevailed in this instance. We also have seen that the launch of the A320 involved not just the penetration of a new market segment but also a major technological leap. By introducing a fully computerized flight control system and redesigning the cockpit around the new technology, AI sought to take a major step in differentiating its products from those proposed by its competitors. But such an advance would have implications beyond the merely technological: "With this airplane . . . [AI] attempted, in making a generational advance, to impose upon the market its own rhythm of generational change, and to establish in its turn the 'market standard,' which would confer upon it leadership in that segment."[24]

The lengthy delays in gaining final funding approval for the A320 allowed AI's American competitors, especially McDonnell Douglas, to introduce derivatives of existing aircraft with proven technology and to reap substantial sales in the 150-seat segment.[25] But despite this shortcoming, the wisdom of the European move was vindicated as the order book for the new aircraft grew rapidly, including major purchases from important airlines in the United States. So, with the A320, AI confronted the American manufacturers not only with competition in an additional market segment but also with a product that promised to set new industry standards. This wresting of the technological initiative from the industry's dominant players was thus a very significant element in the consortium's overall strategy. After it introduced the A320, AI was no longer merely responding to conditions established by its competitors; now it was influencing directly the very rules under which the competition would take place. "Public funds, so criticized by the American competition, had thus given Airbus the necessary breathing space to acquire sufficient commercial credibility to play its own game in an autonomous manner, with success if one judges by the sales figures for the A320."[26]

With the commercial success of the A320, the technological prowess of the partners had been combined with the financial support and political will of the national governments in implementing a game plan that had begun to pay real dividends. As discussed in chapter 8, Airbus Industrie wasted no time in following the initiatives of the A320 with the launch of not one but two new products in 1987. But with the A330/A340 program, a technological leap of the magnitude realized with the A320 was rejected in favor of a more conservative tack. In keeping with its earlier strategy, the consortium sought to implement another major piece of the "family of aircraft" concept while incurring little additional technological risk. By basing two versions of a long-range aircraft on a single wing and fuselage, AI hoped to gain access to a lucrative market segment (and one that was projected to grow steadily as traffic on the long-distance routes to Asia increased) dominated up to that point entirely by the Americans, while keeping development costs low and aircraft commonality high. With the A330/A340, the technological risks taken in the A320 program would bear additional fruit with a prudent and calculated extension of the product line into the last remaining U.S.-monopolized segment: "Airbus Industrie sought above all to consolidate its position by imposing the technological breakthroughs of the A320 as new standards."[27]

Even as AI has in the 1990s rounded out its product offerings to include three main types of aircraft, it has continued to consolidate these three types with the introduction of derivative products, including the A300-600, the A310-200 and A310-300, the A321 and, most recently, the A319. Now able, like its major competitor Boeing, to offer airlines a range of aircraft across the major market segments, AI has attained the stature of the world's second largest civil airframe manufacturer. But concomitant with this stature, and from the perspective of this study more important than the achievements in technology and marketing themselves, is the fact that AI has thoroughly and permanently altered the very structure of the industry in which it now competes. Even if Boeing continues to be the market leader and remains the single most significant force in the industry, American hegemony in the civil airliner market has been broken decisively.[28]

But it must be recalled that AI's ability in attaining this stature within 25 years is due not only to the organizational skill of the consortium's management, or evidence simply of the partners' design and production capabilities, but testament also to the sustained political will of the national governments that funded the programs. As a result of this constancy, national and even European political and economic goals have been realized through the commercial strategy employed by Airbus Industrie. From inception right through its recent successes, AI's "mission was to keep Europe in the technological forefront in commercial aviation and related industries to bolster export and provide employment in a key sector."[29] Understood as an instrument forged to meet the political and industrial ends of national governments, AI has served its purpose well. Sequential product development according to the family-of-aircraft concept comprised the operational or tactical level of this strategy, which first penetrated a neglected market segment and then followed this opening wedge with innovations that gradually took the technological initiative from the established market leaders. Now positioned to be a major player in developing the next generation of commercial aircraft, perhaps even in collaboration with its American rivals, Airbus Industrie had rewritten the rules and indeed redefined the very shape of the arena for a strategic contest that is certain to continue into the next century.

## THE AIRBUS SYSTEM: CREATIVE TENSION OR INSTITUTIONALIZED INEFFICIENCY?

As a creature of the environment from which it emerged, and due to the very nature of its purpose and tasks, the Airbus Industrie consortium embodies contradictory forces and logics, and there is little prospect that these will ever be fully reconciled. Indeed, "it is likely that Airbus will live quite awhile with this ambiguity inherent in the very structure of its organization."[30] But with seven products, four partners, two associate members and an international network of subcontractors, the Airbus system has become increasingly difficult to manage in its current form. The growing need for efficiency and rationality reinforces outside pressures from its competitors and critics for the consortium to reorganize itself into a fully integrated company with a single system of cost accounting and financial oversight.

Therefore, at the most fundamental level, the challenges confronting Airbus Industrie as it looks to the future revolve around the issue of control: who is to exert authority over the government monies and industrial assets that have been combined so effectively through the Airbus system to produce the aircraft that have spelled the end American dominance of the world civil airframe industry. Presently, that authority is divided among the governments, the industrial partners and the GIE in a way that, from the perspective of this study, reflects the necessity of reconciling distinctive national interests with the commercial imperatives of the industry as it has developed. Yet, paradoxically, the consortium's success in accomplishing the larger objectives of the governments and partners has brought into sharp relief the twin problems of transparency and accountability, which bear directly on questions of how best to assure that the interests of all the consortium's participants are served as completely and equitably as possible.

During the course of interviews with executives within the consortium, I asked about the effectiveness of the current configuration of Airbus Industrie, its prospects and probable future structure and its usefulness as a model for other collaborative ventures. The answers I received revealed not only the complexity of the problems the organization now confronts but also the inherently indeterminate or open-ended nature of the road ahead. Yet, while it is clear that nothing can be taken for granted concerning the further success of the consortium, or even its continued existence in its present form, nonetheless it seems safe to draw some conclusions based on these informative conversations.[31]

As discussed at length in the earlier analysis, both the structure and operation of Airbus Industrie reflect the separation within the consortium of the functions of development and production from those of marketing and after-sales support. The result is a system in which the industrial partners act essentially as prime contractors to an entity of their own making: the GIE. In their dual capacity as both owners and major suppliers, the member firms have interests that both coincide and conflict. As a part owner, each partner wishes to see overall costs remain low and profits high, creating strong incentives for the exercise of effective oversight of the entire operation. On the other hand, however, as contractors each member seeks to maximize income from its share of the work by receiving the highest possible price for the components it builds, placing upward pressure on production costs while perpetuating the dispersal of authority and retarding the formation of a comprehensive oversight capability within the consortium.

In addition, each partner wishes to see the greatest possible number of Airbus aircraft sold in order to generate demand for its components; yet none wishes to see Airbuses sold at prices so low as to make their design and construction inherently unprofitable. Thus the partners are divided among themselves concerning the transparency of the component's costs and also individually and collectively at odds with the GIE concerning its accountability for sales agreements negotiated with airlines, which commit the partners to cost and performance guarantees that may be difficult to meet.

The system of "business control" developed by the consortium reflects these tensions and necessarily embodies a set of compromises made in order to balance them. Perhaps the single most important element of the business control system within Airbus Industrie is the set of "contracting rules" that determine exactly what portion of the aircraft each partner will design and build and precisely how much it will receive as compensation. At one level, these rules must find a satisfactory and effective means of addressing the "permanent trade-off" that exists between the partners in their role as monopoly suppliers of the aircraft's major components and their position as owners who want to see total costs driven down as low as possible.

More specifically, the contracting rules bring down to an operational level the more general industrial agreements signed by the partners at the launch of a new aircraft type. The precise content of these rules is decided at meetings in which exact work shares are defined and each partner presents to the others its assessment of how much building its own components will cost. Just as each partner tries to extract from these negotiations the maximum possible allowance for its portion of the aircraft, in their position as owners, all of the partners have strong incentives to question why costs should be so high.

Predictably, these meetings often are both lengthy and acrimonious. But my interlocutors stressed that the claims made and the aspersions cast in these negotiations are moderated both by an overriding commonality of interest and especially the presence of a third party, the GIE. The latter serves as arbitrator if not arbiter by reminding everyone present that the market in which it and the partners must operate will bear only so much and that the total cost of the aircraft must remain within a given range in order to retain any hope of commercial viability. Therefore, what become in effect "transfer prices" within the consortium strike a balance between what each partner considers to be a minimum level of profitability and what the market will allow.

And what of relations between the partners and the GIE? How do the partners exert control over its actions as their sales agent without rendering it ineffective? I was told that, facing the hard reality of competitive sales campaigns in which the pressure to make financial and commercial concessions is intense, the GIE constantly is "walking on the edge" between the need to make deals and abiding by the partners' constraints on its activities. In order to protect themselves from commitments made on their behalf by a zealous and harried sales force, the partners have developed a set of criteria by which to judge the profitability of sales proposals and contracts. Under these restrictions, in their negotiations with customers, the sales force is compelled to work from a "selling price" that is based (using computerized calculations of complex formulae) on a "net income ratio." This ratio is determined by estimating the gross revenue that will derive from the sale of a given aircraft (not including the engines) and then dividing this amount by a "reference price" based on projected sales and costs for that particular model. If the sales team wishes to deviate from the base price, it must receive "a special dispensation," and this process may well entail gaining the approval of the individual partners. In bargaining situations in which speed is of the essence, such constraints can be a liability, requiring that the individuals in decisionmaking positions, even at the Executive Board level, themselves must exhibit the flexibility that the cumbersome consortial structure may militate against.[32]

To what extent does such a system, in which authority is dispersed and tensions between functional roles institutionalized in the very structure of the organization, make the already complex business of building and selling commercial airliners more difficult than need be? Conversely, is it possible that such a system could have any advantages that are finally reflected in the technical or commercial attributes of the products it produces? The responses I received to these questions were at once predictable and surprising, transparently self-serving and extremely compelling. The thrust was that the Airbus system is one driven by "creative tension," in which "the conflict among the partners produces results that are beneficial for the business as a whole." I was assured that having the partners play roles that are at once cooperative and adversarial has been of benefit to the consortium at all levels of its activity, from technical and engineering to sales and product support. Thus Airbus aircraft represent the end result of a decisionmaking process in which numerous and varied options to technical and commercial problems have been considered and the best selected. Rather than stalemate or outcomes of the lowest-common-denominator type, Airbus aircraft are flying proof that the tensions in the system have been channeled into producing superior products.

Such assertions are based on the belief that the capabilities of the partners are ultimately complementary, and I was reminded that despite the specialization of tasks among them, all have retained and even strengthened their own competencies in the major areas of aircraft design, production and marketing, so as not to be placed at a disadvantage in negotiations with their counterparts or the GIE. Therefore, in making its case for the right to build a certain portion of an aircraft and thus receive an agreed-upon compensation, each partner must convince the others that both its methods and its costs are effective and reasonable responses to the challenges inherent in that work.[33] This means that the member firms are continually compelled to justify their approaches and solutions in discussions with counterparts who consider themselves also quite knowledgeable about such challenges and who stand ready, as a matter of pride, principle and self-interest, to raise questions at every turn. Basic assumptions are questioned and elementary contentions challenged; the interests and skills of each partner thus serve as a "reality check" on the others and therefore make the entire program better than it otherwise might be.

Furthermore, the system can be seen as "self-regulating," in that competitive pressures within it combine with the wide availability of outside information (concerning costs of materials and labor used to construct the various components) to insure that partners cannot exaggerate their own claims too wildly. Thus, the argument runs, the incentive of each partner to keep overall costs down while pressing its counterparts to find the most technically and commercially sound means of fulfilling its responsibilities are used in conjunction with market pressures to produce an aircraft of high quality at a low cost. Moreover, market forces are brought to bear throughout the chain of production; because each partner constantly seeks means to reduce the costs it incurs in performing its assigned tasks, extensive use is made of sub-contractors who must bid competitively for the work they receive.[34] Indeed, this practice of competitive bidding has been introduced into the consortium itself. For example, work on the center section of the fuselage of Airbus aircraft had traditionally gone to Deutsche Airbus, yet BAe recently outbid its partner/competitor for the right to build the plugs that are inserted into the A320 aircraft to produce the A321 model. Thus, both the GIE and the member firms cite the increase in such practices as evidence that market forces constantly are brought to bear throughout the entire organization, making Airbus Industrie as rational in its goals and methods as its American competitors.

If Airbus Industrie is so rational and responsive to market forces, why doesn't the consortium take what would seem to be the logical step of merging the civil aircraft divisions of the member firms into a single company? I was told that placing the appropriate divisions of the partners "inside the fence" and forming an integrated business concern would be quite difficult and indeed constitute a decision as "important and controversial as the initial formation of the consortium." First, separating out Airbus operations from other activities within each of the member firms would not be so easy as it might seem. Each of the partners engages in a variety of aeronautical programs, both civil and military, and many of these are collaborative. Given these overlapping obligations, design and production facilities and personnel are not strictly segregated among programs—indeed, given the nature of aerospace technology and products, it is not clear that such a separation is desirable or even possible. Second, such a move would necessarily entail the elimination of at least some of the separate functional capacities maintained by each partner (whether in R&D, engineering or marketing and after-sales support) and thus mean a substantial reduction in employment at each national facility. Understandably, those affected would stoutly resist moves in that direction.

Thus powerful technical and organizational forces militate against the formation of a fully integrated civil airframe manufacturing firm from the existing assets and arrangements that constitute Airbus Industrie. Moreover, if the claims made concerning the creative tensions at work within the consortium are to be taken seriously, integrating the partners' respective capacities would undermine the very basis for the technical and commercial success of Airbus Industrie. Full merger would imply the loss of the distinctive perspectives and capabilities that have generated the innovative solutions to design and engineering challenges which have allowed the consortium to wrest the technological initiative from their American competitors and in turn reestablish a permanent European presence in the world civil airframe industry.

But beyond the danger of killing the goose that laid the golden egg, integrating the distinctive elements that make up Airbus Industrie may not be advisable or even possible for the very fundamental reasons discussed throughout this study. AI was formed as a GIE in order to coordinate the efforts and realize the goals of governments and partners that, while convergent, are not necessarily identical. The consortial structure embodies a delicate balance between national interests that remain distinctive, and these interests continue to be served by maintaining substantial and separate capabilities in an economic sector whose technological and industrial characteristics place it at the heart of national security. Forged in the competitive struggle among industrialized states, the aerospace sector combines political priorities and the most advanced technologies and processes into formidable new capabilities. Airbus Industrie also combines these distinct yet complementary forces, and perhaps it is the tensions between them that continue to generate important and innovative responses to the most daunting challenges of our day.

## AIRBUS INDUSTRIE: A MODEL FOR COOPERATION?

Given that AI has emerged as an important actor and in a crucial industry and thus has served well the interests of those who created it, does it offer any lessons for collaborative efforts in other industries, or perhaps even for the process of international cooperation more generally? What generalizations might be drawn from the case of Airbus Industrie regarding the circumstances under which the interests and abilities of governments and firms can be combined most fruitfully in producing economic and industrial outcomes that serve the interests and realize the objectives of the parties involved? More specifically, is it possible to establish a set of criteria that might indicate those situations most conducive to collaboration between government and business?

In the first place, the story of Airbus Industrie's successful penetration of the global commercial airframe market demonstrates the importance of there being a challenge of a scale sufficient to motivate a major collective effort among parties with interests that are less than fully congruent. In the case of the postwar aerospace industry, American dominance was so complete and the industrial, technological and commercial implications of this imbalance so stark that European political and industrial leaders had no difficulty in agreeing on the need for a response and recognized that collaboration was requisite to its success. Moreover, the barriers to entry (or more accurately to European reentry) in the commercial aerospace sector were so high and the learning curves so steep that state involvement was required to provide risk capital that no private firms could hope to borrow or generate on their own.

Second, the success of Airbus relative to other ventures (collaborative or otherwise) involving governmental support for industrial undertakings is due in part to the clear and specific nature of the task at hand. The challenge to Europe was embodied quite concretely in the design, production and sales organizations of the major American aircraft firms, McDonnell Douglas and especially Boeing, and indeed in the very aircraft themselves. Therefore, what had to be done was quite evident, if still daunting: design, build, market and support a line of aircraft that would appeal to customers already loyal to the products of established incumbents. The clarity and lack of ambiguity inherent in the situation provided the governments and industrial partners alike with a focus and a means of measuring progress toward the common goal that was crucial to defining and then maintaining the momentum of the cooperative program.

Third, the case of AI shows that in order for the resources and talents of government and business to be combined smoothly and fruitfully, the dividing line between their separate competencies should be clear and stable. Early on in the Airbus project, it was realized that the only prospect for the market success requisite to achieving larger political objectives was for state officials to defer to the technical and commercial expertise of the industrial partners regarding the aircraft's design, construction and marketing. If overtly political considerations had been allowed to influence the characteristics of the consortium's products or service, the governmental political and financial support so crucial to AI's eventual success would have meant almost certain failure. Here again, the technically and commercially specific nature of the American challenge meant that the roles and functions of financial support and actual business decisionmaking could be and were kept distinct from one another, allowing the pursuit of political goals without direct governmental involvement in the strategy devised to achieve these ends.

These lessons indicate that truly productive collaboration involving governments and firms is made much more likely if the objectives are clear and the stakes high. Without a compelling rationale to undertake specific action, it is difficult for such parties to justify incurring the expense, risk and frustration inherent in collective action. Predictably, and perhaps unfortunately, experience has shown that firms seek financial help and governments are willing to provide it when existing jobs are at stake, in contrast to situations in which new chances must be taken to provide uncertain future benefits. Therefore, most industrial policies are of the "negative" type, in which a given industry or firm receives government aid to forestall a disruptive collapse. Furthermore, many of the rest are cases in which hope and vision have badly outrun any real or clearly identifiable prospects for success, and these usually result in early abandonment or expensive failure. Much fewer are circumstances such as those surrounding Airbus Industrie, in which the danger was clear and present, the scale of the undertaking prohibitive to private capital and the nature of the task so specific that all could agree upon a rational division of responsibility. Thus, the forces that converged in the creation and subsequent success of AI are unlikely to recur with great frequency. This should serve to caution those prematurely enamored of the prospects for collaborative projects involving a substantial degree of government participation.

But while the salience and specificity of the challenges in civil aerospace might have made international industrial collaboration an understandable and perhaps even predictable response, the mechanism adopted to attain the desired ends remains unusual in both its structure and effectiveness. While stopping far short of the full integration of national aeronautics capabilities, the Airbus consortium did much more that simply coordinate separate interests and assets. More specifically, it has turned differences in national perspectives, abilities and even rivalries into a powerfully creative force, a result sought but certainly not yet attained at the political level in Europe. Its success in this regard points both to the necessity of cooperation in Europe and to the virtue of not seeking to achieve the unattainable goal of completely submerging national priorities and aspirations in the process. Airbus Industrie thus has made a virtue of necessity in creating a structure of collaboration that recognizes the validity of distinctive national perspectives while effectively harnessing the commonality of interest that informs all participants.

## INDUSTRY STRUCTURE, INTERNATIONAL TRADE AND COMPETITIVE ADVANTAGE: THE CASE OF AIRBUS INDUSTRIE

The strategic success of Airbus Industrie in breaking the American lock on the global civil airliner industry is important for a number of reasons. First, by reestablishing a permanent European presence in the large commercial airframe industry, AI has stimulated the growth of a large base of European firms that act as its subcontractors and components suppliers. Second, the decisive shift in the industry's competitive balance has had a negative impact on political relations between the United States and Western Europe, although the two sides seem to have recognized the potential of the "subsidy dispute" to damage transatlantic relations more generally and thus have agreed to disagree on the issue for the time being.

But beyond such immediate effects, the emergence of AI as a major player in the commercial airframe industry is also significant for larger questions of international trade and competition. This section will therefore assess the Airbus Industrie consortium in its connection to recent theoretical and empirical work on these issues. Not only is this work relevant to understanding the creation and development of AI, but the case of AI also has contributed directly to the elaboration of these new approaches in political economy that emphasize the impact that the strategic interaction of powerful business organizations can have in shaping the industries and markets in which they operate.

Several recent and mutually reinforcing developments in the global economy, including the growing volume and salience of trade in similar industrial goods among economically advanced states, the emergence of oligopolistic structures and excess capacity in many sectors, and the growing trend toward managed trade, have led to an important reassessment of traditional thinking on the nature of international trade and the bases of comparative advantage. In particular, the idea that nations should specialize production and exchange in those industries in which they hold cost advantages due to naturally occurring factor endowments has been called increasingly into question. Although quite formal and mathematically precise, in essence this orthodox theory rests on the late eighteenth and early nineteenth century assumptions of Adam Smith and David Ricardo, and models based on these ideas make "no allowance for the possibility that a country's comparative advantage could change as a function of private economic activity or might even be shaped by government policy."[35]

In response to the perceived inadequacies of neoclassical economics in explaining patterns of trade and competition observed in the late twentieth century, new theories and models have been developed recognizing that many industries and markets bear no resemblance to the atomistic "perfect competition" posited by traditional theory. These new models explicitly assume that in many important sectors firms are not simply passive actors operating under given technological constraints and reacting to movements in effective demand merely by changing production and/or prices, or by substituting one productive factor for another. Rather, it is assumed that firms can gain and exert significant market power and earn substantial "rent" by exploiting so-called market imperfections such as oligopoly and economies of scale.[36] Not merely fleeting, such benefits can be cumulative and long term, as firms build on past advantages to increase market share and lower unit costs, thereby reinforcing an already powerful competitive position. In addition to economies of scale and learning effects, some industries may generate significant "externalities," ancillary or "spin-off" benefits that accrue to other economic actors or society as a whole as a result of activity in them. Taken together, these assumptions and the models of trade and competition based on them suggest that simply allowing the market to work may not automatically produce optimal outcomes.

Furthermore, many recent models of trade and comparative advantage are accurately characterized as strategic because they "incorporate international interdependence of policy actions in an oligopolistic environment."[37] Such theories therefore suggest that firms or even countries could not only extract substantial and long-run "rent" or "externalities" from certain types of economic activity, but do so at the expense of their rivals.[38] Thus, models of strategic interaction such as the well-known Brander-Spencer variant posit profit-shifting between firms or even countries in industries in which economies of scale are large, learning curves steep and thus barriers to entry high. If a firm can gain an initial advantage in capturing market share, these industry characteristics allow that firm to increase turnover and generate economies of scale and move along the learning curve. Lower unit costs and prices gradually will eliminate rivals and bring additional market share in a self-perpetuating process, thereby raising barriers to potential entrants and further strengthening the early leader's competitive position.

These models of strategic trade and international competition suggest that a firm's competitive position in the type of market just described can be altered permanently by its own actions or by the policies of other actors (especially governments) that might affect, directly or indirectly, its costs. This type of thinking is a far cry from the neoclassical notions of mutually beneficial specialization and exchange and suggests (although usually not explicitly addressed in the theoretical literature) policies diametrically opposed to the standard prescription of open markets and increased competition as the means to economic efficiency and the maximization of welfare. Therefore, once it is accepted that not all economic activities are equal in terms of employment and technological benefits that derive from them, and that the realization of substantial rents and externalities is possible under conditions of imperfect competition, the interests of business organizations and political authorities may well converge around a mutual desire to see one or more national or local firms succeed in these special industries. Indeed, in this neomercantilist conception it might be possible through appropriate actions for firms or countries to create conditions that result in the establishment of a favored or even dominant position in an industry, or perhaps even to redress an existing competitive imbalance: "Particularly with dynamic increasing returns, current policy can have important permanent effects on trade because temporary learning advantages can lead to long-term comparative advantage."[39]

Clearly, the assumptions and policy implications of these new models of international trade and competition have direct applicability to the civil airframe industry and the place of Airbus Industrie within it. The scale of the resources, the complexity of the technology and the organizational skill required to design, build, market and support large civil airframes successfully all help to create the economies of scale and learning effects that generate powerful tendencies toward oligopoly in the industry.[40] Its global scope and importance for both the military and economic dimensions of national security along with other externalities also make the industry inherently strategic, meaning that governments will not be indifferent to developments affecting relative national performance in the sector.

These new models of trade and competition are relevant to understanding the European strategic rationale for responding to the American challenge by creating Airbus Industrie. Clearly, the current situation in the world civil airframe market certainly would look quite different if it were not for the creation and development of AI. Given the oligopolistic and strategic characteristics of the industry and the trends in market share clearly in evidence since the early 1960s, a Boeing monopoly was a real possibility had the market as constituted before the emergence of AI had been allowed to operate according to its own logic.

Not surprisingly, the case of AI has received substantial attention from the same theorists and analysts who have advanced the new thinking on international trade and competition. Predictably, there have been several attempts to model AI's entry into the large civil airframe market as a strategic game, in order to analyze the impact that entry has had upon the welfare of the producers and consumers who make up the market.[41] As efforts to represent in formal economic terms a complex and dynamic situation, they necessarily encounter difficulties in capturing precisely strategic patterns of interaction between the European and American producers. More important from our perspective, by focusing on the putative welfare gains or losses that may or may not have accrued to producers and consumers in Europe, North America and elsewhere, these analyses often miss much more significant points. Irrespective of gains or losses as conceptualized and measured by statistical techniques, Airbus Industrie did in fact enter the market for large civil aircraft and has permanently altered its structure and dynamics.[42] Whether or not "welfare," either overall, consumer or European, had been increased is somewhat beside the point since the motivation for the AI program has been more political and industrial rather than economic in the formal sense. More important for economic theory and practice is that AI's continued presence "will provide one more example of how publicly-aided, selective initiatives can lead to sustained economic activities in targeted industries."[43] In this case, the root of the initiative was to reestablish a European presence in civil airframe construction, and this goal has been attained. Therefore, more significant than any purported "welfare effects" is that Airbus Industrie is an example of how political will can be combined with technological skill, industrial capability and commercial savvy to create a new entity able to produce long-term changes in the very environment that brought it into being.

## LESSONS FOR THE RELATIONSHIP
## BETWEEN STATE AND MARKET

The ability of European governments and aeronautics companies to effect structural change in a major global industry in only 25 years raises even broader questions regarding the relationship among states, firms and markets. Specifically, developments in airliner manufacturing challenge accepted notions of firms as passive economic actors that respond to autonomous changes in demand and of states as merely providing the framework for market activity. Rather, the civil airframe industry and the place of Airbus Industrie within it shows both firms and governments to be active agents in generating new possibilities for economic undertakings, indeed creating entire new markets and industries.

Traditional thinking holds that markets emerge as a natural consequence of the desire of individuals and groups to produce and exchange for mutual benefit. Firms produce goods to meet existing and anticipated demand, and governments provide the legal and physical infrastructure, or the public goods framework, in which this economic activity can occur. In this conception, as markets operate over the long run, resources, including capital and labor, will be drawn to their most optimal use; an increase in demand for a given good or service will draw resources into that particular activity by holding out the possibility of higher sales and profits for firms. Firms respond by competing for the new business, and those most efficient at combining inputs to meet that demand will gain market share. In this orthodoxy, governments can enhance the efficiency of economic activity by extending the reach of markets, allowing firms to compete for more customers, raising turnover and further specializing internal corporate functions. The process of market extension will encourage a deepening and broadening of the division of labor throughout the economy, raising rates of productivity and further increasing economic efficiency.

Furthermore, this division of labor can and should be extended to the international level, where countries will specialize in production and exchange in industries in which they have a naturally occurring comparative advantage. Thus traditional theory holds that any attempt by governments to favor local or national industries by protecting them from outside competition with tariffs or other restrictions will reduce economic efficiency and ultimately be counterproductive, since relatively high-cost local producers will be rewarded and consumers thus forced to pay higher prices.

As argued earlier, for all of its mathematical sophistication, modern neo-classical economics clearly owes a major intellectual debt to Adam Smith and David Ricardo. But the focus on the extension of markets as the main motor of economic expansion leaves little room for a consideration of how firms actually create economic value and how states can act both domestically and internationally to favor some firms over others in gaining access to the resources necessary to a superior value creation capability. "It makes no sense for economists to concern themselves with the 'optimal way' to slice a 'scarce' economic pie if they have no understanding of what determines the changing size of the pie."[44] The new thinking on trade and international competition just outlined emphasizes that industries, markets and the relative positions of firms within them are shaped by business organizations that plan and implement strategies to change the economic, industrial and technological environment around them.[45] Rather than "distorting" an idealized environment or creating "imperfections" in a hypothesized market, business organizations that gain influence over market outcomes by securing privileged access to resources can, at least potentially, create novel economic possibilities.[46]

What are the implications of this approach for the relationship between state and market? As discussed, clearing away barriers to market exchange is the standard prescription for enhancing economic performance at the level of the firm and thus in the larger economy; sales volume can be increased, unit costs lowered, and the division of labor intensified and extended. But while these measures may be effective at creating "external economies of scale" and thus lowering costs in an existing business activity, more important for the creation of valuable goods, processes and services are new technologies, enhanced organizational capabilities and more efficient production processes—the internal economies of scale that innovative firms generate in response to competitive pressures.[47] While "public authorities can help firms respond to these pressures by providing a technological infrastructure to facilitate innovation by individual producers," to be really effective such efforts may have to go beyond even sector-specific industrial policies.[48] More precisely, under conditions of international oligopoly resulting from large economies of scale and barriers to entry, "the more dominant the existing organizations and the greater the capital investments required to enter the global industry, the more necessary will it be for a national strategy to give privileged access to public resources to those national business organizations that can best develop and utilize these resources."[49]

From the perspective of this study, precisely such a strategy explains the creation of Airbus Industrie. The governments of France, Germany and later Great Britain acted in concert to insure that their respective national aeronautics firms, whether nationalized or privately owned, had sustained access to the quite substantial financial resources that made possible their reentry into the global civil airframe market. But money alone was not enough. Reestablishing a permanent and significant European presence in civil aerospace required the creation of a novel means of balancing the separate national interests of the partners against the technological and commercial imperatives that embodied American dominance in aeronautics and in the Cold War era more generally. Thus the structure and operation of Airbus Industrie assume crucial importance, because it was through the GIE formulation that the partners' resources and skills could be harnessed in pursuing a common end. Product development and marketing became the focal point of a long-term strategy to wrest technological leadership from the American firms and thus reestablish a European presence in the industry. While breaking American hegemony in civil aerospace was a long and costly process and relied heavily on public funding, as an instrument of larger European political and economic goals, the consortium succeeded in its mission by making the "integration of technical innovation and the needs of the market central to its decision-making system."[50]

## EUROPEAN CHALLENGE, AMERICAN RESPONSE?

The emergence of Airbus Industrie as an innovative business organization that serves as the chosen instrument of a larger European political and industrial strategy presents theorists and practitioners of foreign economic policy, especially in the United States, with both theoretical and practical difficulties. Due to the intrinsic characteristics of Airbus Industrie, it may well be that political and industrial elites in the United States lack both the conceptual and institutional apparatus to respond effectively to what is in essence a strategic challenge to American interests. AI's unusual configuration as a GIE, its heavy reliance on public funding, indeed, its very reason for being, all fly in the face of accepted American business theory and practice.

Furthermore, the creation and subsequent commercial success of AI run counter to American assumptions about the proper relationship between government and business, between state and market. Manifesting this confusion is the use of inappropriate categories and analogies in analyzing the development of the aerospace industry and the place of Airbus Industrie within it, habits that only breed further misunderstanding of the situation as it actually exists and inhibit formulation of an appropriate policy.[51] As revealed in our discussion of the subsidy issue in chapter 8:

> In the final analysis, civil aerospace in Europe is a public policy issue, whereas in the United States this is not the case—or at least not yet. As a result, any dispute between the United States and the Europeans will be underpinned by a fundamental difference of philosophy about the rightful place of the state in the promotion of civil industry and technology.[52]

Dealing effectively with the challenges presented by Airbus Industrie will require, above all, new thinking in the United States and moving beyond the "persistent intellectual dominance of an outmoded market mentality that systematically fails to make use of our knowledge of the history and theory of capitalist development."[53]

Closely held and unquestioned perceptions and prejudices, however inappropriate to reality, can inform behavior long after having outlived whatever usefulness they might once have served. The history of the aeronautics industry, the development of the commercial airframe sector, the emergence of Airbus Industrie within that industry—all show that juxtaposing political authority and market forces as contending modes of directing economic activity provides no guide to understanding the real forces operating in the modern political economy. Rather, a most salient feature of international relations in the twentieth century has been the inexorable interpenetration of political authority and market structures, with the driving force behind their confluence ideological and geopolitical competition among powerful states in a context increasingly dominated by industry, science and technology. Seeking the material means of self-preservation in this environment, these states selectively channeled huge volumes of resources—financial, material, human and otherwise—into particular industries such as telecommunications, information processing and aeronautics. Those resources were directed to these specific ends according to political criteria and accomplished through bureaucracies created expressly for those purposes, thus creating technological and organizational capabilities that have made entire new industries and markets possible.

The growth of the postwar commercial aerospace sector represents just such a situation. The American firms and their products made manifest the formative impact that governments can have on commercial conditions when their political priorities are translated through procurement policies into new technological and industrial facts. During the Cold War, the authority of the American state to direct resources for military procurement was the single most important factor in shaping what is now called simply the "market" for commercial airliners, as if that term referred to a set of relationships that somehow emerged from the "natural" interaction of the forces of supply and demand. Facing the daunting conditions prevailing in the "market" for large civil aircraft, European governments sought a means to translate their own priorities into an effective riposte, and the unique structure of Airbus Industrie allowed the distinctive aeronautical capabilities of each country to be combined without relinquishing national control of these valuable industrial assets. By providing the financial backing for, while not intervening directly in, the consortium's response to the engineering and commercial challenges posed by American products and their dominant market position, these same governments made possible the effective combination of political will, technical competence and commercial savvy that has reshaped the world market for civil aircraft.

# APPENDIX

**Figure A.1: Aerospace Industry Consolidation, 1940–1970**

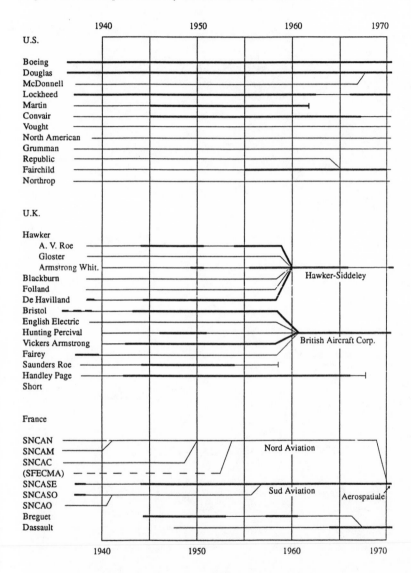

Source: Reprinted by permission of the publishers from M. S. Hochmuth, "Aerospace," p. 156, in *Big Business and the State: Changing Relations in Western Europe*, edited by Raymond Vernon, Cambridge, Mass.: Harvard University Press, copyright © 1974 by the President and Fellows of Harvard College.

*Appendix*

**Figure A.2: British Aerospace Industry Consolidation, 1957–1977**

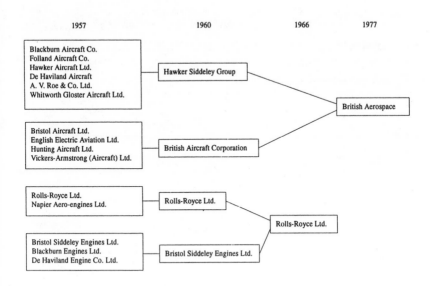

Source: Keith Hayward, *The British Aircraft Industry* (Manchester, UK: Manchester University Press, 1989), p. 76.

**Figure A.3: French Aerospace Industry Consolidation, 1936–1976**

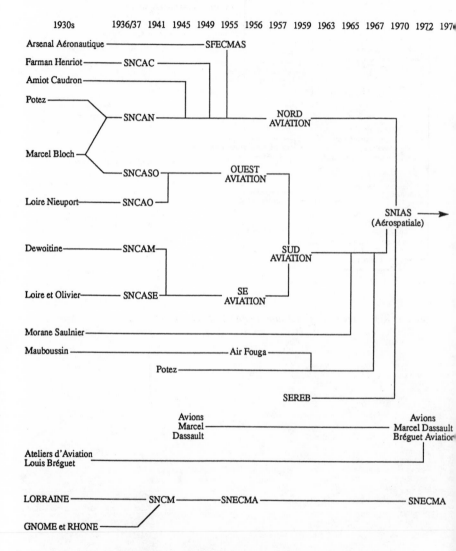

## Figure A.4: Airbus Industrie

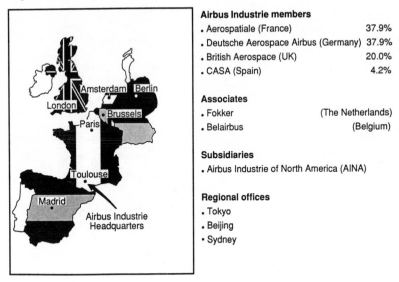

**Airbus Industrie members**
- Aerospatiale (France) 37.9%
- Deutsche Aerospace Airbus (Germany) 37.9%
- British Aerospace (UK) 20.0%
- CASA (Spain) 4.2%

**Associates**
- Fokker (The Netherlands)
- Belairbus (Belgium)

**Subsidiaries**
- Airbus Industrie of North America (AINA)

**Regional offices**
- Tokyo
- Beijing
- Sydney

Source: Airbus Industrie, 1993. Reprinted by permission.

## Figure A.5: Order Buildup

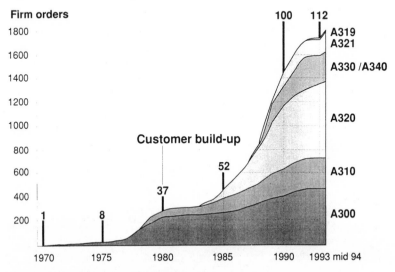

Source: Airbus Industrie, 1993. Reprinted by permission.

**Figure A.6: Delivery Buildup**

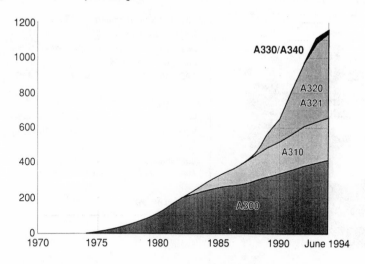

Source: Airbus Industrie, 1993. Reprinted by permission.

**Figure A.7: Airbus Order Share**

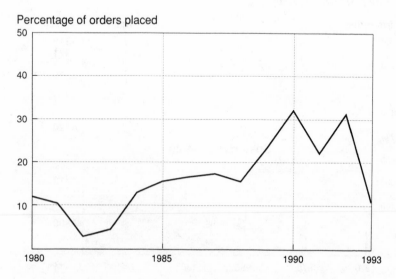

Source: Airbus Industrie, 1993. Reprinted by permission.

**Figure A.8: Airbus Industrie Corporate Structure**

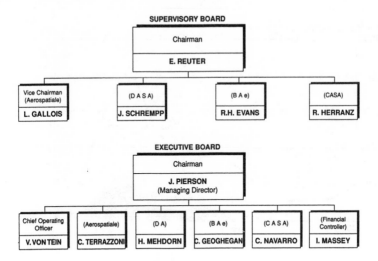

Source: Airbus Industrie, 1993. Reprinted by permission.

**Figure A.9: Airbus Industrie Organization**

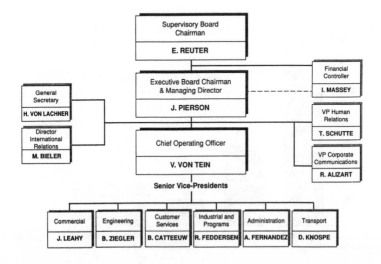

Source: Airbus Industrie, 1993. Reprinted by permission.

**Figure A.10: Order Development, 1980–1993**

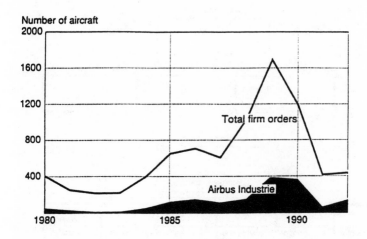

Source: Airbus Industrie, 1993. Reprinted by permission.

**Figure A.11: Comparative Aircraft Orders, 1992**

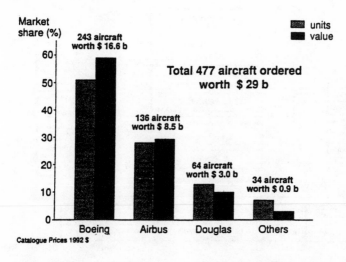

Source: Airbus Industrie, 1993. Reprinted by permission.

**Figure A.12: Airbus Product Line—Equal Seat Spacing**

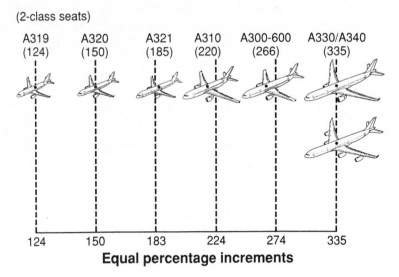

Source: Airbus Industrie, 1993. Reprinted by permission.

**Figure A.13: Competing Product Lines**

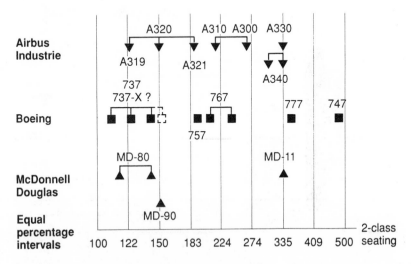

Source: Airbus Industrie, 1993. Reprinted by permission.

**Table A.1 Aircraft Deliveries, 1958–1984**

| | 1958 | '59 | '60 | '61 | '62 | '63 | '64 | '65 | '66 | '67 | '68 | '69 | '70 | '71 |
|---|---|---|---|---|---|---|---|---|---|---|---|---|---|---|
| **707** | 8 | 77 | 91 | 80 | 68 | 34 | 38 | 61 | 83 | 118 | 111 | 59 | 19 | 10 |
| **727** | | | | | | 6 | 95 | 111 | 135 | 155 | 160 | 115 | 54 | 33 |
| **737** | | | | | | | | | | 4 | 105 | 114 | 37 | 29 |
| **747** | | | | | | | | | | | | 4 | 92 | 69 |
| **DC-8** | | 21 | 91 | 42 | 22 | 19 | 20 | 31 | 32 | 41 | 102 | 85 | 33 | 13 |
| **DC-9/MD-80** | | | | | | | | 5 | 69 | 152 | 203 | 121 | 54 | 44 |
| **DC-10** | | | | | | | | | | | | | | 13 |
| **L-1011** | | | | | | | | | | | | | | |
| **880/990** | | | 14 | 33 | 33 | 16 | 4 | 2 | | | | | | |
| **757** | | | | | | | | | | | | | | |
| **767** | | | | | | | | | | | | | | |
| **U.S. Manufacturers Subtotal** | 8 | 98 | 196 | 156 | 122 | 75 | 157 | 210 | 319 | 470 | 681 | 498 | 289 | 211 |
| **Comet** | 7 | 19 | 20 | 14 | 13 | 2 | 2 | 1 | | 1 | | | | |
| **Caravelle** | | 18 | 39 | 39 | 35 | 23 | 22 | 18 | 18 | 21 | 14 | 11 | 9 | 4 |
| **Trident** | | | | | | | 12 | 18 | 11 | 1 | 11 | 9 | 2 | 13 |
| **VC-10** | | | | | | | 14 | 11 | 7 | 10 | 9 | 2 | 1 | 12 |
| **BAC-111** | | | | | | | 34 | 46 | 20 | 26 | 40 | 22 | | |
| **F-28** | | | | | | | | | | | | 9 | 11 | 10 |
| **Mercure** | | | | | | | | | | | | | | |
| **A300** | | | | | | | | | | | | | | |
| **A310** | | | | | | | | | | | | | | |
| **BAe 146** | | | | | | | | | | | | | | |
| **VFW-614** | | | | | | | | | | | | | | |
| **Concorde** | | | | | | | | | | | | | | |
| **Non-U.S. Manufacturers Subtotal** | 7 | 37 | 59 | 53 | 48 | 25 | 50 | 74 | 82 | 53 | 60 | 71 | 45 | 39 |
| **TOTAL** | 15 | 135 | 255 | 209 | 170 | 100 | 207 | 284 | 401 | 523 | 741 | 569 | 334 | 250 |

*Table A.1 (continued)*

|  | '72 | '73 | '74 | '75 | '76 | '77 | '78 | '79 | '80 | '81 | '82 | '83 | '84 | Total |
|---|---|---|---|---|---|---|---|---|---|---|---|---|---|---|
| **707** | 4 | 11 | 21 | 7 | 9 | 8 | 13 | 6 | 3 | 6 | 8 | 8 | 8 | 969 |
| **727** | 41 | 92 | 91 | 91 | 61 | 67 | 118 | 136 | 131 | 97 | 26 | 11 | 8 | 1834 |
| **737** | 22 | 23 | 55 | 51 | 41 | 25 | 40 | 77 | 92 | 111 | 95 | 82 | 67 | 1070 |
| **747** | 30 | 30 | 22 | 21 | 27 | 20 | 32 | 67 | 73 | 58 | 25 | 23 | 16 | 609 |
| **DC-8** | 4 |  |  |  |  |  |  |  |  |  |  |  |  | 556 |
| **DC-9/MD-80** | 32 | 29 | 48 | 42 | 50 | 22 | 22 | 39 | 23 | 73 | 44 | 50 | 44 | 1166 |
| **DC-10** | 52 | 57 | 47 | 43 | 19 | 14 | 18 | 36 | 40 | 23 | 11 | 4 | 2 | 379 |
| **LC-1011** | 17 | 39 | 41 | 25 | 16 | 11 | 8 | 14 | 24 | 29 | 14 | 6 | 4 | 248 |
| **880/990** |  |  |  |  |  |  |  |  |  |  |  |  |  | 102 |
| **757** |  |  |  |  |  |  |  |  |  |  | 2 | 25 | 18 | 45 |
| **767** |  |  |  |  |  |  |  |  |  |  | 20 | 55 | 29 | 104 |
| **U.S. Manufacturers Subtotal** | 202 | 281 | 325 | 280 | 223 | 167 | 251 | 369 | 386 | 397 | 243 | 264 | 196 | 7082 |
| **Comet** |  |  |  |  |  |  |  |  |  |  |  |  |  | 112 |
| **Caravelle** | 5 | 3 |  |  |  |  |  |  |  |  |  |  |  | 279 |
| **Trident** | 11 | 7 | 4 | 6 | 9 | 7 | 4 |  |  |  |  |  |  | 117 |
| **VC-10** |  |  |  |  |  |  |  |  |  |  |  |  |  | 54 |
| **BAC-111** | 7 | 2 | 4 | 2 |  | 6 | 3 |  | 3 | 2 | 2 |  |  | 231 |
| **F-28** | 13 | 19 | 9 | 20 | 17 | 13 | 11 | 13 | 13 | 13 | 11 | 19 | 17 | 218 |
| **Mercure** |  |  | 6 | 4 |  |  |  |  |  |  |  |  |  | 10 |
| **A300** |  |  | 4 | 9 | 13 | 16 | 15 | 24 | 40 | 45 | 46 | 21 | 19 | 252 |
| **A310** |  |  |  |  |  |  |  |  |  |  |  | 17 | 29 | 46 |
| **BAe 146** |  |  |  |  |  |  |  |  |  |  |  | 7 | 11 | 18 |
| **VFW-614** |  |  |  | 1 | 4 | 5 |  |  |  |  |  |  |  | 10 |
| **Concorde** |  |  |  | 1 | 6 | 2 |  |  | 3 | 2 |  |  |  | 14 |
| **Non-U.S. Manufacturers Subtotal** | 36 | 31 | 27 | 43 | 49 | 49 | 33 | 38 | 59 | 62 | 59 | 64 | 76 | 1361 |
| **TOTAL** | 238 | 312 | 352 | 323 | 272 | 216 | 284 | 412 | 445 | 450 | 302 | 328 | 272 | 8443 |

Source: Richard Baldwin and Paul Krugman, "Industrial Policy and International Competition in Wide-Bodied Aircraft," in *Trade Policy Issues and Empirical Analysis*, ed. Robert E. Baldwin (Chicago: University of Chicago Press, 1988), pp. 45-71, copyright © 1988, National Bureau of Economic Research.

# NOTES

## Introduction

1. Robert Gilpin is one of the best-known and most credible proponents of an approach in which state and market are juxtaposed as ideal types. In *The Political Economy of International Relations* (Princeton, NJ: Princeton University Press, 1987, 10) he states: "Students of international political economy. . . must attempt to understand how these contrasting models of organizing human activity and of decision making affect one another and thereby determine social outcomes."

2. The authors cited in this part draw on a much deeper and broader literature that emphasizes the importance of states as coherent and purposeful actors in the international system. This realist perspective sees competition and conflict among states as the unavoidable consequence of their interaction in a system in which no higher authority exists to guarantee their individual or collective security.

3. Gautam Sen, *The Military Origins of Industrialization and International Trade Rivalry* (New York: St. Martin's Press, 1984), 66, provides a particularly unambiguous statement of this view of international relations: "the dominant reality is rivalry and competition between national actors, and the currency of transaction between them is power; and the highest denomination of this currency of power is military capability."

4. Andrew Bard Schmookler, *The Parable of the Tribes* (Los Angeles: University of California Press, 1984), 21. Schmookler defines power as "the capacity to achieve one's will against the will of another" or also as "the ability to restrict the range of another's choices" (p. 20).

5. In his powerful allegory of international relations, Schmookler (op. cit.: 21) depicts "four possible outcomes for the threatened tribes: destruction, absorption and transformation, withdrawal, and imitation."

6. Sen (op. cit.: 11). Later Sen notes that the adoption of industrial processes elicits similar behavior on the part of other states, initiating a self-perpetuating process in which "all countries are obliged to join once the phenomenon begins to spread" (p. 84).

7. Sen (ibid.: 69-70) asserts that "Thus, the history of the industrial revolutions of the past two centuries can also be seen as the history of international political rivalries."

8. Ibid. "It is this apprehension of industrial backwardness in a world of industrially and, therefore, militarily advanced nations that prompts the State to intervene and speed

up the process of industrial transformation. Thus, at bottom the motivation for rapid industrial change is almost invariably of a military nature" (ibid.: 7-8).

9. William Lazonick, *Business Organization and the Myth of the Market Economy* (Cambridge: Cambridge University Press, 1991). Lazonick identifies the value-creating capabilities of innovative firms rather than the extension of markets as the motor of capitalist economic development. He argues that planned coordination has gradually displaced market coordination in generating the "internal economies of scale" that create competitive advantage within firms and, by extension, in national economies.

10. Ibid.: 88. Similarly, Sen (op. cit.: 75) notes: "The State, unlike private entrepreneurs, is willing to bear the burden of temporary losses by building excess capacity in the interest of economies of scale, which would be justified by the future growth of the market."

11. Sen (op. cit.: 73-74) goes as far as to claim that "The creation of industries for military purposes lays the basis on which the civilian manufacturing economy subsequently grows."

12. Lazonick (op. cit.) argues that orthodox economic theory is wholly inadequate for understanding the process of capitalist economic development. Concerned as it is with idealized conditions of perfect competition and market equilibrium, neoclassical liberalism fails to address the forces that produce shifts in competitive advantage.

13. Paul Krugman, "Introduction: New Thinking about Trade Policy" in *Strategic Trade Policy and the New International Economics*, ed. Paul Krugman, pp. 1-22 (Cambridge, Mass.: MIT Press, 1986): 7.

14. Michael Borrus, Laura D'Andrea Tyson and John Zysman. "Creating Advantage: How Government Policies Shape International Trade in the Semiconductor Industry," in *Strategic Trade Policy and the New International Economics*, ed. Paul R. Krugman, pp. 91-113 (Cambridge, Mass.: MIT Press, 1986): 92.

## Chapter 1

1. Paul Kennedy, *The Rise and Fall of the Great Powers* (New York: Random House, 1987): 357.

2. Anton DePorte, *Europe Between the Superpowers* (New Haven, Conn.: Yale University Press, 1979): ix.

3. Kennedy (op. cit.: 368).

4. Benjamin J. Cohen, "The Revolution in Atlantic Economic Relations: A Bargain Comes Unstuck," in *The United States and Western Europe*, ed. Wolfram Hanrieder, pp. 106-133 (Cambridge, Mass.: Winthrop Publishers, 1974): 127-128. Cohen argues convincingly that the political leadership of the United States was increasingly willing in the 1960s and early 1970s to sacrifice the interests of its Atlantic Community "partners" in Europe in order to preserve its eroding position in the international system.

5. David Calleo and Benjamin Rowland, *America and the World Political Economy* (Bloomington: Indiana University Press, 1973): 123.

6. Ibid.: 162.

7. Ibid.: 165.

8. Jacques Servan-Schreiber, *Le Defi Americain* (Paris: DeNoel, 1967).

9. M.S. Hochmuth,"Aerospace," in *Big Business and the State*, ed. Raymond Vernon, pp. 145-169 (Cambridge, Mass.: Harvard University Press, 1974): 145.

10. Daniel Todd and Janice Simpson, *Aerospace and Development: A Survey* (Winnipeg: University of Manitoba, 1985): 33.

11. Jacob A. Vander Meulen, *The Politics of Aircraft: Building an American Military Industry* (Lawrence: University Press of Kansas, 1992), argues that Congress was successful in keeping the early American aircraft industry "a bastion of republican political economy"(p. 3). Influential members used their control of funding to maintain ruinous price competition among aircraft builders in an attempt to impose on the young industry an inappropriate ideology based on free enterprise, the individual innovator, small firms and a limited role for the state.

12. Ann Markusen et al., *The Rise of the Gunbelt* (London: Oxford University Press, 1991): 56.

13. The following paragraphs rely on the selections by Mingos (originally published in 1930) and Freudenthal (originally published in 1940) contained in G.R. Simonson, ed., *The History of the American Aircraft Industry* (Cambridge, Mass.: MIT Press, 1968).

14. Also see David C. Mowery and Nathan Rosenberg, "The Commercial Aircraft Industry," in *Government and Technical Progress*, ed. Richard R. Nelson, pp. 101-161 (New York: Pergamon Press, 1982): 128-131.

15. Freudenthal in Simonson (op. cit.: 91).

16. See Mowery and Rosenberg (op. cit.) and Freudenthal in Simonson (op. cit.) for data on the sales profiles of the major U.S. aviation manufacturers during the 1930s.

17. Vander Meulen (op. cit.: 218) argues that this so-called military Keynesianism would prove "a potent and attractive solution to the contradiction between voluntarist American political culture and the need for ongoing state intervention to encourage demand, which the depression had made clear."

18. Charles D. Bright, *The Jet Makers* (Lawrence: Regents of Kansas Press, 1978): 4.

19. These figures are taken from a study by the Aircraft Industry Association of America, which is reproduced in Simonson (op. cit.: 161-178). Similar and supporting data can be found in Bright (op. cit.: 7-11).

20. Jacob Vander Meulen (op. cit.: 188) argues that "Unlimited demand during World War II temporarily relieved the tensions of a contracting business artificially geared to produce for the mass market. After the war it would be up to cold war planners to produce such a market for a vastly expanded industry."

21. Bright (op. cit.: 15).

22. For a detailed treatment of the development of the jet engine, including profiles of the major innovators as well as illuminating technical information, see Edward W. Constant II, *The Origins of the Turbojet Revolution* (Baltimore: Johns Hopkins University Press, 1980).

23. Anthony Sampson, *The Arms Bazaar* (New York: Viking Press, 1977): 99.

24. Mowery and Rosenberg (op. cit.: 133).

25. Gregory Hooks, *Forging the Military-Industrial Complex* (Urbana: University of Illinois Press, 1991): 235.

26. Markusen et al. (op. cit.: 230).

27. Mowery and Rosenberg (op. cit.: 140).

28. Ibid.: 131.

29. Hochmuth, "Aerospace," (op. cit.: 152).

30. Edward Kolodziej, *Making and Marketing Arms*, (Princeton, NJ: Princeton University Press, 1987). Kolodziej examines the impact of French arms exports upon the domestic political economy of France as well as on the larger international system. He argues that while these sales initially were intended to provide economies of scale and

lower military procurement costs to the French government, they took on a logic and importance of their own that ultimately was damaging to French democracy and civil society. Kolodziej asserts that arms sales gradually became so important to national prestige and societal welfare that "the arms complex has become a government within a government with its own rules, interests, aims and priorities"(p. 213).

31. Sampson (op. cit.: 128). His account of the intense competition between the American and European protagonists reveals clearly the close connection between the political and industrial dimensions of defense contracting.

32. Ibid.: 260.

33. Ibid.: 269.

34. Keith Hayward, *The British Aircraft Industry* (Manchester, UK: Manchester University Press, 1989:) 3.

35. Hochmuth, "Aerospace," (op. cit.: 148).

36. Ibid.: 155. Much of Hochmuth's data has been drawn from a report issued by the Commission of the European Communities in July 1972 entitled "A Policy for the Promotion of Industry and Technology in the Aeronautica."

37. Mowery and Rosenberg (op. cit.: 112). See in particular Table 3.5.

38. Ira Magaziner and Daniel Patinkin, *The Silent War* (New York: Random House, 1989): 374. See especially chapter 8 (pp. 231-263) and its notes (pp. 373-394). Exact numbers of commercial aircraft deliveries per year differ slightly among sources, but Table 1 gives a clear picture of the extent of U.S. mastery of the industry at this time.

39. Hochmuth, "Aerospace," (op. cit.: 153).

## Chapter 2

1. Stephen Blank, "Britain: The Politics of Foreign Economic Policy," in *Between Power and Plenty: Foreign Economic Policies of Advanced Industrial States*, ed. Peter J. Katzenstein, pp. 89-137 (Madison: University of Wisconsin Press, 1978): 132.

2. Ibid.: 108

3. Ibid.: 122.

4. Ibid.: 102.

5. Alec Cairncross, *The British Economy Since 1945* (Oxford: Blackwell, 1992): 78.

6. Peter A. Hall, *Governing The Economy* (New York: Oxford University Press, 1986): 67. Hall emphasizes historical factors such as Britain's early industrialization and the imperial legacy of the sterling era as well as institutional characteristics of the British political economy, all of which combined to make an effective response to the economic challenges of the postwar era especially difficult.

7. Ibid.: 73.

8. Ibid.: 87.

9. Ibid.: 56.

10. Prime Minister Wilson promised to "reforge Britain in the white hot heat of the scientific revolution." Quoted in ibid.: 87-88.

11. D.J. Morris and D.K. Stout, "Industrial Policy," in *The Economic System in the UK* 3rd ed., ed. Derek Morris, pp. 851-894 (Oxford: Oxford University Press, 1985): 871. Emphasis in original.

12. Aubrey Silbertson, "Industrial Policies in Britain 1960-1980," in *Industrial Policy and Innovation*, ed. Charles Carter, pp. 39-51 (London: Heinemann, 1981): 46.

13. Morris and Stout (op. cit.: 873).

14. Stephen Young and Neil Hood, "Industrial Policy in the United Kingdom," in *National Industrial Policies*, eds. Robert E. Driscoll and Jack N. Behrman, pp. 197-214 (Cambridge, Mass.: Oelgeschlager, Gunn and Hain, 1984): 200.

15. Keith Hayward, *The British Aircraft Industry* (Manchester, UK: Manchester University Press, 1989): 13.

16. While some of the so-called Brabazon types showed technical and commercial promise, many (like Brabazon 1, which first flew in 1949) were already obsolete upon reaching the prototype stage. See ibid.: 52-55.

17. Ibid.: 51.

18. M.S. Hochmuth, "Aerospace," in *Big Business and the State*, ed. Raymond Vernon, pp. 145-169 (Cambridge, Mass.: Harvard University Press, 1974): 159.

19. Ibid.: 159.

20. Hayward, *British Aircraft Industry*, (op. cit.: 53).

21. Ronald Miller and David Sawers, *The Technical Development of Modern Aviation* (New York: Praeger, 1970). The authors characterize World War II and the years just after as a "plateau" in the technical and economic development of civil aviation, a period in which major innovations of the 1930s (monoplanes, pressurized cabins, tricycle landing gear, stronger and more efficient piston engines and high octane fuels) were put into wide practice. Although their implementation reduced costs and improved performance, the industrial and financial impact of jet technology was yet to come and would confer substantial benefits to American manufacturers. See especially chapter 5, pp. 128-148.

22. The de Havilland Comet entered commercial service in May 1952 with BOAC and was the symbol of British technical competence in commercial aviation. Two mysterious crashes (10 January and 8 April 1954) were fatal to all aboard and later were found to be caused by cabin explosions due to metal fatigue. The plane was taken out of service for four years, giving the Boeing 707 and the Douglas DC8 the time needed to insure American dominance in the emerging jet airliner market. See ibid.: 179ff. Also Arthur Reed, *Britain's Aircraft Industry* (London: J.M. Dent & Sons, 1973), especially chapter 3. In showing the extent of the British lead in jets, Reed notes on p. 34 that "as the first Comet made its maiden flight, the Americans were literally sketching out the first Boeing 707 design."

23. Hochmuth, "Aerospace," (op. cit.: 162).

24. Hayward, *British Aircraft Industry*, (op. cit.: 64).

25. Ibid.: 67.

26. Ibid.: 71.

27. The "Blue Streak" was cancelled in favor of the U.S. "Skybolt" system, itself unceremoniously terminated by the Kennedy administration in 1962. The incident was highly embarrassing for British officials and brought into sharp relief the extent of British political and military dependence on U.S. financing and technology for weapons systems development.

28. Aubrey Jones, *Britain's Economy: The Roots of Stagnation* (Cambridge: Cambridge University Press, 1985). His book helps one to appreciate the philosophical and cultural difficulties that the very ideas of economic planning or industrial policy presented for British political and business leaders during this time. Jones is also quite critical of governments, Labour and Conservative alike, for their failure to lead a rational restructuring of the British aeronautics sector in the postwar period.

29. Hayward, *British Aircraft Industry*, (op. cit.: 80).

30. Ibid.: 81.

31. Jenkins also pressed for the dissolution of the Ministry of Aviation (MoA), seen by Labour as an overly powerful bureaucracy run amok. It was incorporated into the new Ministry of Technology (MinTech) in November 1966 mostly intact, prompting some to "wonder exactly who was absorbing whom." See Keith Hayward, *Government and British Civil Aerospace* (Manchester, UK: Manchester University Press, 1983): 73.

32. See "Report of the Committee into the Aircraft Industry." Command Paper 2853 (London: HMSO, 1965).

33. In May 1966 a holding company (SEPECAT) based in France was created to manage the combined efforts of BAC and Bréguet in designing and marketing the Jaguar fighter.

34. Hayward, *British Aircraft Industry*, (op. cit.: 110). Also see chapter 3 of this study on Henri Ziegler's role in the Jaguar program; he later became the first managing director of Airbus Industrie.

35. Ibid.: 110-111.

36. Ibid.: 111.

37. Ibid.: 114.

38. Ibid. In fact, Hayward cites (p. 115) a British MoD official as saying "if we had attempted any other solution it would probably have meant the complete domination and absorption by the American aircraft industry." And the Tornado continues to be a bright spot in the otherwise bleak picture of British and European aerospace. Prime Minister John Major announced recently that Saudi Arabia (the only country outside the consortium to have bought Tornados) had ordered an additional 48 aircraft. This second stage of the ongoing Al Yamamah deal will benefit BAe and numerous subcontractors in Britain and Europe.

39. Official British sentiment in favor of engaging in international collaboration to realize a questionable technology had been slim. Aubrey Jones, an early Conservative advocate of British cooperation with its cross-channel neighbors, recalls: "Accordingly in June 1959 I went to Paris and proposed to the French government that we study together the possibility of building jointly a supersonic civil aircraft. I was warmly received, and a committee was set up comprising three experts from each side. When I reported back to London that technical collaboration with the French was possible, the Cabinet, consistently with their scorn for Europe, laughed with derision. Nonetheless, I was allowed 250,000-300,000 [pounds sterling] to conduct a feasibility study. Thus was Concorde born." Jones (op. cit.: 80).

40. Elliot J. Feldman, *Concorde and Dissent* (Cambridge: Cambridge University Press, 1985): 89.

41. Hayward, *British Aircraft Industry*, (op. cit: 102).

42. Hayward, *Government and British Civil Aerospace*, (op. cit.: 68).

43. Hayward, *British Aircraft Industry*, (op. cit: 103).

44. Roger Williams, *European Technology: The Politics of Collaboration* (London: Croon Helm, 1973), cites British government figures showing that between 1962 and 1972, estimates of Concorde's cost ballooned from £150 to £970 million sterling, with the bulk of the increase coming in the period from 1965 to 1968. See chart and figures, p. 118).

45. Hayward, *Government and British Civil Aerospace*, (op. cit.: 63).

46. Ibid.

47. Keith Hayward emphasizes the conflict that inevitably arises between project stability and accountability when political commitments undertaken have no mechanism for

review or cancellation in the event of rising costs or technical failures. See especially chapter 5, "Controlling Concorde", in ibid.: 124-151.

48. Reed, *Britain's Aircraft Industry*, (op. cit.: 13).

49. Hayward, *Government and British Civil Aerospace*, (op. cit.: 98).

50. BA operates now a few Airbus A310s that it inherited from its purchase of British Caledonian.

51. Hayward, *British Aircraft Industry*, (op. cit.: 108).

52. Christopher Layton, "The High-Tech Triangle," in *Partners and Rivals in Western Europe: Britain, France and Germany*, eds. Roger Morgan and Caroline Bray, pp. 184-204 (Brookfield, VT: Gower, 1986): 189.

## Chapter 3

1. Richard F. Kuisel, *Capitalism and the State in Modern France* (Cambridge: Cambridge University Press, 1981): 277. In his study of twentieth century French economic policy, Kuisel notes that the Communists, Socialists, Catholics (MRP) and Gaullists all had different views on what economic reform, especially nationalization, could and should accomplish. He argues convincingly that a neoliberal and technocratic variant of traditional French *étatisme* eventually won out in directing the development of the postwar French economy.

2. Ibid.: 202.

3. Christian Stoffaes, "French Industrial Strategy in the Sunrise Sectors," in *European Industry*, ed. Alex Jacquemin, pp. 274-292 (Oxford: Clarendon Press, 1984): 280.

4. The literature on French postwar economic and industrial policy is extensive, and economic planning is an especially well-documented topic. One of the better sources for appreciating the inherently political nature of the planning process is Stephen S. Cohen, *Modern Capitalist Planning: The French Model* (Berkeley: University of California Press, 1977).

5. Kuisel (op. cit: 213). Kuisel and others have noted the skill with which Monnet and his successor, Etienne Hirsch, convinced the heads of government ministries and industry alike that it was in their own interest to cooperate with the plan. Kuisel argues that their success in doing so is in some ways more similar to religious conversion than to the effect of rational argumentation.

6. Ibid.: 251.

7. Cohen (op. cit.: 67).

8. Kuisel (op. cit.: 257).

9. See John Zysman, "The French State in the International Economy," in *Between Power and Plenty*, ed. Peter J. Katzenstein, pp.255-293 (Madison: University of Wisconsin Press, 1978). Zysman says on p. 271 that in postwar France: "The institutional instrument of a state-led economic strategy, an effective and independent bureaucracy with tools to affect the business decisions of industrial enterprise, was constructed."

10. Peter Hall, *Governing the Economy*, New York: Oxford University Press, 1986): 168.

11. Christian Stoffaes, "Industrial Policy in the High-Technology Industries," in *French Industrial Policy*, eds. William James Adams and Christian Stoffaes, pp. 36-62 (Washington, DC: The Brookings Institution, 1986): 43. Numerous observers have noted the frequency of movement of managerial staff among government agencies, nationalized industry and private business in France, summed up in the term *pantouflage*.

12. The period from 1945 to 1975, known as "Les Trente Glorieuses," saw annual aver-

age GDP growth rates of 6.8 percent in France, a performance that compares favorably with both the United States and Germany and is nearly three times that of Great Britain during the same period.

13. Stoffaes, "French Industrial Strategy," (op. cit.: 280).

14. William J. Adams, *Restructuring the French Economy* (Washington, DC: The Brookings Institution, 1989).

15. Edward Kolodziej, *Making and Marketing Arms* (Princeton, NJ: Princeton University Press, 1987): 33.

16. For an excellent summary of Gaullist thinking and aims, see Anton Deporte, *Europe Between the Superpowers* (New Haven, Conn.: Yale University Press, 1979).

17. Hall (op. cit.: 149).

18. Ibid.: 168.

19. Stoffaes, "French Industrial Strategy," (op. cit.: 279).

20. Adams (op. cit.: 54).

21. See Zysman (op. cit.). He provides an interesting comparison of the relative success of French strategy in various industrial sectors. He argues that French methods were appropriate and effective in mature, capital-intensive industries to which the state could channel resources and realize economies of scale (oil and steel), but produced much less favorable results where market conditions changed rapidly because of constant technological innovation (computers).

22. Stoffaes, "French Industrial Strategy," (op. cit.: 279).

23. A most interesting and exhaustive study of the early history of the French aviation industry is Emmanuel Chadeau's *De Blériot à Dassault* (Paris: Fayard, 1987).

24. Herrick Chapman's *State Capitalism and Working Class Radicalism in the French Aircraft Industry* (Berkeley: University of California Press, 1990) provides valuable insight into the character of industrial relations as they evolved in France during the crucial period from 1936 to 1950. He argues persuasively that the aviation industry was both "unique and exemplary"–unique in its importance in the history of French labor relations and exemplary for understanding the development of the peculiar form of state-directed capitalism that developed in Fourth Republic of France.

25. Ibid.: 306.

26. Kolodziej (op. cit.: 45).

27. In *The Arms Bazaar* (New York: Viking Press, 1977), Anthony Sampson delves into the personalities and intrigues that characterized the world of defense contracting and arms sales (especially aircraft), not only in France but in all of Europe as well as in the United States. His portrayal of Marcel Dassault is especially revealing, both of the man himself and of his influential place in the postwar French political economy. Sampson argues: "By the time de Gaulle had returned to power in 1958 Dassault's position in French politics had become almost institutionalised as kind of one-man embodiment of the military-industrial complex" (p. 158).

28. M.S. Hochmuth, "Aerospace," in *Big Business and the State*, ed. Raymond Vernon, pp. 145-169 (Cambridge, Mass.: Harvard University Press, 1974): 166.

29. SNECMA (Société National d'Étude et Construction de Moteurs d'Aviation) was formed in the immediate postwar period primarily from the assets of the collaborationist and later nationalized engine builder Gnome & Rhone, and was given a virtual monopoly in providing engines for French commercial and military aircraft alike.

30. Hochmuth, "Aerospace," (op. cit.: 167).

31. Kolodziej's (op. cit.) main thesis is that postwar France developed the most tightly knit military-industrial complex in the West, a process he argues has had pernicious effects on both French democracy and the international system. He says that the highly integrated French bureaucracy for arms sales and exports, whose initial raison d'être was to reduce the cost of procurement to the French armed services, was progressively transformed into "a state within a state" and arms exports increasingly became identified with national prestige and economic well-being.

32. Ibid.: 236.

33. Kolodziej (ibid.) asserts that an overweening concern with designing products with export markets in mind began to affect adversely both the mission appropriateness and the timeliness of the delivery of weapons systems to the French armed forces. (Also see note 30, chapter 1.)

34. Mark Lorell, *Multinational Development of Large Aircraft* (Santa Monica: RAND, 1980): 8.

35. Lorell (ibid.) notes that the Germans built both the Nord NorAtlas military transport and the Fouga Magister jet trainer on license from the French government.

36. Société Européenne pour la Construction du Bréguet Atlantic (SEBCAT) was created in December 1959 with Ziegler as managing director to oversee project funding and work shares. See Lorell (op. cit.: 20-24) for a detailed discussion of the structure of these arrangements. And as we shall see in Part II of this study, Henri Ziegler would transfer a great deal of what he learned on the Atlantic to the Airbus program.

37. Lorell (op. cit.: 32).

38. See ibid.: 45, for a chart directly comparing the two aircraft.

39. Ibid.: 46.

40. Ibid.: 47.

## Chapter 4

1. Michael Kreile, "West Germany: The Dynamics of Expansion," in *Between Power and Plenty*, ed. Peter J. Katzenstein, pp. 191-224 (Madison: University of Wisconsin Press, 1978): 195.

2. This discussion of German postwar economic policy draws on Karl Hardach, *The Political Economy of Germany in the 20th Century* (Berkeley: University of California Press, 1980). Hardach notes that Erhard was increasingly influential after March 1948 when he became the first German director for economic administration in the "Bi-zone." The term *Sozialmarktwirtschaft* was coined by his chief advisor, Muller-Armack.

3. Malcolm Maclennan et al., *Economic Planning and Policies in Britain, France and Germany* (New York: Praeger, 1968): 54.

4. Joanne Gowa, "Bipolarity and the Postwar International Economic Order," in *Industry and Politics in West Germany*, ed. Peter J. Katzenstein, pp.33-50 (Ithaca, NY: Cornell University Press, 1989): 33.

5. Some observers have argued that the famous German emphasis on currency stability has served an integral part of a larger strategy for enhancing international economic and industrial competitiveness. "Only recently did we learn that German monetary policy does not have its origins in a special German fear of inflation, or a national preference for stability, but was conceived from the very beginning as a means of improving competitive-

ness in world markets." Horst Tomann, "Germany," in *Current Issues in Industrial Economic Strategy*, eds. Keith Cowling and Roger Sugden, pp. 183-187 (Manchester, UK: Manchester University Press, 1992): 185.

6. Most estimates place annual rates of economic growth in Germany for the period from 1950 to 1980 at over 5 percent, with the industrial and manufacturing sectors at annual rates of over 6 percent. But average annual growth in the volume of exports exceeded 9 percent, thus leading Germany's economic resurgence.

7. These ideas became widely accepted as the SPD's major light on economic issues, Karl Schiller, moved away from the socialist rhetoric of the centrally planned economy. At the Party Congress in 1954, the SPD adopted a mainstream Keynesian position, with Schiller walking the line between laissez-faire and *dirigisme:* "As much competition as possible, as much planning as necessary." Cited in Hardach (op. cit.: 201).

8. Maclennan et al. (op. cit.: 73).

9. Hardach (op. cit.: 201).

10. An OECD report published during this period noted that "German industrial policy is only a special aspect of the general economic policy aimed at maintaining full employment with stable prices, balanced foreign trade and satisfactory expansion." *The Industrial Policies of 14 Countries* (Paris: OECD, 1971): 27.

11. Jeffrey A. Hart, "West German Industrial Policy," in *The Politics of Industrial Policy*, eds. Claude E. Barfield and William A. Schambra, pp. 161-186 (Washington, DC: American Enterprise Institute, 1986): 165. Hart goes on to note that the debate over the wisdom of direct state intervention in industry became a major point of contention between the coalition partners, especially between SPD leader and Chancellor Willy Brandt and FDP leader Otto von Lambsdorff, and contributed directly to the fall of the coalition government in 1982.

12. Ernst-Joachim Mestmacker, "Competition Policy and Antitrust: Some Comparative Observations," *Zeitschrift fur die gesamte Staatswissenschaft*, Vol. 136, No. 3 (1980): 389.

13. Ibid.: 389.

14. "Economic competition in Germany has always been intimately bound up with the international issues of obtaining sufficient natural resources and gaining access to world markets." Christopher S. Allen, "Germany: Competing Communitarianisms," in *Ideology and National Competitiveness*, eds. George C. Lodge and Ezra F. Vogel, pp. 79-102 (Boston: Harvard Business School Press: 1987): 87.

15. Mestmacker (op. cit.: 392).

16. Hardach (op. cit.: 149).

17. J.R. Cable et al., "Federal Republic of Germany 1962-1974," in *The Determinants and Effects of Mergers*, ed. Dennis C. Mueller, pp. 99-132 (Cambridge, Mass.: Oelgeschalger, Gunn and Hain, 1980): 116.

18. Cited in Mestmacker (op. cit.: 397).

19. Georg H. Kuster, "Germany," in *Big Business and the State*, ed. Raymond Vernon, pp. 64-86 (Cambridge, Mass.: Harvard University Press, 1974): 80.

20. Juergen B. Donges, "Industrial Policies in West Germany's Not so Market-oriented Economy," *The World Economy*, Vol. 3, No. 2 (1980): 185-204: 191.

21. Kreile (op. cit.: 199).

22. Kuster (op. cit.: 78).

23. Streit (op. cit.: 134).

24. Ronald Miller and David Sawers, *The Technical Development of Modern Aviation* (New

York: Praeger, 1970). On pages 169 to 173 the authors summarize some of the more important theoretical and technical German aeronautical innovations during the 1920s and 1930s.

25. Edward L. Homze, *Arming the Luftwaffe* (Lincoln: University of Nebraska Press, 1976): 40. Homze recalls the importance of aerial technology in Hitler's rise to power, as he barnstormed the country in aircraft and descended godlike from the clouds in the Leni Riefenstahl film *Triumph of the Will*.

26. Ibid.: 143. Homze later observes that "who owned the industry was not as important as how it operated and was controlled": 261.

27. Homze (ibid.: 262-263) argues persuasively that the structure and patterns of production in the German aerospace industry at this time reflected the nature of political authority in the Third Reich: competing centers striving to extract maximum benefit from a resource-rich but chaotic situation.

28. Miller and Sawers (op. cit: 169).

29. Volker R. Berghahn, *The Americanisation of West German Industry* (Leamington Spa, UK: Berg Publishers, 1986): 278.

30. OECD Report (op. cit.: 29). Also see Kuster (op. cit.: 77).

31. See *Aviation Week and Space Technology (AWST)*, 24 April 1972, as the special report on German aerospace profiles some of the major firms and outlines this early phase of industrial consolidation.

32. The United States instead opted to develop its own antisubmarine warfare aircraft, the Lockheed P-3A Orion, and eventually sold these to NATO members Norway, Holland, Canada and Spain, and to other foreign buyers as well. Great Britain went ahead with its own program, the Nimrod, in 1965. For a detailed history of the Atlantic and other European collaborative programs see Mark Lorell, *The Multinational Development of Large Aircraft* (Santa Monica: RAND, 1980).

33. Ibid.: 22. See Tables 2 and 3.

34. Ibid.: 32.

35. Lorell (ibid.) notes that the French probably made this concession to induce the German government to reject the U.S. government's proposal of the Lockheed C-130A Hercules transport.

36. Ibid.: 42. The firms were Siebel and Messerschmitt.

37. Ibid.: 47.

38. Ibid.: 46.

39. Jean Picq, *Les Ailes de l'Europe* (Paris: Fayard, 1990): 25, credits Franz Joseph Strauss in particular with having a "political vision" of the importance of Germany's industrial participation in the Airbus program.

40. It is interesting to note that, despite the liberal rhetoric of the German political and industrial elite, Germany today has the most concentrated aerospace sector of all the major European nations. Almost all important aeronautical assets are grouped under the single corporate banner of Germany's most powerful industrial firm, Daimler-Benz.

## *Chapter 5*

1. A brief and somewhat anecdotal recounting of the inception and development of the Airbus products and consortium can be found in: Ira Magaziner and Daniel Patinkin, *The Silent War* (New York: Random House, 1989). See chapter 8, "Europe: The Race for the Skies," pp. 231-263, and notes pp. 373-394.

2. Bill Gunston, *Airbus*, (London: Osprey, 1988) and Arthur Reed, *Airbus: Europe's High Flyer* (St. Gallen, Switzerland: Norden, 1991) both provide informative and amply illustrated descriptions of the forerunners of the A300.

3. Jean Picq, *Les Ailes de l'Europe* (Paris: Fayard, 1990), notes that representatives of 11 European airlines met in London in October 1965 at the suggestion of the technical director of Air France, Paul Besson, to discuss future aircraft requirements. Interestingly, Frank Kolk, the technical director for American Airlines, would later, in April 1966, also specify the design of an aircraft that looked remarkably similar to the eventual Airbus design. Called "the Kolk machine," on the drawing boards of the American airframe designers it metamorphosized into the tri-jets later produced by Lockheed (L-1011) and Douglas (DC-10). (See also note 23 in this chapter).

4. As seen in chapter 4, tracing the process of consolidation within the German aerospace industry is complicated by the complex pattern of cross-holdings and partial mergers that characterized this period. As a result, authors differ in precisely how they refer to the various firms. For his part, Gunston (op. cit.: 14) lists the seven firms in the Studiengruppe Group as ATG Siebelwerke, Bolkow, Dornier, Flugzueg-Sud, HFB, Messerschmitt and VFW. (See also notes 4 and 11 in this chapter).

5. Pierre Muller, *Airbus: L'ambition Européenne* (Paris: L'Harmattan, 1989): 48, says that "In December 1965, the Germans transformed the study group into a more formal structure regarding the Airbus project (Arbeitgemeinschaft [sic] Airbus) which brought together the principal industrial firms (Dornier, Hamburger Flugzeugbau, Messerschmitt-Bolkow, Siebel and later, VFW). Picq (op. cit.: 27) attributes the initiative for German cooperation at this stage to Ludwig Bolkow and Dr. Bernhardt Weinhardt.

6. Muller (op. cit: 50).

7. I will not pretend to resolve the dispute over the exact parentage of the A300. Gunston (op. cit.: 19) has "no hesitation in stating that the HBN.100 and its successor, the A300, had their genesis principally at Hatfield" (the location of the HSA main design facility). But Muller (op. cit.) specifically takes Gunston to task on this, saying there is no single antecedent aircraft.

8. Picq (op. cit.: 28-29) observes that the May 1966 meeting between British transport Minister Fred Mulley and his French counterpart Edgar Pisani produced a selection of partners for the Airbus notably lacking in "industrial rationality." He also notes the British choice of HSA followed a simple pattern of alternation; since BAC had been given the work on the most recent collaborative project, the Concorde, the Airbus would go to HSA.

9. This meeting brought together: for Great Britain, John Stonehouse (minister of state for technology); for France, Andre Bettencourt (minister of state for foreign affairs); and for Germany Dr. Johann Schollhorn (state secretary at the economic ministry).

10. Mark Lorell, *Multinational Development of Large Aircraft* (Santa Monica: RAND, 1980): 55.

11. Muller (op. cit.: 47).

12. Ibid.: 49, observes: "At the beginning of 1967, the structure was again transformed with the creation of the company Deutsche Airbus which brought together (20%) each, the five principal firms involved in the Airbus project." Lorell (op. cit.: 61) lists the five firms comprising Deutsche Airbus as VFW, Messerschmitt, Siebel, Hamburger and Dornier, which matches Muller's list.

13. Keith Hayward, *Government and British Civil Aerospace* (Manchester, UK: Manchester University Press, 1983), notes that after the BSE merger, Rolls-Royce was

able to dominate the British aerospace scene because it faced no effective industrial counterweight, especially since merger negotiations between HSA and BAC had collapsed earlier in 1966. See in particular chapter 3 (pp. 69-98) on the pernicious influence of Rolls-Royce on British aerospace policy.

14. Ibid.: 82. Similarly, Muller (op. cit: 59) asserts that "British participation, from the beginning was built around the use of Rolls-Royce engines."

15. Hayward, *Government and British Civil Aerospace* (op. cit.: 89), notes that knighthoods were given to two Rolls-Royce executives for their efforts in the L-1011 deal.

16. Gunston (op. cit.: 22).

17. Lorell (op. cit.: 53).

18. Ibid.: 56.

19. Picq (op. cit.: 33) notes that Roger Beteille, the technical director of the A300 project, paid a visit to Rolls-Royce headquarters at Derby in the spring of 1968. He came away convinced that the British engine builder hoped to have the Airbus program defray the costs of developing the RB-211 for the American market by overcharging their European collaborators on the RB-207.

20. Ziegler had been Chief of Staff of the Free French forces in London during World War II, the first director-general of Air France and head of Bréguet Aviation before coming to Sud.

21. Henri Ziegler, "Les technologies avancées vecteur du développment économique," *Bulletin de l'institut d'histoire du temps présent*, Supplement No. 6, Paris (1984): 30, recalls this as a crucial stage in the Airbus program. Having to make the case that the French government fund the A300 instead of Dassault's proposed Mercure civil aircraft, Ziegler says: "Believing my choice the better one, I talked, I explained, and ended up convincing." He characterized the role of interlocuter between the industrial and political sides of the program as "an extremely complex and permanent dialog in which the role of the man at the level of decision-maker is fundamental."

22. This episode is recounted in virtually all sources on Airbus Industrie and occupies a prominent place in the lore of the consortium.

23. Picq (op. cit.: 32) notes that Beteille paid a visit to the United States in early 1968 to "get a feel for the market." He went to Dallas and met with Frank Kolk of American Airlines, who gave to Beteille the technical proposal for the so-called Kolk machine, a large-capacity, twin-engine aircraft (also see note 3 this chapter).

24. Muller (op. cit.: 60).

25. Picq (op. cit.: 37) recalls that de Gaulle's scheduled referendum, ostensibly on reforming the French Senate, was scheduled for 28 April 1969 and was intensifying political uncertainty in France, as were the impending elections scheduled for September of that year in Germany.

26. Gunston (op. cit.: 25).

27. See Lorell (op. cit.: 60) for a listing of some of these. Picq (op. cit.: 41) also recalls that Airbus, in the interest of "not inventing what already exists," decided to purchase the engine housings (nacelles) from the American firm Douglas. This not only saved on development costs, but also gave the A300B additional commonality with the popular Douglas DC-10.

28. Lorell (op. cit.: 59).

29. Ibid.: 61.

30. Muller (op. cit.: 70). Picq (op. cit.: 35) credits F.J. Strauss, the powerful leader of the

Bavarian CSU, with having a clear understanding of the political importance of German industrial participation in collaborative programs in general and the Airbus program in particular, even without project leadership.

31. Muller (op. cit.: 71). Further, Ian McIntyre, *Dogfight: The Transatlantic Battle over Airbus* (Westport, Conn.: Praeger, 1992): 24, notes: "Karl Schiller, the SPD finance minister in the grand coalition, and Franz Joseph Strauss, who was defence minister at the time, gave their backing to the idea that West Germany should not only match the French contribution but also find the 60 percent of the development cost of the wing that Hawker-Siddeley was not able to meet."

32. Picq (op. cit.: 37) estimates that the financial commitment of HSA represented about 40 percent of the wing's development costs, or about 7 percent of the aircraft's total development cost. He credits Sir Arnold Hall and Sir John Lidbury of HSA with recognizing that the company's interests lay with the Airbus project.

33. Ibid.: 38. Picq notes that this situation created an odd spectacle at the signing ceremonies where all three national flags of the industrial participants were displayed, yet representatives of only two governments were present. For Picq, this is compelling evidence of the importance of "the Franco-German 'couple' in constructing Europe."

34. Muller (op. cit.: 72).

35. Ibid.

36. Throughout this period there were attempts to bring the British back into the project on a formal basis, culminating in a final British refusal in December 1970.

37. This unique form of business organization is defined and explained more fully later in Part II.

38. As will be explained in greater detail in Part II, members of a GIE retain ownership and management of productive assets yet agree to be jointly and severally responsible for any obligations incurred as the result of their mutual participation in designated projects. For its part, the GIE proper coordinates the activities of the partners relative to the project, and may assume specified management functions as required.

39. Muller (op. cit.: 74).

40. Ibid. This juxtaposition of one "logic" with the other provides the analytical framework for his insightful analysis of the Airbus project.

41. Ibid.: 53.

## Chapter 6

1. P. Gianni, "L'Airbus Européen," *Revue général de l'air et de l'espace*, Vol. 34, No. 4 (1971): 401-443: 411. Gianni further notes that: "In the longer term, that failure would have put the countries of Europe in a position of dependence on the US for their needs in civil and commercial aircraft."

2. See ibid.: 429-437 for a complete text, including annexes 1 and 2, of the 29 May 1969 Franco-German agreement.

3. Ibid.: 413.

4. Keith Hayward, "Politics and European Aerospace Collaboration: The A300 Airbus," *Journal of Common Market Studies*, Vol. 14, No. 4 (June 1976): 354-367: 355.

5. Keith Hayward, *International Collaboration in Civil Aerospace* (New York: St. Martin's Press, 1986): 64, asserts that "The Concorde provided a clear example of how not to organise cooperation in a large-scale civil programme." Gianni (op. cit.: 405) notes that on the Concorde, "despite the close relations between the industrial partners of the two coun-

tries, in fact England and France had each constructed, under *separate contracts* approximately half and airframe and half a propulsion system. . . ."

6. Gianni (op. cit.: 412).

7. Ibid.: 421.

8. Ibid.

9. Keith Hayward, *International Collaboration in Civil Aerospace* (op. cit.: 65), observes (as does Gianni) that the privately owned members of Deutsche Airbus felt at a disadvantage relative to the state-owned Aérospatiale, regarding especially the unlimited liability of the partners insisted upon by the French. But Hayward says that the financial worries of the Deutsche Airbus firms "were also eased by Federal guarantees."

10. The GIE was established as a legal form of business organization in France by Ordinance No. 67821 of 23 September 1967. See Gianni (op. cit.): 421.

11. Ibid.: 422.

12. Ibid.

13. See ibid.: 436-443 for a text of the December 1970 agreement. Subsequent parenthetical references will make note of specific articles and items contained in those statutes.

14. Gianni (ibid.: 423) notes that "This joint and several responsibility is completely logical considering its [AI's] constitution without capital and the importance attached to the entity." In a similar vein, Keith Hayward, *International Collaboration in Civil Aerospace* (op. cit.: 65), notes that "Unlimited liability, backed by intergovernmental agreements against default, provided a firm legal and psychological basis for operation."

15. Gianni (op. cit.: 426) notes that Roger Beteille was appointed technical director (and was in charge of coordination), Felix Kracht was director of production, Friedrich Feye was in charge of administration and finances and Didier Godchot was commercial director.

16. These regulations are expressly mentioned in Article 14 of the statutes, but not described in detail. Gianni does not include these in the appendix to his article as part of the text of the agreement.

17. Gianni (op. cit.: 425).

18. Ibid.

19. Bill Gunston, *Airbus* (London: Osprey, 1988): 31. Chapters 1 and 2 of his book provide an informative history of the A300/A300B project, including photographs, diagrams and other technical information. Gunston sees British policy toward the aircraft industry in general and toward the Airbus program in particular as shortsighted and ultimately damaging to the country's industrial and economic health. He notes that British withdrawal from the A300 project "resulted in a large and sustained flow of the very best British engineering and sales talent to the A300B management centers, initially in Paris and Munich and later in Toulouse" (p. 28). The pullout also "resulted in a massive expansion of the French and German equipment and accessory industry, in almost every case duplicating products that could have been obtained from Britain" (p. 28).

20. Subsequent versions of the A300 have extended this range to over 4,000 nautical miles. For descriptions of the various versions of the A300B and the evolution of their design and capability, see ibid., and especially *Jane's All the World's Aircraft* (Surrey: Jane's Information Group), beginning with the 1971-72 edition and in subsequent annual volumes.

21. As described in chapter 5, both SNECMA of France and MTU of Germany won important subcontracting roles from GE on the CF6, including work on parts destined for

DC-10s as well as the Airbus. Gunston (op. cit.: 30) notes that SNECMA captured about 27 percent of the value of work on the CF6, and MTU 12 percent, leaving 61 percent for GE itself.

22. Following the merger between Fokker and VFW in May 1969, Fokker-VFW contracted in December 1970 to manufacture flaps, spoilers and ailerons for the A300B. In exchange for the work, the Dutch government agreed to provide 6.6 percent of the development funding for the aircraft, but Fokker-VFW did not become a member of the AI consortium.

23. CASA is the acronym for the state-owned Spanish aeronautics firm Construccionnes Aeronauticas S.A. CASA came into the A300B program on 23 December 1971 by joining Airbus Industrie as a partner with a 4.2 percent share, reducing the holdings of the French and German partners to 47.9 percent each. For background on CASA and its rationale for joining AI, see Arthur Reed, *Airbus: Europe's High Flyer* ( St. Gallen, Switzerland: Norden Publishing House, 1991): pp. 29-30 and pp. 118-124.

24. This section relies on Gunston (op. cit.). See especially pp. 31-32 on the A300B flight testing and certification process.

25. Pierre Muller, *Airbus, L'ambition Européenne* (Paris: L'Harmattan, 1989): 81, notes that the Airbus was now a physical reality, and "particularly significant from this point of view was the fact that henceforth Airbus would be written with a capital letter. What had been up until then a common name had become a proper name." For a detailed account and photos of the occasion, see Reed, *Airbus* (op. cit: 31-33).

26. Muller (op. cit.: 81).

27. As noted earlier, the A300B was not a particularly innovative aircraft from a technical standpoint, utilizing as it did a number of standard components and proven systems. However, its designers had undertaken (rather late in the definition process) a commercially motivated decision to expand the diameter of the fuselage to 5.64 meters (18 ft. 6 in.) so as to accommodate the LD-3 cargo containers used in the Boeing 747. Both Gunston (op. cit.) and Muller (op. cit.) observe that this modification, which increased cargo capacity, would be an important factor in selling the A300B.

28. Muller (op. cit.: 55).

29. The fleet of so-called "Super Guppy" transports used to ship the massive Airbus subassemblies are derived from Boeing 377s, civil versions of Stratocruisers that had been owned and operated by Aero Spacelines, a company formed by former Boeing test pilot A. M. "Tex" Johnston. That company went out of business and sold the drawing and production rights for the Super Guppy 201 to AI. These nose-loading aircraft had transported NASA rocket boosters and DC-10 sections, and now carry AI wings and sections of fuselage between production and assembly sites. See Gunston (op. cit.: 118-119).

30. This 4 percent figure is mentioned throughout Airbus internal and promotional literature and is cited as well by outside observers as credible. For example, see Hayward, *International Collaboration in Civil Aerospace* (op. cit.: 71), where he also notes that "Airbus Industrie has pioneered the pre-fabrication of large sub-assemblies, and the relative compactness of Europe insures that they are in transit for no more than 48 hours."

31. Ibid.: 79.

32. Ibid.

33. Ibid.: 71.

34. Ibid.: 80.

35. Both Airbus literature and secondary sources put the overhead expenses at approxi-

mately 2 to 3 percent of total sales. As noted above, purchases of major components outside the consortium amount to 20 to 25 percent of the total cost of the aircraft, leaving
approximately 70 percent of sales revenues to "flow through" to the partners.

36. Hayward, *International Collaboration in Civil Aerospace*, (op. cit.: 70).

37. Ibid.

38. Ibid. Hayward goes on to say that "In many cases, governmental decision is simply a
question of vetoing or ratifying choices made by Airbus industrie and its members."

39. Muller (op. cit.: 87).

40. Muller (ibid.: 88) cites a very interesting internal memo to this effect.

41. Ibid.: 86. Muller also notes that, paradoxically, the growing independence of Airbus
Industrie from the partners and especially Aérospatiale occurred even though AI moved in
January 1974 from its location in Paris to a new site at the Toulouse Blagnac airport, very
near the Aérospatiale assembly facilities there.

42. "Between 1971 and 1976, five major U.S. airlines, which accounted for about 30%
of the world's passenger traffic, placed only 4 percent of the orders for new aircraft." M. Y.
Yoshino, "Global Competition in a Salient Industry: The Case of Civil Aircraft," in
*Competition in Global Industries*, ed. Michael E. Porter, chapter 16, (pp. 517-538) (Boston:
Harvard Business School Press, 1986): 525.

43. Muller (op. cit.: 87).

44. See Gunston (op. cit.: 73) for a more detailed description of these trips, including
specific time and distances covered on the latter tour.

45. These sales efforts were successful enough to inspire this enthusiastic assessment:
"AI had become the dominant twin-aisle builder for Europe, the Middle East and Far
East," Gunston (op. cit.: 81). Some of the more important of these sales were: Korean Air
Lines (October 1974), Indian Airlines (January 1975) and South African Airways (August
1975). Although accounts of precise numbers and options vary slightly among the secondary sources on the placing of orders of A300B aircraft, *Jane's All The World's Aircraft*
(op. cit.) keeps a running total and is generally considered authoritative. The 1975-76 edition says that as of May 1975, AI had orders and options for 52 aircraft (see p. 106 for a
complete listing of sales up to that point).

46. Muller (op. cit.: 87).

47. Arthur Reed, *Airbus* (op. cit.), entitles chapter 6 of his book "Through the Marketing
Desert," as it was a very trying time for all involved in AI.

48. Typifying these disappointments was the collapse of the promising prospect of a substantial sale to Western Airlines of the United States, which elected in January of 1977 to
purchase additional DC-10s and 727s. See Gunston (op. cit.: 78).

49. See ibid.: 78-80 for a thorough account of the Eastern deal.

50. Not only did the Eastern sale render the product credible, it also "gave evidence of
the commercial savoir-faire of Airbus Industrie which did not hesitate to go blow-for-blow
in the competition." Muller (op. cit.: 105). Also see Ira C. Magaziner and Mark Patinkin,
*The Silent War* (New York: Random House, 1989): 248, on the details and significance of
the Eastern deal.

51. Gunston (op. cit.: 80) notes that "AI entered 1979 with a firm order book of 123 aircraft, of which 70 were gained in 1978!"

52. The period from 1976 to 1978 had been a real test for the partners and their commitment to AI, including the French. Dassault had attempted to return to the civil market
and in June 1976 announced a cooperative arrangement with McDonnell Douglas to pro-

duce a version of the new Mercure 200, the so-called ASMR (Advanced Short/Medium Aircraft). Aérospatiale also had considered working with the Americans on the ASMR and even had discussions with Boeing on a version of the proposed B-10 variant of the A300B. For more on these Franco-American flirtations, see Muller (op. cit.: 92-104), Jean Picq, *Les Ailes de l'Europe* (Paris: Fayard, 1990): 71-87 and Hayward, *International Collaboration in Civil Aerospace*, (op. cit.: 96-102).

53. Commercial Fan Moteur (CFM) International had been formed in 1971 by the American and French companies to fill what they saw as a gap in the offerings of the major engine manufacturers, the so-called 10 tonne (22,000 lb.) motor that would be used to retrofit existing single-aisle aircraft or to power the next generation.

54. Gunston (op. cit.: 88) notes that by "9 June 1978, Swissair and Lufthansa defined their joint specification for the A310, and a month later these airlines announced their intention to place launch orders."

55. Gunston (ibid., 86) notes that this view had considerable support within AI. "Many, including Roger Beteille and Commercial Director Dan Krook, were of the opinion that the best solution was to put fewer seats on an A300B2 or B4.". . . Even the Production Director, famed engineer Felix Kracht . . . had grave misgivings about trying to design a totally new wing to support a cut-down fuselage."

56. Picq (op. cit.: 113-114) points out that the design of an aircraft is never "fixed once and for all" and that designers must try to anticipate the evolving needs of airlines by retaining in any aircraft a measure of adaptability regarding possible changes (usually increases) in range and payload.

57. It should not go unnoticed here that the governments that ultimately would have to put up the money for whatever was decided did not try to influence the outcome of this debate. Muller (op. cit.: 111) observes that "the A310 was defined according to strictly industrial and commercial criteria, which is an additional indication of the real power of decision of the industrialists relative to the politicians."

58. For a full recounting of the formation of BAe, see Keith Hayward, *The British Aircraft Industry* (Manchester, UK: Manchester University Press, 1989): 148-153. As Hayward notes, Labour had long argued for the technological and financial desirability of the nationalization and merger of BAC and HSA. Originally set to take effect on 1 January 1976, the official creation of BAe did not occur until 29 April 1977, and the deal was a rich source of uncertainty and misunderstanding in Britain, Europe and elsewhere concerning the new firm's role in the Airbus program.

59. Hayward, *International Collaboration in Civil Aerospace*, (op. cit.: 105). The competing studies were based in Bremen and included engineers from Aérospatiale as well in the Integrated Wing Design Team (IWDT). Also see Gunston (op. cit.: 88).

60. Picq (op. cit: 116-117).

61. Hayward, *British Aircraft Industry*, (op. cit.: 156).

62. Ibid.

63. The absence of a firm governmental opinion certainly was not from lack of advice. The Boeing/Airbus issue was hotly debated in the press, with the *Economist* for one coming down squarely on the side of the American option and railing against the Airbus as a political airplane. For representative articles, see the following issues: 4 June 1977: 92-93, 18 June 1977: 93-94, 22 April 1978: 87-88, 12 August 1978: 63-64, 2 September 1978.

64. High political considerations again came to the fore concerning the possible return of the British through participation in the A310 program; Muller (op. cit.: 113) refers to a

12-13 December 1977 meeting between Callaghan and Giscard and then a February 1978 meeting between Giscard and Schmidt.

65. Gunston (op. cit.: 89-90) observes that the competition between the two wing design groups was settled amicably, with German and French engineers coming to Hatfield (HSA's main design center) and hammering out a compromise configuration. He quotes Roger Beteille as saying: "The discussions between the different wing schools have been very fruitful, and the final wing will be significantly better than the best originally achieved. . . ."

66. Christopher Layton,"The High-Tech Triangle," in *Partners and Rivals in Western Europe: Britain, France and Germany*, eds. Roger Morgan and Caroline Bray, pp. 184-204 (Brookfield, VT: Gower, 1986).

67. Hanns H. Schumacher, "Europe's Airbus Programme and the Impact of British Participation," *The World Today*, Vol. 35, No. 8 (August 1979): 332-339, observes that the alternative would have been equally costly: "the failure of efforts to secure British participation would have had a damaging effect on AI's reputation and re-awakened the memory of previous failures in European cooperation."

68. See Gunston (op. cit.: 164); Hayward, *British Aircraft Industry*, (op. cit.: 155).

69. Hayward, *British Aircraft Industry*, (op. cit.: 154).

## Chapter 7

1. Bill Gunston, *Airbus* (London: Osprey, 1988): 132, recalls: "AI sold four aircraft in 1974, nine in 1975, one in 1976 and only 41 from early 1972 until early 1978." See chapter 6 herein for a discussion of the lease and sale of Airbus aircraft to Eastern Airlines.

2. See ibid.: 85-114 on the evolution, configuration and precise specifications of the A310.

3. As described in chapter 6, there had been discussion of the new wing being built in Germany, but all involved were relieved that the experienced British team would have the responsibility for it. See Gunston (op. cit.: 99-104) for a thorough description of the A310 wing and its characteristics, including diagrams and pictures.

4. Lew Bogdan, *L'Épopée du Ciel Clair* (Paris: Hachette, 1988): 345, recalls that, beginning in September 1977, Lufthansa and Swissair had held mutual discussions with AI concerning their design preferences for the A310. Gunston (op. cit: 88-90) notes that Swissair had placed an order on 15 March 1979 for ten A310s. With his typical enthusiasm for Airbus Industrie and its products, he notes: "On 1 April 1979 Lufthansa signed for not 10 of the new jetliners but for 25, with another 25 on option!" and also that KLM followed two days later with a 10/10 order, its first for any non-American jet.

5. See Gunston (op. cit.: 92) on the formation of Belairbus.

6. Bogdan (op. cit.: 359) notes that Bernard de Lathière and Sir Kenneth Keith signed for their respective companies on 11 June 1979 at the Le Bourget air show.

7. Gunston (op. cit.: 97) quotes P&W President Richard Carlson as lamenting: "The French government wasn't on our side."

8. Gunston (ibid.: 94) notes: "At this difficult period AI stood out as leader of the bad guys who were actively promoting the FFCC."

9. Bogdan (op. cit.: 377-381) describes "La Guerre du Cockpit" and the influence that Garuda's adoption of the FFCC had upon other airlines, including Varig, Tunis Air, Finnair and Saudia, in their eventual decisions to use the new technology.

10. While the tailplane is formally the Spanish partner CASA's responsibility, MBB

undertook the design studies for the in-tail tank. These in turn were based on the British and French experience with the Concorde, which had a similar feature. MBB also made extensive use of carbon fiber construction material and techniques in producing the vertical tailplane; Gunston's (op.cit.) photo caption on p. 100 claims that "is the largest carbon primary structure in production in the world."

11. Keith Hayward, *International Collaboration in Civil Aerospace* (New York: St. Martin's Press, 1986): 59.

12. Bogdan (op. cit.: 349).

13. Bogdan (ibid.) notes that the announcement was accompanied by a $1.8 billion order by United Airlines for 30 767s, launching the new aircraft.

14. Jean Picq, *Les Ailes de l'Europe* (Paris, Fayard, 1990): 125, notes that air traffic grew 15 percent in 1978 and 14 percent in 1979, and that in 1978 orders for aircraft exceeded 600 units for the first time ever. For additional data on annual rates of growth in air traffic, also see Picq, Appendix 22, p. 303.

15. See ibid.: 124-125. As an example of the consortium's success during this period, Picq notes that in September 1979 Airbus Industrie broke into the Japanese market for the first time with an order from TOA for 9 A300s.

16. Ibid.: 129.

17. Bogdan (op. cit.: 351).

18. Picq (op. cit.: 135) recalls that "the most celebrated of these fare wars was between the two Texas companies, Braniff and American Airlines," with the latter promising not to be undersold on any route that it considered vital.

19. In September 1980 the Airbus consortium had announced the launch of another wide-bodied, medium-range aircraft, the A300-600. This modified version of AI's original product was based on the same wing and fuselage as the A300 but had greater range and capacity because of new and more powerful engines, and, as in the A310, incorporated advances in flight control technology and the use of composite materials.

20. Picq (op. cit.: 120-123) observes that Boeing had anticipated the need for this sort of flexibility and had designed the 767, particularly its wing, to be capable of carrying larger loads over longer distances than had been initially promised to airlines. Airbus, on the other hand, had designed its wing for maximum efficiency at lower weights and shorter ranges, and to match Boeing had to rely on its British engineers' "prowess in obtaining the best performance from the wing" (p. 122). Utilizing the fuel tank-in-tail, the longest-range A310-300s carry around 200 passengers and can fly as far as 5000 nautical miles, almost exactly matching the 767 in payload and range.

21. John Newhouse, *The Sporty Game* (New York: Alfred A. Knopf, 1982). Newhouse places the sales contest between Boeing and Airbus in a larger context that stresses the highly competitive nature of both the manufacturing and operating sides of the airliner business. Through numerous interviews with aerospace industry executives, he shows that risks inherent in the business compel firms to "bet the company" in seeking returns in a highly uncertain commercial environment.

22. In late November of 1979, Lathière and AI appeared to have scored a major coup in Boeing's home market with an order from TWA for ten A310s with another 45 on option. But the decision was swung in Boeing's favor by the very favorable financing terms offered by the American manufacturer in its determination not to allow a situation similar to that of the Eastern Airlines sale in April 1978. See Newhouse (op. cit: 34) and Bogdan (op. cit.: 368) for detailed accounts of the TWA deal.

23. Bogdan (op. cit.: 380) recalls that in March 1980 the president of France, Valery Giscard-d'Estaing, was in Kuwait signing a statement favoring self-determination for the Palestinians of the West Bank at the same time that Jimmy Carter's government was confronting a crisis before the UN on this same issue. Newhouse (op. cit.: 39) observes that after the incident, "Boeing, although completely unaware of it, could no longer compete in the Middle East on equal terms with a French-led European consortium."

24. Gunston (op. cit.: 52-55, 140, 147) notes that the first flight of the A300-600 was on 8 July 1983. The new model was certified on 29 February 1984 and entered revenue service with Saudia in April 1984. See p. 54 for a diagram showing work shares on the new aircraft, which are almost identical to the A300B.

25. Newhouse (op. cit.: 41-42). Newhouse says that because of the "commonality factor", the MEA board assigned a $2.6 million "penalty" to the 767 in making the comparison with the A310, with the predictable outcome in favor of the former.

26. All sources on the industry confirm this characterization of the competition for commercial airline sales, with Newhouse (op. cit.) providing perhaps the most insightful study.

27. Hayward, *International Collaboration in Civil Aerospace*, (op. cit.: 58).

28. Gunston (op. cit.: 31-32) notes that, of the proposed designs, the B1 served as the A300 prototype and was subsequently lengthened and became the B2 and B4 production models. The B3 was to have an even greater take-off weight, but was never built. The B5 and B6 were freighters that were never realized purely as such, and the B7 and B8 were slightly stretched A300 models that were supplanted by the even larger B9 and B11, which would become the A330 and A340 respectively. The B10, a shortened A300, became the A310 described above.

29. Picq (op. cit.: 145) notes that Prime Minister Jacques Chirac announced at the 1975 Le Bourget air show France's intention to launch a commercial airliner of approximately 150-seat capacity, the first of no less than five times over the next nine years a major French political figure would do so in the same venue.

30. It is worth noting that Fokker and McDonnell Douglas created quite a stir as they announced plans in 1981 to develop and market together a new jet of 150-seat capacity to be called the MDF-100. Despite a seeming convergence of complementary interests and talents, the Dutch-American project went nowhere and was cancelled in February 1982.

31. Pierre Muller, *Airbus: L'ambition Européenne* (Paris: L'Harmattan, 1989): 125.

32. Newhouse (op. cit.: 217).

33. Ian McIntyre, *Dogfight: The Transatlantic Battle over Airbus* (Westport, Conn.: Praeger, 1992): xxiv, notes that the new "MD" designation was first used in 1983, and that the series now consists of the MD-81, MD-82, MD-83, MD-87 and MD-88.

34. Picq (op. cit.: 153) observes that in introducing its series of derivative aircraft, McDonnell Douglas had "anticipated the crisis and the needs of the market, and at the relatively light cost of modernizing its old DC-9. The results were measure of both its audacity and its lucidity."

35. Hayward, *International Collaboration in Civil Aerospace*, (op. cit.: 58).

36. Newhouse (op. cit.: 214) notes that Delta said it would buy 100, United declared for 150, and Eastern 100 as well of a new generation 150-seat airliner.

37. Picq (op. cit.: 147) recalls that the German, British and Spanish transport ministers were apprehensive upon their first meeting on 17 July 1981 with their new French Communist counterpart, Charles Fiterman. He soon assuaged their fears, saying: "It is by

the will of universal suffrage to undertake a policy of change, but that change should pursue what is good for the country, for example the Airbus venture."

38. As noted in chapter 5, Commercial Fan Moteur (CFM) International had been formed in 1971 as a joint venture owned 50% each by GE of the United States and SNECMA of France to build a "ten-ton"(22,000lb.) thrust engine to power the anticipated new generation of single-aisle aircraft. The CFM56-3 was adopted by Boeing for its 737-300.

39. Hayward, *International Collaboration in Civil Aerospace*, (op. cit.: 59).

40. Gunston (op. cit.: 171) notes that this "was the first time since 1947 that Rolls-Royce and Pratt and Whitney had collaborated on an engine, and the result could hardly fail to be important." The ownership of IAE is as follows: P&W (30 percent), Rolls-Royce (30 percent), JAEC (23 percent), MTU (11 percent), Fiat (6 percent).

41. Picq (op. cit.: 155).

42. Muller (op. cit.: 130). "In reality things were a bit more complicated, but it is true that the ministerial intervention probably helped in breaking the vicious circle. . . ." Picq (op. cit.: 157) relates that Roger Beteille and Bernard de Lathière reminded the assembled group that despite its interest in proceeding quickly with the A320, the consortium was not in the business of building gliders.

43. Hayward, *International Collaboration in Civil Aerospace*, (op. cit.: 60).

44. Ibid.: 62.

45. Hayward (ibid.: 62) notes that it was Morgan Grenfell, the merchant banking concern that patched together the various elements of the British financing package for the A320.

46. Ibid.: 63.

47. Ibid. Muller (op. cit.: 127) agrees: "In reality, nothing better illustrates the emergence of Airbus Industrie as an actor-leader than that subtle balancing game between diverse partners having interests which were not perfectly coincidental."

48. Hayward, *International Collaboration in Civil Aerospace*, (op. cit.: 63). He goes on to note that "the programme had generated a powerful industrial momentum which made it hard, even if clearly not impossible, to resist demands for further investment."

49. "White-tails" are aircraft lacking the livery of any airline painted on their tails, indicating that the planes were built without solid prospects for sales. Picq (op. cit.: 138-140) notes that the "queues blanches" created something of a scandal in France, with the newspaper *Le Monde* playing a central role in criticizing the consortium for failing to adjust production schedules quickly enough, thus incurring unnecessary inventory carrying costs at Aérospatiale.

50. Picq (ibid.: chapter 9, 162-176) recounts in detail the circumstances surrounding the Pan Am deal. He notes that Pan Am was convinced to take Airbuses in part because the A300/310 line offered freight commonality with its fleet of 747s, which, ironically, the Boeing 767 did not. With its narrower fuselage, the 767 cannot accommodate two LD-3 containers, a capability explicitly included in the design of the A300B and its successors. See chapter 5 herein for discussion of this and numerous other commercial considerations that influenced the A300's design.

51. Picq (op. cit.: 169-170) recalls that Acker met with Otto von Lambsdorf, the German economics minister, and also with French premier Pierre Mauroy. But Picq devotes more detail to Acker's conversation with F. J. Strauss, who assured him that "'the major axis in Europe for the next 50 years is the Franco-German axis. And Airbus is an integral part of the Franco-German axis.'"

52. Gunston (op. cit.: 135).

53. Ibid.: 152.

54. Ibid.: 182.

55. For years there had been discussion in the aeronautics industry of the possibility of designing an engine that would combine the simplicity of a propeller with the power and supersonic capability of a gas turbine. The answer seemed to reside in the unducted fan (UDF), in which counterrotating propellers would push the aircraft at great speeds without the complexity and expense of existing high-bypass ratio superfan engines. Despite extensive research by GE and others, the commercial prospects of the UDF seem dimmer today than before.

56. Picq (op. cit.: 161) recounts this dramatic episode in which Princess Diana of the United Kingdom officially and elegantly launched the A320 with the traditional magnum of champagne. Also see the full-page color photo of the A320 roll-out ceremony in Gunston (op. cit: 153).

57. Gunston (op. cit.: 182). Muller (op. cit.: 132) notes that by the end of 1987, orders for the A320 stood near 500, 309 of these firm.

58. The A320 continues to sell well, although the precise figures are subject to change, especially in today's uncertain commercial environment. As an example of the current industry upheaval, Guiness Peat Aviation (GPA), until its recent troubles the world's largest aircraft leasing firm, announced on 23 September 1993 that it would probably be forced to cancel orders placed with Airbus Industrie with a estimated value of $2.5 billion. Most of these planes are the A320, A321 or A330 models. See *Financial Times*, Friday, 24 September 1993: 21.

59. The A320-100 has a shorter range than the A320-200, and the precise distances each can fly depend primarily on takeoff weight and the engines used (either the CFM56-5 of the IAE V2500). See Gunston (op. cit.: 173) for a diagram illustrating these differences.

60. Ibid.: 175.

61. See Ira C. Magaziner and Daniel Patinkin, *The Silent War* (New York: Random House, 1989): 254, on the technical and commercial significance of the cockpit and instrumentation of the A320.

62. Gunston (op. cit.: 174). Also see pp. 174-179 for more detail on the A320's avionics and flight control systems. It is worth noting that the A320 cockpit is of interest not only to pilots and engineers. On my tour of the Airbus assembly lines in Toulouse in May 1993, I had the good fortune to be accompanied by a student of psychology from a university in Denmark conducting doctoral research on the "man-machine interface," who found the entire A320 flight deck, including everything from the instrumentation to the ergonomics, to be fascinating.

63. Gunston (op. cit.: 177).

64. Picq (op. cit.: 160).

65. Muller (op. cit.: 175).

*Chapter 8*

1. The first flight of the A320 was on 22 February 1987 and, by "mid 1987, 15 airlines and three leasing companies had signed for 287 A320s, plus 160 on option a total of 447." Bill Gunston, *Airbus* (London: Osprey, 1988): 182.

2. Jean Picq, *Les Ailes de l'Europe* (Paris: Fayard, 1990): 251, observes that the Airbus "system was in some ways a victim of its own success."

3. Ian McIntyre, *Dogfight: The Transatlantic Battle over Airbus* (Westport, Conn.: Praeger, 1992): 209.

4. The members of the committee were known as the "four wise men" or simply "les sages." See both Picq (op. cit: 248-268) and McIntyre (op. cit.: 209-233) for a discussion of the "wise men" and their report.

5. McIntyre (op. cit.: 209). "If there was anyone in the industry Bechinou did not know, it could be taken that it was an acquaintance not worth cultivating."

6. Ibid.: 210.

7. Picq (op. cit: 251). Here Picq quotes from the report.

8. McIntyre (op. cit.: 212).

9. Ibid.: 229.

10. McIntyre (ibid.) notes: "Hans Friderichs had something of a chequered career." A member of the FDP, he had from 1972 to 1977 been federal minister of economics and the party's leader from 1974 to 1977. He gave up politics in 1977 for the chairmanship of the Management Board of Dresdner Bank and later oversaw the restructuring of AEG Telefunken. Legal problems arose in 1985 concerning the funding of the FDP, and although cleared of bribery charges, Friderichs was fined for tax evasion in 1987. On Friderichs appointment, see also *AWST,* 21 November 1988.

11. As described above, Hans Friderichs had been named chairman of the Supervisory Board of Airbus Industrie in November 1988. Friderichs was now to be joined on the reconstituted board by: Henri Martre (as vice-chairman), chairman and CEO of Aérospatiale; Hans-Arnt Vogels, president and CEO of MBB; Sir Raymond Lygo, CEO of BAe; and Javier Alvarez Vara, president of CASA. (See *AWST,* 27 March 1989: 91).

12. In his position as managing director of AI and chair of the Executive Committee, Jean Pierson was joined by Heribert Flosdorff (former engineering director of MBB and already AI's vice-president) as chief operating officer; Jacques Plenier, managing director of Aérospatiale's aircraft division; Hartmut Medhorn, managing director of MBB's transport aircraft group; Sydney Gillibrand, chairman of British Aerospace Commercial Aircraft Ltd.; and Alberto Fernandez, managing director of CASA's aircraft division. They were joined by Robert Smith (formerly of BAe's Royal Ordinance subsidiary) in the newly created position of financial director. See *AWST,* 27 March 1989: 91.

13. McIntyre (op. cit: 219) quotes Martre as saying "the conclusion must be that Airbus would disappear at the end of four or five years. It does not make any sense to think of separating the commercial side from the military side of an aerospace company."

14. The *Economist,* 16 February 1991: 52, would later characterize the situation this way: "This peculiar system encourages each member to charge as much as possible to the consortium, shifting losses onto Airbus itself and so on to other members. At least that is the way the system seems to work. Airbus's accounts are such a mystery, nobody knows for sure."

15. McIntyre (op. cit: 218).

16. Ibid.: 219. Martre goes on to add: "Transparency in the matter of costs simply does not exist. We would also have to have common accounting conventions. That would take an enormous amount of work. Would it apply to subcontractors? To the suppliers of engines? I don't see the object of the exercise."

17. *Business Week,* 18 December 1989: 47. The article cites Jacques Plenier, head of Aérospatiale's aircraft division and member of the Airbus Executive Board, as saying "I know my Airbus costs very, very well, but I'm not going to disclose them."

18. Picq (op. cit.: 252). He goes on to observe that "transparency of costs and resale prices supposes in effect that each of the partners wholly agrees to play the game. Such is not the case today."

19. Formal launch approval for the 186-seat A321 was given by the Airbus Industrie Supervisory Board at its monthly meeting on 24 November 1989. See *AWST,* 4 December 1989: 31.

20. The working group was established on 27 October 1989. See *AWST,* 6 November 1989: 57.

21. Pierson said: "British Aerospace has to settle this issue and to settle it now. This strike is going into its 10th week, and enough is enough." See *AWST,* 15 January 1990: 64.

22. See *AWST,* 22 January 1990: 92; *AWST,* 5 February 1990: 82. First flight of the A321 took place on 11 March 1993, and following flight testing the new aircraft won European JAA certification on 17 December 1993. As of 31 December 1993, 153 A321s had been ordered by 11 customers. (See *Insider's Report,* January 1994.)

23. It was estimated that MBB would spend $40 to $47 million and Aérospatiale around $72 million on new facilities. But Jacques Plenier, head of Aérospatiale's aircraft division and member of the AI Executive Board, said: "Collocating final assembly with passenger cabin outfitting will lead to a reduction in the planned A330/340 production cycle." See *AWST,* 12 March 1990: 27.

24. On the TWA order, see *AWST,* 3 April 1989: 64-65.

25. At this point in mid-1989, orders, options and MoUs for the A330/A340 line stood at 266: 144 A330s and 122 A340s. See *AWST,* 10 April 1989: 91.

26. *AWST,* 8 May 1989: "Orders for the A300 and A310 have surpassed the 540 mark from 65 customers."

27. *AWST,* 6 November 1989: 18.

28. *AWST,* 19 June 1989: 159. The Northwest delivery also marked the consortiums's five hundredth. "Total firm orders for all Airbus aircraft types reached 1,153 from 77 customers during the show."

29. *AWST,* 15 January 1990: 64-65.

30. "By the end of February 1990 the strike was estimated to have cost the consortium $200 million." *Aerospace America,* April 1990: 14. Also see *AWST,* 15 January 1990, on the strike and the tensions it caused within the consortium.

31. See AWST, 16 July 1990: 52-54, for a survey of the subcontractor network established by AI, including an interview with Heribert Flosdorff, AI's chief operating officer.

32. The incident was as controversial as it was tragic, because for a considerable time the Indian authorities refused AI officials access to the crash site or to the flight recording devices. See *AWST,* 26 February 1990: 30.

33. *AWST,* 18 December 1989: 63-65. The article also notes: "The consortium recently completed the best nine months in its history, taking orders for 293 aircraft from 38 customers."

34. Assessing the damage, the International Air Transportation Authority (IATA) estimated that the organization's member airlines lost $2.7 billion in 1990 and another $4.7 billion in 1991. See *Financial Times,* 7 July 1992: 20. The large financial losses caused a wave of bankruptcies and corporate reorganizations among some of the world's best-known airlines, including Continental, TWA and Northwest. Also, a number of controversial strategic alliances have been rumored or actually concluded, including British Airway's taking a minority stake in financially troubled USAir.

35. These figures are taken from *Le Monde* (version hebdomidaire #2254), 9-15 January 1990: 11.

36. *AWST,* 4 November 1991: 36-48, contains a review of the A330/A340 program, including specifications and a detailed account of the A340's first test flight from Toulouse Blagnac Airport on 25 October 1991. It notes: "The A340 is the largest transport developed by Airbus Industrie, and is the biggest commercial aircraft ever put into series production by Europe's aerospace industry." For its part, the A330 received simultaneous certification from the U.S. Federal Aviation Administration (FAA) and the European Joint Airworthiness Authority (JAA) on 21 October 1993. This followed a year-long flight test program conducted with GE CF6-80E engines (see *Insider's Report,* November 1993: 1). However, the A330 certification procedure with P&W engines was tragically interrupted on 30 June 1994 by a crash at Toulouse fatal to seven crew members. Also see note 118.

37. The A319, a 112 to 124-seat version of the A320, was not officially launched until June 1993.

38. Heribert Flosdorff, AI's chief operating officer, observed: "We spent a lot of money and effort to recover the lost production . . . With hindsight, maybe it would have been wiser to let the production build up normally after the strike rather than to have accelerated it." A320 production had slowed to 1.2 per month in January 1990 and had gradually been raised to 11.25 per month over the course of 1991. It was progressively reduced to 10 per month by April 1992 and was projected to go still lower. See *AWST,* 15 January 1990: 64-65; 6 April 1992: 29.

39. In July 1992 United Airlines, formerly a loyal Boeing customer, surprised the aviation world by announcing its intention to buy 50 Airbus A320s with options on 50 more. See *Financial Times,* 9 July 1992: 1; 10 July: 17.

40. See *New York Times,* 8 December 1992: C1. Also see *Financial Times,* 8 December 1992: 16; 9 December 1992: 15.

41. While the GPA saga was followed closely in the trade and business press, the *Financial Times* devoted especially extensive coverage to both the company and the larger issues raised by its meteoric rise to prominence and its even faster demise. Even the after company's rescue in the summer of 1993 by GE Capital (the investment unit of the U.S. conglomerate), the fate of GPA and its ability to take delivery of the 130 Airbus aircraft it has on order remains in question. Indeed, recent reports indicate Airbus may well lose up to $2.5 billion in orders for 51 aircraft from GPA. Especially vulnerable are the 40 scheduled for delivery after 1994, including A320's, A321s and A330s. As of December 1992, GPA had been AI's biggest single customer, with a backlog of 123 aircraft, so these developments have serious implications. As a result of the continued slump, AI production growth rates are projected to be cut from 150 in 1993 to 170 in 1995, compared to the 225 initially hoped for 1995. See *Financial Times,* 24 September 1993: 21.

42. McIntyre (op. cit.) provides a detailed description of both the issues and personalities involved in the political wrangling between the United States and Europe that took place concerning Airbus Industrie.

43. McIntyre (ibid.: 169) draws this quotation from United States Trade Representative (USTR) Clayton Yeutter's own characterization of these discussions in an April 1987 letter to British trade minister Paul Channon.

44. Indeed, many in the United States were frustrated with the pace and direction of the discussions: "As the impasse continued, U.S. industry officials said that the talks were becoming institutionalized." *AWST,* 5 September 1988: 65.

45. McIntyre (op. cit.: 170) cites from a April 1987 letter sent by USTR Yeutter to the respective trade ministers in France, Britain and Germany regarding the commercial prospects of the A330/A340 program. "Our preliminary economic analyses do not persuade us that there is a solid economic basis for providing government aid to launch these aircraft programs."

46. McIntyre (ibid.: 178-184) notes that these hearings were before the House Committee on Energy and Commerce under a subcommittee chaired by James J. Florio. McIntyre's account of the grilling of Alan S. Boyd, chairman of Airbus Industrie of North America, is especially revealing of the disagreeable turn the dispute was taking.

47. McIntyre (ibid.: 191) notes that the delegations to the December 1987 meeting in Brussels were headed by George Schultz, the United States secretary of state, and Willy deClerq, European commissioner for external affairs.

48. A report entitled "Airbus Industrie: An Economic and Trade Perspective" was prepared by the Congressional Research Service for the Subcommittee on Technology and Competitiveness of the Committee on Science, Space, and Technology of the United States House of Representatives. The coordinating author is John W. Fischer and it is dated 20 February 1992. It contains sections on the nature of the commercial aircraft market, subsidies policy in the EC, the Airbus dispute and the GATT, and an analysis of the impact of Airbus activities on the U.S. economy. The report is available through the U.S. Government Printing Office in Washington, DC, and hereafter is cited as CRS.

49. McIntyre (op. cit.: 248-260) offers a detailed account of the maneuvering, both between Daimler-Benz and the shareholders of MBB and between the governing CDU/CSU-FDP coalition and the Cartel Office, on the final terms of the MBB takeover. To say the least, the issue was a divisive one in Germany; the Cartel Office rejected the eventual plan but found its ruling overturned by the government, and the chairman of the Monopolies Commission resigned over the issue.

50. Daimler-Benz reorganized its internal structure to accommodate its new holdings. A new division, Deutsche Aerospace (DASA), was created to combine the aerospace activities of MBB with those of Dornier, AEG and MTU, all of which had been partially or wholly acquired in the mid-1980s. Deutsche Airbus would then constitute an operating unit of DASA, which would control 80 percent. The remaining 20 percent would be held by the Kreditinstalt fur Wideraufbau (KfW), a government bank established after World War II, although this share was to be purchased gradually by Daimler-Benz. For more detail on the corporate restructuring of Daimler-Benz and the creation of DASA, see *AWST*, 29 January 1990: 74-77; 5 November 1990: 96. See also Helga L. Hillebrand, "What Is Deutsche Aerospace?" *Armed Forces Journal International* (May 1990): 37-39.

51. Picq (op. cit.: 283, note 3 to chapter 14) says that the forex protection would "cover exchange risk in the 1.60-2.00DM/dollar range for the A300/A310/A320 programs, and the 1.60-1.80DM/dollar range for the A330/340 programs, up to 100% until 1996, 75% in 1997-1998 and 50% in 1999-2000."

52. The CRS report (op. cit. 32-33) includes a citation from the commission's (CEC) *Nineteenth Report on Competition Policy* (1990): "In view of the economic and technological importance of the aviation industry to the Community, the Commission considered that the proposed measure would strengthen the overall competitiveness of the sector and thus concretely serve the general interest."

53. While the CEC view had some basis in fact, the ownership situation of MBB remained quite complex. In addition to Daimler-Benz's 50 percent share, Lander govern-

ments (Bavaria, Bremen and Hamburg) and private companies (Siemens and Aérospatiale) still owned pieces of MBB. See *AWST,* 18 September 1989: 31; 27 November 1989: 28.

54. The CRS Report (op. cit.: 35) notes that "The aircraft code included many provisions to liberalize aircraft trade; for example it eliminated tariffs, prohibited licensing requirements, and banned discriminatory procurement. However, it did not include clear rules covering aircraft subsidies and said only that the multilateral subsidies code, which was negotiated at the same time, would apply to aircraft."

55. The CRS report (ibid.: 39) notes that both the structure and pace of the GATT negotiating mechanisms were at fault in this case. Of special concern was the overlap between the Aircraft and Subsidies Codes with respect to the issue of government support, especially regarding forex guarantees. Thus the parties engaged in so-called forum shopping: "Each party wanted the dispute considered in the Committee most likely to uphold its position."

56. Gellman Research Associates, Inc., *An Economic and Financial Review of Airbus Industrie.* Report prepared for the U.S. Department of Commerce, International Trade Administration (Jenkintown, Penn.: September 1990). Cited hereafter as GRA.

57. Ibid.: ES-1.

58. Ibid.

59. Ibid.: 1.11. Note 12 (on that same page) says: "More precisely, commercial viability means that the expected activities' present discounted value of the net cash flows, using the private sector cost of funds, exceeds zero after repayment of all government supports."

60. It should be noted that the Congressional Research Service report cited above (see note 48) relies heavily on the data and methodology of GRA.

61. GRA (op. cit.: 2.3). As shown in Figure 2.1, "West Germany accounted for over half if the committed government support while France committed 25% and the UK 16%." Appendix B of the GRA report contains detailed data for each country, including numerous charts and tables, on the amount and type of subsidies granted by the three national governments, including estimates concerning repayment.

62. Ibid. GRA uses the nominal aid committed figure of $13.5 billion to calculate an adjusted value at government opportunity costs (given an average government borrowing rate of 8.7 percent) of $19,367.6 billion, and an adjusted value of $25,851.5 billion at private borrowing cost. However, it is important to note that not all of the money committed has been disbursed by the governments. GRA Table 2.1 shows $5.430.5 billion in launch aid disbursed, $2.843.4 billion in other support disbursed, for a total aid disbursed figure of $8.274 billion, of which $462.4 million has been repaid.

63. Ibid.: 2.13.

64. GRA (ibid.: 4.4) says "nominal cash flow totals are the sum of cash inflows and outflows without consideration of the opportunity cost of the funds."

65. GRA (ibid.: 4.7) concludes, however, that because of these projected positive incremental flows, "there does not appear to be any need for additional financial support for AI programs from the governments of the AI member firms."

66. Ibid.: 4.4.

67. Ibid.: 5.7.

68. GRA (ibid.: 5.2) asserts that "Based on the material presented above, AI clearly represents the less efficient competitor in the market for civil transport aircraft. Without long-standing government subsidies, AI would not be able to compete with the more efficient producers" (5.3).

69. Ibid.: 5.4.

70. Ibid.

71. Ibid.

72. McIntyre (op. cit.: 247) notes that the Bush administration delayed publication of the GRA report so as not to disrupt the ongoing negotiations. Its conclusions were seen as so damning of Airbus and the European governments that its release might inflame sentiments in Congress for retaliatory action: "The administration therefore found itself in the bizarre position of having fashioned a weapon that was too powerful to be used."

73. Jean Pierson, *Henry Ford II Scholar Award Lecture*, delivered Tuesday, 23 April 1991, at the Cranfield School of Management. See his similar remarks at a speech given to the European Club of the Harvard Business School, 6 March 1991.

74. The Continental members of Airbus, especially the French, had long been trying to obtain an order from the British carrier, even having unsuccessfully attempted to make British entry into AI in 1979 conditional upon such a purchase. (See chapter 6.) BA does today operate Airbus aircraft, but the ten A320s were acquired in the 1988 merger with British Caledonian. AI and especially Jean Pierson were sufficiently upset at the BA/Boeing 777 situation that they considered legal action and also forbid AI staff to fly BA. See *Economist*, 9 November 1991: 80.

75. Arnold and Porter, *U.S. Government Support of the U.S. Commercial Aircraft Industry*. Report prepared for the Commission of the European Communities. (Washington, DC: November, 1991). Cited hereafter as AP.

76. In their analysis, AP use a variety of official documents and government sponsored reports, as well studies by private research institutes and company financial reports. For example, for historical data they cite extensively a report issued by DoD, NASA and the U.S. Department of Transportation (DoT) that reviews the contributions of military R&D to civil aviation since 1925. It was published in 1972 and entitled *Research and Development Contributions to Aviation Progress (RADCAP)*. AP also relied on a report issued by the Office of Science and Technology Policy, Executive Office of the President, entitled *Aeronautical Research and Technology Policy*. It was published in November 1982.

77. AP (op. cit.: 7-8) estimated that "Boeing received at least $5.8 billion of DoD R&D contracts between 1976 and 1990 and McDonnell Douglas received at least $6.6 billion. Of these amounts, $1.79 billion of the DoD funds Boeing received were for aircraft related R&D" and $4.55 billion of the DoD funds McDonnell Douglas received were for aircraft related R&D."

78. Ibid.: 12.

79. Ibid.: 20.

80. Ibid.: 34-35.

81. The four programs analyzed are:

(1) Boeing 707/KC-135: The Boeing 707 was a slightly larger and heavier version of the KC-135 tanker, thus essentially a commercial version of a military aircraft. But the transfer of technology and expertise was not only direct, as in the tooling, jigs, parts and production processes used to build the airframe, but indirect in that all the testing done on the KC-135 was applicable to the 707 as well. Also, AP asserted that Boeing benefited from information and experience gained in the B-47 and B-52 bomber programs, especially in wing-design and wind-tunnel testing. Also, the 707 engine was a P&W JT-3C, a commercial derivative of the military J-57 engine, and its Bendix autopilot was a military derivative as well.

(2) Boeing 747/C5-A: Although Boeing did not win the design competition for the C5-A, AP argued that the 747 benefited directly from C5-A R&D, including aerodynamic design studies conducted at government expense. The engines developed by GE (CF-6) and P&W (JT9D) also had direct commercial application, the latter on the 747. Flight control and avionics systems, landing gear and experience in titanium forgings were also of indirect benefit to the 747.

(3) DC-10/C5-A: The DC-10 tri-jet was powered by the GE CF-6 engine, developed for the C5-A, and AP asserted that Douglas gained information and expertise in wing and nacelle design on the C5-A, which was incorporated into the DC-10. Moreover, both McDonnell Douglas and Boeing were able to use the design teams assembled for the military bidding and procurement process to work on these civilian aircraft.

(4) National Aerospace Plane (NASP) and High Speed Civil Transport (HSCT): The point of both programs is to encourage basic research into technologies and processes that have application in military and civil aviation, and possibly other high-technology industries. Phase I of NASP began in 1986 with $7 million in funding by DoD, NASA, USAF, and USN. Contracts were awarded to U.S. aeronautical firms for design studies. The program has been in Phase II since February 1991 when $502 million was granted to validate these studies. HSCT began in 1986 (but drew on prior Supersonic Transport [SST] research, and since 1989 the program has been aimed at determining the commercial feasibility of new technologies. Research on two programs overlaps regarding propulsion systems and fuels, material and structures.

82. AP (op. cit.: 62).

83. Ibid. Exhibit 2 contains an organizational chart for NASA.

84. The four programs are: Aircraft Energy Efficient Program, Aircraft Noise Reduction Program, Supercritical Wing Program, High-Lift System Program.

85. AP (op. cit.). Exhibit 3 contains 1976 to 1990 figures from the total NASA budget and for the Aeronautics Division.

86. Ibid.: 82-85. For example, AP discuss the NASA-sponsored program to redesign the Pratt and Whitney (P&W) JT8D engine to make it quieter. AP assert that not only P&W benefited from NASA money, but so did Boeing and McDonnell Douglas, because the improved engine was offered on their 727 and DC-9 aircraft, respectively.

87. Ibid. Exhibit 4 contains a summary of the tax benefits that AP claim Boeing and McDonnell Douglas received between 1976 and 1990.

88. Ibid.: 92. AP state: "These tax deferrals, because of the time value of money, effectively saved Boeing approximately $619.55 million of interest over the same [1976-1990] period . . . and effectively saved McDonnell Douglas approximately $899.26 million over the same period."

89. Ibid. Appendix C explains the legal provisions for DISC's and FSC's. DISCs were eliminated by Congress in 1984 and replaced by FISCs, but AP argue that both have served essentially the same purpose.

90. AP (ibid.: 95-96) estimate the value of these benefits (for the 1985-1990 period) at $282 million for Boeing and $80.2 million for McDonnell Douglas.

91. Ibid. AP describe these facilities extensively, especially those of NASA, which include: the Ames Research Center in Moffett, California, the Lewis Research Center in Cleveland, Ohio and Langley Research Center in Hampton, Virginia. See in particular pp.97-103 and Appendix D.

92. Ibid.: 104.

93. Ibid.: 104-105.

94. Ibid.: 108. AP quote Frank Schrontz, Boeing's chairman, as saying in 1991 that "[A] defense-commercial mix provides long-term stability and a testing ground for new technologies lacking immediate commercial application. Financially, there have been times when the defense side carried the commercial business." (Original cite from *Wall Street Journal*, 30 July 1991: 1.)

95. AP (op. cit.: 112).

96. Ibid.: 6.

97. The official name of the accord is the *Agreement Concerning the Application of the GATT Agreement on Trade in Civil Aircraft.*

98. The agreement states (Section 5.3): "Benefits from indirect support shall be deemed to arise when there is an identifiable reduction in costs of large civil aircraft resulting from government-funded research and development in the aeronautical area...."

99. Agreement (op. cit: 4). The same article went on to say that these infusions "will not, however, be provided in such a manner as to undermine the disciplines foreseen in the Agreement."

100. Ibid.: 7.

101. Ibid.: 8. This article further specifies in footnote 1: "For the purposes of this paragraph, 'Parties' shall be deemed to include any of the individual Member States of the EC."

102. See *Financial Times*, Friday, 7 January 1994: 6. Orders in 1993 included 13 A320s, three A310s, six A300-600Rs, one A330 and 15 A340s. Deliveries included 71 A320s, 22 A310s, 22 A300s and 22 A340s. See *Insider's Report*, January 1994, pp. 2-3, for detailed accounting of 1993 deliveries and orders, and pp. 4-5 for cumulative orders, deliveries and operators as of 31 December 1993. Also see *AWST*, 10 January 1994: 33-34 and *AWST*, 30 June 1994: 30-31 for a detailed breakdown of deliveries and projected production rates.

103. Among the most important appointments to the Clinton administration regarding economic policy, especially in its foreign dimensions, were: Robert Reich as secretary of labor, Laura D'Andrea Tyson as the chairman of the Council of Economic Advisers. As discussed more thoroughly in chapter 9, the conclusion to this volume, these appointees advocate in varying degrees a partnership between American government and business in responding to challenges posed by overseas economic competition.

104. In a televised "town meeting" in Detroit on 9 February 1993, Clinton said: "Either the Europeans are going to have to quit subsidizing Airbus . . . or we're going to have to take on the competition. I'm not going to roll over and play dead." See *Financial Times*, 13 February 1993: 2.

105. *AWST*, 1 March 1993: 18. Clinton spoke to about 5,000 Boeing employees before meeting with aerospace industry executives. Regarding American aerospace job losses, Airbus spokesman David Venz said: "We have nothing to with the layoffs at Boeing. They're the result of the poor financial standing of the world's airline industry; we're losing orders too." Cited in *Wall Street Journal*, Friday, 26 February 1993: A2.

106. See *Financial Times*, Wednesday, 3 March 1993: 13, for an extensive article that used the occasion of the A321 rollout to survey European and U.S. executives on conditions in the global aerospace business; none expressed any interest in a transatlantic trade war. Also see *New York Times*, Thursday, 4 March 1993, for insightful analysis of the divisions being created within the U.S. aerospace industry concerning the aggressive new tack being taken by the Clinton administration toward Airbus.

107. Cited in *Financial Times*, Tuesday, 17 August 1993: 6.

108. See *AWST*, 30 August 1993: 30-33.

109. Pierson noted: "The opportunity for linkage of the two issues is self-evident." See *Financial Times*, Thursday, 30 September 1993: 1.

110. See *AWST*, 7 February 1994: 22. U.S. defense contractors FMC, General Dynamics, Hughes and Raytheon also were involved in the restructuring package.

111. See *Financial Times*, Tuesday, 1 February 1994: 6.

112. French prime minister Balladur, defense minister Leotard, foreign minister Juppé and industry minister Longuet all paid a visit to Saudia Arabia to discuss possible armaments purchases, but the Saudia aircraft buy was reportedly also on the agenda. See *Financial Times*, Monday, 10 January 1994: 4.

113. Clinton called the deal "A gold medal win for America's businesses and workers." Cited in *New York Times*, Thursday, 17 February 1994: A1. Also see *Financial Times*, Thursday, 17 February 1994: 1. It was observed by a U.S. aerospace industry executive that the highly political character of the announcement "is only going to drive the Airbus people berserk, and which could result in our being accused of violating GATT." See *AWST*, 21 February 1994: 33.

114. Cited in *Financial Times*, Wednesday, 2 March 1994: 6.

115. See *Insider's Report*, June 1994: 1; *AWST*, 20 June 1994: 30.

116. Airbus is setting up flight simulation and training programs in Beijing (see *AWST*, 1 November 1993: 43). AI also is creating a new operating unit, Airbus Industrie China, to oversee industrial and commercial activities in that expanding air travel market. AI announced orders for 18 aircraft during 1993 from the People's Republic of China (see *Insider's Report*, January 1994: 3).

117. See *AWST*, 27 June 1994: 29-30, for details on the SIA order. See *AWST*, 11 April 1994, for numerous articles on the 777 rollout.

118. See *AWST*, 4 July 1994: 53, on Cathay's decision to replace its fleet of aging L-1011 with A330s while buying 777s to replace its 747-200/300s.

119. See *AWST*, 16 January 1995: 32. This was five more than Boeing's 120. The article goes on to note that the consortium delivered 123 aircraft in 1994, 30 of which were A340s and 95 of which were of the A319/A320/A321 series. The consortium's backlog of 615 aircraft is valued at $51.8 billion. See also *Financial Times*, Tuesday, 10 January 1995, on AI's 1994 orders.

120. AFC will be headquartered in Dublin, Ireland, and be owned by the four AI partners in the same proportion as their stake in the Airbus consortium. AFC is to provide financing to airlines for the purchase of Airbus aircraft through a revolving line of credit set up with a syndicate of U.S. banks. See *AWST*, 9 January 1995: 36.

121. In a recent interview (*AWST*, 23 January 1995: 52-54), AI managing director Jean Pierson stated that the consortium's goal was to attain a 50 percent market share. When asked about his objectives for the near term, he said: "My absolute priority simply is to compete against Boeing as strongly as possible, thanks to our current seven-aircraft range of products." (p. 53).

122. The 30 June 1994 crash of an Airbus A330 undergoing testing in Toulouse that killed seven flight engineers "raises new questions about the highly automated, state-of-the-art glass cockpit systems, pilot interaction with such systems and the risks tied to flight crew's overconfidence in them." See *AWST*, 8 August 1994: 20-22, along with previous and subsequent issues of *AWST* and other news sources. Hans Krakauer, an official of the International Airline Passengers Association, also expressed fears: "We're very concerned that [such technology] may have gone too far." See *Business Week*, 18 July 1994: 49. The

so-called glass cockpits are likely to be a subject of controversy for years to come; *AWST* has devoted substantial space in recent weeks to problems of the "man-machine" interface. See the two-part report: *AWST*, 30 January 1995; *AWST*, 6 February 1995.

123. "Airbus' application of that process is built on the common foundation of its aircraft in computer-controlled, fly-by-wire flight control and management systems." See *AWST*, 29 August 1994: 25-26.

124. The Boeing overtures to the Airbus partners were called "a brazen move...that could present a new threat to the cohesiveness of the consortium." See *Wall Street Journal*, Tuesday, 5 January 1993: A3. The *Financial Times*, Wednesday, 6 January 1993: 8, also asked if Boeing was trying to drive a wedge between the AI partners and questioned the continued viability of the collaborative effort in its present form as a GIE.

125. *AWST*, 13 June 1994: 32. Regarding the basic 3XX design, AI vice-president for strategic planning Adam Brown says that the Airbus partners are "determined to find a way not to leave Boeing alone in such an important segment of the market." Following the fall 1994 Farnborough air show AI has decided to get the reaction of over a dozen major airlines to its new A3XX design concept, while recognizing that "how soon airlines will be willing to talk about such an airlines is problematical, however." See *AWST*, 5 September 1994: 49. Still, AI has at least four versions of the 3XX under study. See *AWST*, 21 November 1994: 54.

126. See *Financial Times*, Thursday, 9 June 1994: 7; *AWST*, 13 June 1994: 19.

127. See *Financial Times*, Tuesday, 6 September 94: 1. At the Farnborough air show, AI announced the creation of a military equipment subsidiary to manage the development and marketing of the FLA. Exact shareholdings among the prospective partners are yet to be determined, but these arrangements will not affect the existing structure of AI. Dick Evans, the CEO of BAe, was enthusiastic concerning the prospects for the RAF's replacement of its aging transport aircraft and said the FLA program represented for BAe the "only opportunity for 35 years to become a part of a large transport aircraft program."

128. See *Insider's Report*, April 1994: 2.

## Chapter 9

1. Vicki Golich, "From Competition to Collaboration: The Challenge of Commercial-class Aircraft Manufacturing," *International Organization*, Vol. 46, No. 4 (Autumn 1992): 899-934: 902.

2. M.Y. Yoshino: "Global Competition in a Salient Industry: The Case of Civil Aircraft," in *Competition in Global Industries*, ed. Michael E. Porter, pp. 517-538 (Boston: Harvard Business School Press, 1986): 518.

3. Although not a specific subject of this study, these same industry characteristics also have generated enormous pressures on firms and states to sell aircraft, especially military versions, on overseas markets so as to lower their own production and procurement costs. Pierre Muller, *Airbus: L'ambition Européenne* (Paris: L'Harmattan, 1989): 221, observes: "Paradox: the necessity of selling high tech products abroad has become a condition of technological independence." Edward A. Kolodziej, *Making and Marketing Arms* (Princeton, NJ: Princeton University Press, 1987), has examined in detail the deleterious impact this dynamic, which exists in the armaments industry more generally, has had both upon the French political economy and the international system.

4. The Gulf War amply demonstrated the importance of commercial aviation to military

operations, as the United States called upon domestic airlines to provide vital transport capability for both troops and materiel to the theater of operations.

5. Laura D'Andrea Tyson, *Who's Bashing Whom?: Trade Conflict in High-Technology Industries* (Washington, DC: Institute for International Economics, 1992): 171.

6. Yoshino (op. cit.: 520). He goes on to observe (p. 521) that Boeing's mastery of the market also created "significant entry barriers for would-be rivals."

7. "Up to the mid-1970s, the US had 96% of the market for civil aircraft in the non-Communist world; in 1980 the US still provided 86% of the world's airline fleet." Keith Hayward, *International Collaboration in Civil Aerospace* (New York: St. Martin's Press, 1986): 22.

8. "Before 1969, the Airbus venture had been influenced (or immobilized) by the desire of both France and Great Britain to utilize the venture as a keep-up strategy as a support for their aircraft, engine and components industries." David C. Mowery, *Alliance Politics and Economics* (Cambridge, Mass.: Ballinger, 1987): 131.

9. Badiul A. Majumdar, "Upstart or Flying Start? The Rise of Airbus Industrie," *The World Economy*, Vol. 10, No. 4 (December 1987): 487-518: 506.

10. Yoshino (op. cit.: 523). Majumdar (op. cit.: 504) notes as well that in the early 1970s, "there was no wide-bodied aircraft designed specifically to fly over medium-to-short hauls. Hence there was a market gap. Airbus Industrie, by introducing the A300 series, filled this void."

11. Keith Hayward, "Airbus: Twenty Years of European Collaboration," *International Affairs*, Vol. 64, No.1 (Winter 1987-88): 11-26: 19.

12. Yoshino (op. cit.: 522).

13. Majumdar (op. cit.: 508-510) analyzes the fuel economy of the A300 at the time of its introduction relative to its nearest competitors and notes that "A300s were the most fuel efficient aircraft for carrying around 250 passengers over a distance of 1,000 nautical miles."

14. Yoshino (op. cit.: 523).

15. Ibid.: 524. Majumdar (op. cit.: 502) also observes that beyond the limited early sales of the A300, "What is more significant about Airbus Industrie's success is that, although it was a new producer in the market, it was able to convince airlines quickly of its ability to provide quality after-sales service, a remarkable feat in and of itself."

16. Gernot Klepper, "Entry into the Market for Large Transport Aircraft," *European Economic Review*, Vol. 34, No.4 (1990): 775-803: 780.

17. Muller (op. cit.: 179).

18. Ibid.: 180-81.

19. Ibid.: 180.

20. Majumdar (op. cit.: 515).

21. Yoshino (op. cit.: 523).

22. Ibid.: 525.

23. Ibid.: 527.

24. Muller (op. cit.: 183).

25. See Table A.1 on yearly deliveries (1958-1984) of commercial aircraft, including the DC-9 and the Boeing single-aisle aircraft.

26. Muller (op. cit.: 175).

27. Ibid.: 185.

28. The writing on the wall had been legible for some years. As Keith Hayward observed in 1986, "European industry is better placed now than at any other time since 1945, to

effect a strategic shift in the commercial balance of power in civil aerospace." Hayward, *International Collaboration in Civil Aerospace*, (op. cit.: 26).

29. Yoshino (op. cit.: 524). Other observers share this view: Mowery, *Alliance Politics* (op. cit.: 135), says: "Much of the motivation for the Airbus Industrie venture stems from the desire of European governments to maintain, for reasons of national security and economic development, a substantial aircraft design and production capability." Similarly, Hayward, *International Collaboration in Civil Aerospace* (op. cit.: 166), notes: "From this perspective, the money invested in Airbus represents a strategic commitment to maintain a basic, and technologically important industry in Europe."

30. Muller (op. cit.: 189).

31. While I do not cite at length directly from these interviews, I have placed in quotation marks certain terms or phrases to indicate that their usage is widely employed within the organization or is perhaps is an especially important individual characterization.

32. I was told that on a practical level, this system means personal visits and frequent and rushed phone, telex and fax communications at all hours—in general, a highly pressurized environment that has little regard for the demands of one's personal life.

33. It was stressed by an engineer of one of the partners that the "contacting rules" which govern the exact working arrangements among the partners and the GIE confer both rights and responsibilities. Through them, each partner comes to "own a part of the airplane and the consequences of that."

34. This has proven especially beneficial for parts and components suppliers whose prices are in denominated in U.S. dollars. AI receives its revenues and maintains all partner accounts in dollars, exposing the partners to heavy forex risks to the extent that their input prices are in other currencies; thus the partners seek out supplies from "dollar-zone" countries.

35. Klaus Stegemann, "Policy Rivalry Among Industrial States: What Can We Learn from Models of Strategic Trade Policy?" *International Organization*, Vol. 43, No.1 (Winter 1989): 73-100: 73.

36. For an introduction to the new thinking on trade, see Paul R. Krugman, ed., *Strategic Trade Policy and the New International Economics* (Cambridge, Mass.: MIT Press, 1986). In the introduction (p. 12) Krugman defines rent as "payment to an input higher than what that input could earn in an alternative use." Conventional theory assumes that such rents will be competed away as new capital and participants are drawn into the relatively profitable activity.

37. Stegemann (op. cit.: 75).

38. Stegemann (ibid.: 77) notes that in these strategic models, "everything hinges on the assumption that increasing the domestic production of some tradable good or service means increasing a country's share in potential monopoly rents or external benefits associated with this activity."

39. Ibid.: 89. Stegemann is citing James A. Brander, "Shaping Comparative Advantage: Trade Policy, Industrial Policy and Economic Performance," in *Shaping Comparative Advantage*, eds. R.G. Lipsey and W. Dobson, Policy Study No. 2 (Toronto: C.D. Howe Institute, 1987).

40. Klepper (op.cit.: 777) discusses the magnitude of the learning effects in aircraft manufacturing and notes: "There is world-wide consensus that aircraft production exhibits a learning elasticity of 0.2, i.e. production costs decrease by 20% with a doubling of output . . . , and that these learning effects amount to 90% of the overall economies of scale. . . ."

41. Richard Baldwin and Paul Krugman, "Industrial Policy and International Competition in Wide-Bodied Aircraft," in *Trade Policy Issues and Empirical Analysis*, ed. Robert E. Baldwin, pp. 45-71 (Chicago: University of Chicago Press, 1988). See also Klepper (op. cit.) on this topic. For a critique of both the Baldwin and Krugman and Klepper pieces, see Richard Pomfret, "The New Trade Theories, Rent-Snatching and Jet Aircraft," *The World Economy*, Vol. 14, No. 3 (September 1991): 269-277. See as well Majumdar (op. cit.) and Yoshino (op. cit) for less formal discussions.

42. Baldwin and Krugman (op. cit.) find that both Europe and North America experience a drop in overall net welfare, while the rest of the world benefits from having more choices and lower prices for civil air transport. While Klepper (op. cit.) finds that Airbus entry is preferable to a Boeing monopoly for every region but North America, he notes that only North America benefits from Airbus entry as compared to a duopoly with two mature producers. Pomfret (op. cit.) argues that such models are not needed for explaining developments in the industry, that (p. 274) "these models' conclusions follow from their assumptions."

43. Majumdar (op. cit.: 516).

44. William Lazonick, *Business Organization and the Myth of the Market Economy* (Cambridge: Cambridge University Press, 1991): 69. Lazonick argues that the static methodology and individualistic ideology of conventional economics ignores the creative potential of firms. This body of theory posits price-taking firms operating under a given set of constraints, and their collective behavior yields a market-determined equilibrium. Lazonick argues that this orthodoxy lacks a theory of change or economic development and proposes instead: "whereas the textbooks asks how strategic decision makers in the firm optimize subject to given cost structures, I ask how business organization can attain and sustain competitive advantage by contributing to the generation of new cost structures" (p. 9).

45. Lazonick (ibid.: 169) argues: "The history of twentieth-century capitalist development shows, however, that as a dynamic process firms create markets, not vice-versa."

46. Ibid. Lazonick's analysis of value creation in capitalist economies is set in a larger theoretical framework that seeks to explain why leadership in the global capitalist system has shifted over time from Great Britain to the United States and now to Japan. His answer lies in the differential technological and organizational capabilities of firms. He argues that the more successful firms, and thus the more dynamic national economies, have used planned coordination rather than market coordination to inform and implement strategic decisions and thus shape their economic future.

47. Lazonick (ibid.) uses Alfred Marshall's distinction between external and internal scale economies to stress that the value creation capability of firms stems mainly from their ability to gain access to resources and then plan and coordinate their use in an innovative fashion, rather than merely lowering production costs for a given set of inputs.

48. Majumdar (op. cit.: 515).

49. Lazonick (op. cit.: 88).

50. Muller (op. cit.: 186).

51. Such an example is found in Ann McKinstry Denman, "Airbus and Its Ilk: Thumbing Their Noses at the GATT?" *Harvard International Law Journal*, Vol. 29, No. 1 (Winter 1988): 111-125: 116. Initially Denman correctly observes that Airbus Industrie "was founded in the early 1970s with the objectives of establishing a permanent European presence in the commercial airplane market and building a technologically advanced aero-

nautics industry." She then goes on to assert that AI is a form of state trading company and decries "the potential for abuse of the free market system. . ." that such companies create. While this study also argues that AI is indeed an instrument of European governments, it has demonstrated that the environment in which AI operates is quite far removed from any theoretical notion or empirical example of an openly competitive market. Clearly, portraying Airbus Industrie as a threat to the "free market" has less to do with the facts of the situation than with setting up an ideologically informed false dichotomy between political authority and market forces in an effort to condemn the European strategy.

52. Hayward, *International Collaboration in Civil Aerospace*, (op. cit.: 168-169). Hayward (p. 157) goes on to observe that "the differences which have appeared between Europeans and Americans about the place of the state in civil aerospace reflect deep-seated political perceptions and prejudices, where high principle inevitably intermingles with commercial and industrial self-interest."

53. Lazonick (op. cit.: 91).

# BIBLIOGRAPHY

Alford, B.W.E. *British Economic Performance 1945-1975*. London: Macmillan Education, 1988.

Adams, William J. *Restructuring the French Economy*. Washington, DC: The Brookings Institution, 1989.

Allen, Christopher S. "Germany: Competing Communitarianisms," in *Ideology and National Competitiveness*, eds. George C. Lodge and Ezra F. Vogel, pp. 79-102. Boston: Harvard Business School Press, 1987: 87.

Arnold and Porter. *U.S. Government Support of the U.S. Commercial Aircraft Industry*. Report prepared for the Commission of the European Communities, November 1991.

*Aviation Week and Space Technology [AWST]*. Various issues.

Baldwin, Richard, and Paul Krugman. "Industrial Policy and International Competition in Wide-Bodied Aircraft," in *Trade Policy Issues and Empirical Analysis*, ed. Robert E. Baldwin, pp. 45-71. Chicago: University of Chicago Press, 1988.

Berghahn, Volker R. *The Americanisation of West German Industry 1945-1973*. Leamington Spa, UK: Berg Publishers, 1986.

Blank, Stephen. "Britain: The Politics of Foreign Economic Policy," in *Between Power and Plenty: Foreign Economic Policies of Advanced Industrial States*, ed. Peter J. Katzenstein, pp. 89-137. Madison: University of Wisconsin Press, 1978.

Bluestone, Barry, Peter Jordan and Mark Sullivan. *Aircraft Industry Dynamics*. Boston: Auburn House, 1981.

Bogdan, Lew. *L'Épopée du Ciel Clair*. Paris: Hachette, 1988.

Bright, Charles D. *The Jet Makers*. Lawrence: Regents of Kansas Press, 1978.

*Business Week*. Various issues.

Cable, J.R. et al. "Federal Republic of Germany 1962-1974," in *The Determinants and Effects of Mergers*, ed. Dennis C. Mueller, pp. 99-132. Cambridge, Mass.: Oelgeschalger, Gunn and Hain, 1980: 116.

Cairncross, Alec. *The British Economy Since 1945*. Oxford: Blackwell, 1992.

Calleo, David, and Benjamin Rowland. *America and the World Political Economy*. Bloomington: Indiana University Press, 1973.

Chadeau, Emmanuel. *De Bleriot à Dassault*. Paris: Fayard, 1987.

Chapman, Herrick. *State Capitalism and Working Class Radicalism in the French Aircraft Industry*. Berkeley: University of California Press, 1990.

Cohen, Benjamin J. "The Revolution in Atlantic Economic Relations: A Bargain Comes Unstuck," in *The United States and Western Europe*, ed. Wolfram Hanrieder, pp. 106-133. Cambridge, Mass.: Winthrop Publishers, 1974.

Cohen, Stephen S. *Modern Capitalist Planning: The French Model*. Berkeley: University of California Press, 1977.

Congressional Research Service. *Airbus Industrie: An Economic and Trade Perspective*. Report prepared for Committee on Science, Space and Technology of the United Staes House of Representatives, 20 February 1992. Coordinating editor, John W. Fischer. Washington, DC: U.S. Government Printing Office, 1992.

Constant, Edward W. II. *The Origins of the Turbojet Revolution*. Baltimore: Johns Hopkins University Press, 1980.

Denman, Ann McKinstry. "Airbus and Its Ilk: Thumbing Their Noses at the GATT?" *Harvard International Law Journal*, Vol. 29, No. 1 (Winter 1988): 111-125.

DePorte, Anton W. *Europe Between the Superpowers*. New Haven: Yale University Press, 1979.

Donges, Juergen B. "Industrial Policies in West Germany's Not so Market-oriented Economy," *The World Economy*, Vol. 3, No. 2 (1980): 185-204: 191.

*Economist, The*. Various issues.

Feldman, Elliot J. *Concorde and Dissent*. Cambridge: Cambridge University Press, 1985.

*Financial Times* (London). Various issues.

*Flight International*. Various issues.

Gellman Research Associates. *An Economic and Financial Review of Airbus Industrie*. Report prepared for the U.S. Department of Commerce International Trade Administration, Jenkintown, Penn.: 1990.

Gianni, P. "L'Airbus Européen," *Revue general de l'air et de l'espace*, Vol. 34, No. 4 (1971):401-443.

Gilpin, Robert. *The Political Economy of International Relations*. Princeton, NJ: Princeton University Press, 1987.

Golich, Vicki. "From Competition to Collaboration: The Challenge of Commercial-class Aircraft Manufacturing." *International Organization*, Vol. 46, No. 4 (Autumn 1992): 899-934.

Gunston, Bill. *Airbus*. London: Osprey, 1988.

Hagrup, Knut. *The Aerospace Industry of Western Europe*. Stockholm: Tekniska Hogskolan I Stockholm, Institutionen for Trafikplanering, 1980.

Hall, Peter A. *Governing the Economy*. New York: Oxford University Press, 1986.

Hart, Jeffrey. "West German Industrial Policy," in *The Politics of Industrial Policy*, eds. Claude E. Barfield and William A. Schambra, pp. 161-186. Washington, DC: American Enterprise Institute, 1986.

Hayward, Keith. *The British Aircraft Industry*. Manchester, UK: Manchester University Press, 1989.

———. *Government and British Civil Aerospace*. Manchester, UK: Manchester University Press, 1983.

———. *International Collaboration in Civil Aerospace*. New York: St. Martin's Press, 1986.

———. "Airbus: Twenty Years of European Collaboration," *International Affairs*, Vol. 64, No. 1 (Winter 1987-88): 11-26.

———. "Politics and European Aerospace Collaboration: The A300 Airbus," *Journal of Common Market Studies*, Vol. 14, No.4 (June 1976): 354-367.

Hochmuth, M.S. "Aerospace," in *Big Business and the State*, ed. Raymond Vernon, pp.145-169. Cambridge, Mass.: Harvard University Press, 1974.

———, ed. *Revitalizing American Industry*. Cambridge, Mass.: Ballinger, 1985.

———. "The European Aerospace Industry," in *European Approaches to International Management*, eds. Klaus Macharzina and Wolfgang H. Staehle, pp. 205-225. Berlin: de Gruyter, 1986.

Homze, Edward L. *Arming the Luftwaffe*. Lincoln: University of Nebraska Press, 1976.

Hooks, Gregory. *Forging the Military-Industrial Complex*. Urbana: University of Illinois Press, 1991.

Jones, Aubrey. *Britain's Economy: The Roots of Stagnation*. Cambridge: Cambridge University Press, 1985.

Katzenstein, Peter J. *Industry and Politics in West Germany*. Ithaca, NY: Cornell University Press, 1989.

Kennedy, Paul. *The Rise and Fall of the Great Powers*. New York: Random House, 1987.

Klepper, Gernot. "Entry into the Market for Large Transport Aircraft," *European Economic Review*, Vol. 34, No 4 (1990): 775-803.

Kolodziej, Edward A. *Making and Marketing Arms*. Princeton, NJ: Princeton University Press, 1987.

Krugman, Paul R. *Strategic Trade Policy and the New International Economics*. Cambridge, Mass.: MIT Press, 1986.

Kuisel, Richard F. *Capitalism and the State in Modern France*. Cambridge: Cambridge University Press, 1981.

Layton, Christopher. "The High-Tech Triangle," in *Partners and Rivals in Western Europe: Britain, France and Germany*, eds. Roger Morgan and Caroline Bray, pp. 184-204. Brookfield, VT: Gower, 1986.

Lazonick, William. *Business Organization and the Myth of the Market Economy*. Cambridge: Cambridge University Press, 1991.

Lorell, Mark. *Multinational Development of Large Aircraft*. Santa Monica: RAND, 1980.

Maclennan, Malcolm et al. *Economic Planning and Policies in Britain, France and Germany*. New York: Praeger, 1968.

Magaziner, Ira C., and Mark Patinkin. *The Silent War*. New York: Random House, 1989.

Majumdar, Badiul A. "Upstart or Flying Start? The Rise of Airbus Industrie," *The World Economy*, Vol. 10, No. 4 (December 1987): 497-518.

Markusen, Ann et al. *The Rise of the Gun Belt*. London: Oxford University Press, 1991.

McIntyre, Ian. *Dogfight: The Transatlantic Battle over Airbus*. Westport, Conn.: Praeger, 1992.

Miller, Ronald, and David Sawers. *The Technical Development of Modern Aviation*. New York: Praeger, 1970.

Morgan, Roger, and Caroline Bray, eds. *Partners and Rivals in Western Europe: Britain, France and Germany*. Brookfield, VT: Gower, 1986.

Morris, D. J., and D. K. Stout. "Industrial Policy," in *The Economic System in the UK*, 3rd ed., ed. Derek Morris, pp. 851-894. Oxford: Oxford University Press, 1985.

Mowery, David C. *Alliance Politics and Economics*. Cambridge, Mass.: Ballinger, 1987.

Mowery, David C., and Nathan Rosenberg. "The Commercial Aircraft Industry," in

*Government and Technical Progress*, ed. Richard R. Nelson, pp. 101-161. New York: Pergamon Press, 1982.

Mueller, Peter. *Airbus*, trans. Richard Van Osten. Vienna: Europa Verlag, 1984.

Muller, Pierre. *Airbus: L'ambition Européenne*. Paris: L'Harmattan, 1989.

Newhouse, John. *The Sporty Game*. New York: Alfred A. Knopf, 1982.

Picq, Jean. *Les Ailes de l'Europe*. Paris: Fayard, 1990.

Reed, Arthur. *Airbus: Europe's High Flyer*. St. Gallen, Switzerland: Norden Publishing House, 1991.

———. *Britain's Aircraft Industry*. London: J.M. Dent & Sons, 1973.

*Report of the Committee into the Aircraft Industry*, Command Paper 2853. London: HMSO, 1965.

Sampson, Anthony. *The Arms Bazaar*. New York: Viking Press, 1977.

Schumacher, Hanns H. "Europe's Airbus Programme and the Impact of British Participation," *The World Today*, Vol. 35, No. 8 (August 1979): 332-339.

Sen, Gautam. *The Military Origins of Industrialisation and International Trade Rivalry*. New York: St. Martin's Press, 1984.

Servan-Schreiber, Jacques. *Le Defi Americain*. Paris: DeNoel, 1967.

Silbertson, Aubrey. "Industrial Policies in Britain 1960-1980," in *Industrial Policy and Innovation*, ed. Charles Carter, pp. 39-51. London: Heinemann, 1981.

Simonson, G. R., ed. *The History of the American Aircraft Industry*. Cambridge, Mass.: MIT Press, 1968.

Stegemann, Klaus. "Policy Rivalry Among Industrial States: What Can We Learn from Models of Strategic Trade Policy?" *International Organization*, Vol. 43, No. 1 (Winter 1989): 73-100.

Stoffaes, Christian. "French Industrial Strategy in the Sunrise Sectors," in *European Industry*, ed. Alex Jacquemin, pp. 274-292. Oxford: Clarendon Press, 1984.

———. "Industrial Policy in the High-Technology Industries," in *French Industrial Policy*, eds. William J. Adams and Christian Stoffaes, pp. 36-62. Washington, DC: The Brookings Institution, 1986.

Todd, Daniel, and Janice Simpson. *Aerospace and Development: A Survey*. Winnipeg: University of Manitoba, 1985.

Tomann, Horst. "Germany," in *Current Issues in Industrial Economic Strategy*, eds. Keith Cowling and Roger Sugden, pp. 183-187. Manchester, UK: Manchester University Press, 1992.

Tyson, Laura D. *Who's Bashing Whom? Trade Conflict in High-Technology Industries*. Washington, DC: Institute for International Economics, 1992.

Vander Meulen, Jacob A. *The Politics of Aircraft: Building an American Military Industry*. Lawrence: University Press of Kansas, 1992.

Williams, Roger. *European Technology: The Politics of Collaboration*. London: Croom Helm, 1973.

Yoshino, M.Y. "Global Competition in a Salient Industry: The Case of Civil Aircraft," in *Competition in Global Industries*, ed. Michael E. Porter, pp. 517-538. Boston: Harvard Business School Press, 1986.

Young, Stephen, and Neil Hood. "Industrial Policy in the United Kingdom," in *National Industrial Policies*, eds. Robert E. Driscoll and Jack N. Behrman, pp. 197-214. Cambridge, Mass.: Oelgeschlager, Gunn and Hain, 1984.

Ziegler, Henri. "Les technologies avancées vecteur du développement économique," *Bulletin de l'institut d'histoire du temps présent*, Supplement No. 6. Paris: 1984, pp. 17-36 and subsequent discussion.

Zysman, John. "The French State in the International Economy," in *Between Power and Plenty*, ed. Peter J. Katzenstein, pp. 255-293. Madison: University of Wisconsin Press, 1978.

# INDEX